MW01204449

Consumption and Public Life

Series Editors: **Frank Trentmann** and **Richard Wilk**

Titles include:

Kate Soper and Frank Trentmann (*editors*)
CITIZENSHIP AND CONSUMPTION

Lyn Thomas (*editor*)
RELIGION, CONSUMERISM AND SUSTAINABILITY
Paradise Lost?

Harold Wilhite
CONSUMPTION AND THE TRANSFORMATION OF EVERYDAY LIFE
A View from South India

Consumption and Public Life
Series Standing Order ISBN 978–1–403–99983–2 Hardback
978–1–403–99984–9 Paperback
(*outside North America only*)

You can receive future titles in this series as they are published by placing a standing order. Please contact your bookseller or, in case of difficulty, write to us at the address below with your name and address, the title of the series and the ISBN quoted above.

Customer Services Department, Macmillan Distribution Ltd, Houndmills, Basingstoke, Hampshire RG21 6XS, England

Culture of the Slow

Social Deceleration in an Accelerated World

Edited by

Nick Osbaldiston
Monash University, Australia

First published 2013 by
PALGRAVE MACMILLAN

Palgrave Macmillan in the UK is an imprint of Macmillan Publishers Limited,
registered in England, company number 785998, of Houndmills, Basingstoke,
Hampshire RG21 6XS.

Palgrave Macmillan in the US is a division of St Martin's Press LLC,
175 Fifth Avenue, New York, NY 10010.

Palgrave Macmillan is the global academic imprint of the above companies
and has companies and representatives throughout the world.

Palgrave® and Macmillan® are registered trademarks in the United States,
the United Kingdom, Europe and other countries.

ISBN 978–0–230–29976–4

This book is printed on paper suitable for recycling and made from fully
managed and sustained forest sources. Logging, pulping and manufacturing
processes are expected to conform to the environmental regulations of the
country of origin.

A catalogue record for this book is available from the British Library.

A catalog record for this book is available from the Library of Congress.

Contents

Acknowledgements

I should like to take the opportunity to acknowledge and thank the Palgrave staff, in particular Philippa Grand, Andrew James and Naomi Robinson, for taking this project on board and running with it. I would also like to thank the contributors to this volume for their hard work and willingness to be a part of this project. It is because of them and their ideas that this was even made possible. In particular I would like to pay special thanks to Juliet Schor and Kate Soper for their initial enthusiasm over the idea when it was just in embryo form. I would also like to acknowledge the contribution of ideas, thoughts and support to this project from Arlie Hochschild, Phil Smith, Clive Hamilton, Laurence Moss, Federica Davolio, Kate Maher, Theresa Petray, Gundars Rudzitis and Gavin Kendall. I would like to thank Michaela Benson for assisting me in the ideas for my own chapter. Lastly, to my family, once more I am in your debt for your patience, dedication, love and belief in this 'slow' process.

Contributors

Barnaby B. Barratt practises psychoanalysis in Johannesburg and is a training analyst with the South African Psychoanalytic Association. He is Senior Research Fellow at the University of Cape Town, where he convenes the PhD programme in psychoanalysis, and also a visiting professor at the University of Witwatersrand. He is on the editorial board of *Psychoanalysis, Culture and Society*, and his most recent book, *What Is Psychoanalysis? 100 Years after Freud's 'Secret Committee'*, was published in 2012.

Kim Humphery is Deputy Dean of the School of Global Studies, Social Science and Planning at RMIT University, Melbourne. Much of his research over the past two decades has focused on the history, theory and politics of consumption and anti-consumerism. He has published widely in this area, including *Shelf Life: Supermarkets and the Changing Cultures of Consumption* (1998), *Excess: Anti-Consumerism in the West* (2009) and the co-edited collection *Consumer Australia: Historical Perspectives* (2010).

Siv B. Lie is a PhD student at New York University. She spent her undergraduate years at Boston University researching and working in food politics and culinary arts. Since then she has shifted her anthropological focus to music, particularly the study of gypsy jazz and improvisation.

Charles Lindholm is Professor of Anthropology at Boston University. He has written extensively on his fieldwork in Pakistan. He has also written books on Islam, psychological anthropology, authenticity, charisma and American culture. His most recent work (co-authored with J.P. Zúquete) is *The Struggle for the World: Social Movements for the 21st Century* (2010).

Nick Osbaldiston is a lecturer in sociology at Monash University, Victoria. His work concentrates on the phenomenon known as Lifestyle Migration or Seachange and he is the author of several publications, including *Seeking Authenticity in Place, Culture and Self* (2012). He is a member of the Australian Sociological Association Executive Committee and co-editor of the *Nexus* newsletter. He is also a former principal convener of the Australian Cultural Sociology Thematic Group.

Angela T. Ragusa is a senior lecturer and discipline coordinator in sociology and programme leader for the BA honours programme at Charles Sturt University in Wagga Wagga, New South Wales, Australia. She serves on the editorial board of three international social science journals in communication, management and sociology, has reviewed four undergraduate textbooks and has authored more than 30 academic publications. Her 2010 edited book, *Interaction & Communication Technologies and Virtual Learning Environments: Human Factors*, highlights her interest in communication and higher education. Her research publications focusing on social inequality, population and cultural change, environmentalism, consumerism, gender and sexuality, and the media evidence her scholarship in social change. Currently she is examining how geography affects life satisfaction among 'treechangers' and the dynamic relationship between the well-being of people and places.

Martin Ryle is a reader in English at the University of Sussex. His work includes articles on recent and contemporary British and European fiction (by Michel Houellebecq, John McGahern, Ali Smith and others), contributions to eco-critical theory and debate, and various writings on the bicycle, including *By Bicycle in Ireland* (1996).

Roberta Sassatelli is Associate Professor of Sociology at the University of Milan. Her research focuses on the historical development of consumer societies, the theory of consumer action and the politics of contemporary consumer culture. She has done empirical research on ethical and sustainable consumption, the commercialisation of sport and leisure, consumer practices and class boundaries, fashion and the sexualisation of the gendered body, and alternative food cultures. Other interests include the history and sociology of the body, gender theory and gender issues, food studies, ethnography and visual methodology, and cultural theory. Recent books in English include *Consumer Culture: History, Theory and Politics* (2007) and *Fitness Culture: Gyms and the Commercialisation of Discipline and Fun* (2010).

Juliet B. Schor is Professor of Sociology at Boston College. Her most recent book is *True Wealth: How and Why Millions of Americans Are Creating a Time-Rich, Ecologically Light, Small-Scale, High-Satisfaction Economy*

(2011). Other books include *The Overworked American* (1993), *The Overspent American* (1999) and *Born to Buy* (2004). She is a co-founder of the Center for a New American Dream, a former Guggenheim Fellow, a winner of the Herman Daly Prize and a member of the MacArthur Connected Learning Research Network, for which she is studying connected consumption.

Kate Soper is Professor Emerita of Philosophy at London Metropolitan University and an honorary visiting professor at Brighton University. She has published widely on environmental philosophy, aesthetics of nature, theory of needs and consumption, and cultural theory. Her books include *What Is Nature? Culture, Politics and the Non-Human* (1995). She is a co-editor of *Citizenship and Consumption* (2008) and *The Politics and Pleasures of Consuming Differently* (2009).

Slow Culture: An Introduction

Nick Osbaldiston

If we carry on at this rate, the cult of speed can only get worse. When everyone takes the fast option, the advantage of going fast vanishes, forcing us to go faster still. Eventually, what we are left with is an arms race based on speed, and we all know where arms races end up: in the grim stalemate of Mutually Assured Destruction.

(Honoré 2004, p. 11)

To keep up in this competition, the average individual needs to earn more money. This means that he or she must work longer hours, take higher-paying but more demanding jobs, and so on. *Ceteris paribus*, these processes will lower the fraction of productivity growth which individuals desire to take as free time, and increase their demands for income.

(Schor 1998a, p. 123)

Introduction

There is a powerful message permeating our social lives today, found in our self-help networks, talkback television and radio shows, and online forums. It is a warning that, through technology and modernisation, our lifestyles have become increasingly hectic, fast, complex and immediate. 'Life', writes online author Leo Babauta (2009, para. 2), 'moves at such a fast pace that it seems to pass us by before we can really enjoy it'. We are encouraged to take a step back, to breathe deeply and 'slow down', in order to recapture the essence of 'real' living. By doing so, we can escape the seemingly endless stresses associated with our multi-tasked, time-compressed and instantaneous speed culture (Tomlinson 2007). This

1

book presents illustrations of how people are beginning to disentangle themselves from a speed culture by embracing slowness. It is not simply a matter of slowing down, as the term implies, but of undertaking changes in the way we do things at an everyday level. Underpinning these transformations is a concern, as Babauta (2009) suggests, with the uniquely stressful lifestyles we are living in contemporary culture.

These concerns are certainly not unmerited. The reality of increasing technological advance and the expansion of consumer capitalism is that social life has become increasingly more complex and accelerated. In particular, advances in communication and information technologies in the market, in social networks and in the work place (as well as sport and mass media) have created a culture of 'immediacy' or instantaneity (Tomlinson 2007; Macnaughten and Urry 1998; Featherstone 2007). In other words, we no longer have to wait for information; it is with us 24 hours a day. Devices such as smartphones, in particular, ensure that we are never too far from the network. While we sleep, our non-human counterparts receive emails from across the world, online transactions take place in our bank accounts, newspaper articles appear in our favourite broadsheet 'application' and messages from friends and family are delivered through our social media networks. It is not just a 'culture of speed' that we live in, but a 'culture of immediacy' wherein the gap of time and space is not simply compressed but completely transcended (Tomlinson 2007, p. 91; Giddens 1990; Bauman 2001).

The changing pace and ethical virtues of new telecommunications and 'fast' capitalism (Agger 2004) have been well studied over the past few decades sociologically and theoretically (Lash and Urry 1987, 1994; Beck 1992; Giddens 1990; Virilio 1997; Tomlinson 2007; Bauman 2001; Sennett 1998; Ritzer 2010). For Agger (2004), the market place, the industries and, of course, the technologies which facilitate them have speeded up considerably since the writings of Marx in the nineteenth century. The economies of the world are no longer based on stable, localised and ordered industries which encourage class conflict. Rather, as Lash and Urry (1987, 1994) state in their now dated works, capitalism has become disorganised, flexible, fluid and volatile. The dynamics of the market and a globalised financial system mean that local economies can fall or rise rapidly according to speculation and multi-national corporate activity. The recent global financial meltdown, which is reaching its zenith in the Eurozone as I write this introduction, is a testament to this.

These recent dramatic changes in capitalism have taken many by surprise, including Agger (2004, p. 3) who writes:

The rate of communicating, writing, connecting, shopping, browsing, surfing, and working has increased since the Internet came on the scene. I was correct, in 1989, to notice that capitalism has sped up since Marx's time, and even since the post-World War II period in which the Frankfurt School theorists wrote about domination and the eclipse of reason (see Jay 1973; Wiggershaus 1994). But I didn't foresee the extent of acceleration and instantaneity we have come to know today. Who could have?

It would seem, from Agger's (2004, p. 3) point of view, that the rapid speed with which capitalism has developed has not simply altered market places but also assaulted the boundary 'between personal and public life'. No longer are work, consumption and private lifestyles separated. Information technology means that we are subjected more now than ever to various mediums from social media and email to television, radio and smartphones. As Juliet Schor (1998a) warned a few decades ago, escaping either work or consumption is becoming increasingly difficult. Tourist advertisements depend somewhat on this.

Of course, the triumph of speed over the social had occupied the mindsets of the modernists well before the invention of the mobile phone. Georg Simmel's (1997[1903], p. 175) memorable study into the life of the metropolitan, for instance, demonstrates the growing impact of speed and 'rapid crowding of changing images' on the development of the individual. The overwhelming of the senses by the multitude of signs and symbols found in the city imbues the individual, for Simmel (1997, pp. 178–180), with a 'blasé' attitude toward things and a socially reserved persona toward other people.

Alongside criticism of temporal shifts, there were also the broader debates on the impact of increased consumerism on the individual. Frankfurt scholars such as Marcuse (1976), Fromm (1956) and Adorno and Horkheimer (1972[1944]), for instance, all expressed dismay at the proliferation of the commodity and the slavish influence it had on consumer choice. Marcuse's (1976[1964], pp. 22–23) declaration in *One Dimensional Man* that 'people recognise themselves in their commodities' is demonstrable of the style of thought of this group: that through consumerism, individuals would lose their grip on what was 'true' or authentic. Instead, the commodity lays 'claim' to 'the entire individual' and controls them through a process of reifying 'false needs' as 'true'.

These early remonstrations have continued in recent commentaries and debates on the influence and role of consumerism in Western culture (see, for instance, Schor 1993, 1998b, 2000, 2004, 2010; Soper 2007;

Soper, Ryle and Thomas 2009; Gorz 1999; Hamilton 2004; Hochschild 1990, 1997, 2003; Honoré 2004). Within these there is a common thread which ties consumer capitalism to declining trends in well-being through higher levels of stress. Central to such critiques are the pressures of time management and the penetrating influence of labour on previously protected times, as indicated in Agger's (2004) work also (cf. Adam 1995; Hochschild 1997). Popular figures such as Juliet Schor lament the decline of leisure in the West (in particular) where 'people' have 'become subject to a Prisoner's Dilemma in which they work hard to earn additional income to upgrade their status of living, but everyone else does the same' (Schor 1998a, p. 122). As a result, one's 'relative position' does not change. Rather, individuals continue to be locked into a cycle of dissatisfaction with their material position and return to the market place (Schor 1998a, p. 123). In addition to this sentiment, especially in recent times, there is the growing concern with over-consumption and its contribution to the degradation of the environment. Within this space, several researchers and theorists have begun seeking out strategies that promote sustainable forms of consumerism (see Schor, this volume, 2010; Soper 2007).

These criticisms of both consumerism and the increasingly stressful labour we are enduring are not limited to the academic sphere, however. As this book attests, across the world a growing discontent with the offerings of fast and instantaneous consumer capitalism and the speed of modern life has led individuals to explore alternative approaches to lifestyle. Manifestations of this, it could be argued, can be found in a variety of choices that individuals make in the everyday. Whether it is through food production and consumption, travel in both domestic and international spaces or even within intimate relations, there is broad evidence of a cultural reaction to the velocity, intensity and perceived meaninglessness of life. At times, this revolt is organised in the form of quasi-social movements such as Slow Food, Slow Cities/Towns and Voluntary Simplicity. These, in particular Carlo Petrini's Slow Food, are responsible for popularising the term 'slow' within the everyday rhetoric of public discourse.

It is on the various reactions against the mainstream through the 'slow' that this book uniquely focusses. While it is important to accept that movements such as Slow Food are pinnacle realisations of this, it is also wise to consider the wider narrative within which it is situated. Slowness, it is proposed here, is not simply a term that reflects organised, politically embedded social movements. Rather, the thought of 'living life more slowly' is one that has provoked significant individualised changes within the everyday. From this perspective, slowness is not simply a rebellion against speed. Rather, as key authors Wendy Parkins and Geoffrey Craig (2006, p. 3) write in their work *Slow Living*, slowness reflects a style of living that is dislocated from the norms associated with fast capitalism and is synonymous with meaningfulness. At times, perhaps, it is also demonstrable of a more reflexive individual (Giddens 1990; Bauman 2001). They write:

> At its heart, slow living is a conscious attempt to change the temporal order to one which offers more time, time to attend to everyday life...But slow living should not be thought of simply as a slow-motion version of postmodern life; it does not offer or make possible a parallel temporality for slow subjects to inhabit in isolation from the rest of global culture. Rather, its patterns and practices, like others in contemporary culture, are non-synchronous, albeit deliberately and consciously...'Having time' for something means investing it with significance through attention and deliberation. To live slowly in this sense, then, means engaging in 'mindful' rather than 'mindless' practices which make us consider the pleasure or at least the purpose of each task to which we give our time.
>
> (Parkins and Craig 2006, p. 3)

Subsequently, themes that repeat throughout the slow movements are 'care', 'attention' and 'mindfulness' (Parkins and Craig 2006, p. 4). While Parkins and Craig (2006) focus their analysis on the political/social/cultural complexity of organised movements like Slow Food, it is clear that such narratives resonate with activities found in the everyday. For instance, can we exclude within this space the rise in popularity of cycling in the West? As Ryle and Soper demonstrate in this volume, this particular enactment of slowness is one that we cannot ignore. It is, as Soper (2007) argues elsewhere, another example of alternative actions wherein the individual seeks to reappropriate something subjectively pleasurable, such as the feeling of being out in the 'open air' and enjoying the sensations of riding, which also have some wider ecological benefit. Slowness here is not entirely politically driven, but emerges from a rejection of automobile travel and the lack of pleasure that is derived from it.

By analysing slowness in this manner, there is no doubt a danger of attracting criticism regarding what exactly slow culture involves. If the slow narrative can be reduced to small everyday acts such as cycling (as is analysed in this volume), does this strip away the ethical and revolutionary potential that the vernacular of the more established social movements expresses? In other words, do we risk debasing the whole paradigm of slowness by seeking to see its foundations in areas that are at their heart mostly apolitical? This is certainly a worthy question and should be considered briefly in this introduction.

Exploring slowness – the Parkins and Craig model

The notion of the 'slow' is one that captures the imagination of a disenchanted public. Our relative unease with the ethics of fast-paced life, the ubiquity of consumption and the pervasiveness of technology has many testing the waters of alternative lifestyles. Slow advocate Carl Honoré (2004, p. 47) proposes that this is the motivation behind an increasing interest in spirituality. 'These days', he writes, 'many people are seeking refuge from speed in the safe harbour of spirituality' (Honoré 2004, p. 47). Certainly, we have witnessed an increase in the popularity of pseudo-spiritual activities such as T'ai Chi, Yoga and meditation (cf. Possamai 2005). However, the return to meaningful, attentive and careful activities is not found only in spiritual activities. As a host of authors have demonstrated, numerous people in the West have begun swapping 'materialist values' for a lifestyle change that enables 'more time, less stress, and more balance in life' (Schor 1998b, pp. 113–114; Hamilton 2004; Elgin 1981; Etzioni 2004). Unlike 'decelerators from the hippie generation', these new reactions against the mainstream 'are driven less by political or environmental scruples than by the desire to lead more rewarding lives' (Honoré 2004, p. 47). Across the world, downshifters, seachangers or lifestyle migrants have demonstrated this through their willingness to give up the consumerist life for simpler existences, sometimes in completely new locations (Osbaldiston 2012; Benson 2011; Parkins and Craig 2006; Hamilton 2004; Schor 1998b).

For some, the beauty of the slow revolution is the counter-punch it could in the long term inflict on the culture of speed. Tomlinson (2007, p. 148), for instance, recognises at the end of his treatise on 'speed' that the 'contemporary slow movement in the main deploys a politely dissenting discourse, orientated toward exploring change in personal practices'. While the turn away from dominant forms of lifestyle appears 'unlikely' to 'challenge the institutional grip of the condition of immediacy' in any significant way, it can 'in the longer term be consequential' (Tomlinson 2007, p. 149). Establishing that the 'slow' is in fact a form of providing some 'balance' which is somewhat missing in contemporary governance structures and institutions (that are endlessly caught up in the speed cycle), Tomlinson (2007, p. 154) argues:

> In such a context, ideas of balance, measure and proportion become crucial to the governance of modernity. Whilst there are no guarantees that these values will prevail, the hope must be that the attractions of personal balance may resonate in the political cultures of democracies. Thus, in establishing a cultural politics of immediacy, it may be the value of balance that provides a bridge between the personal-existential and the political realms.

The 'culture of immediacy' can be 'disturbed' through cultural reasoning and transformation of normal everyday practices, which can in turn have a long-term influence on how we view speed in both personal or social settings and within our institutions. For instance, a broader collective revaluation of our environment could create a collective re-evaluation of institutional dealings with our ecology (cf. Szerszynski 2005).

While some slow movements appear less politically focussed than broader complex social movements or, as Lindholm and Zúquete (2010) describe them, 'aurora movements' (such as anti-globalisation movements), there are those which have political and ethical undertones. Parkins and Craig (2006), who have written extensively on the analysis of the slow, appear to focus on the latter. The complexity of their argument, however, is not entirely bound up in political motivation. Rather, the essence of their project lies in the potentiality of slow living to alter the landscape of consumption and production in a global capitalist society (not just local politics), similar to others already discussed above. Specifically, the two authors concentrate on the 'creative and ethical potential' that is found within everyday practice (Parkins and Craig 2006, p. 7). Closely aligned to Beck's (1992) individualisation thesis, Parkins and Craig (2006) propose that in contemporary culture individuals are opened up further to a negotiation of lifestyles and a need to construct their own 'biographies' in the wake of a waning of traditional structures and institutions (such as churches). They contend:

> Such practices of individualization which throw into question the assumptions and practices of everyday life have seen the category of the everyday take on a new currency, both in popular culture and political discourse (Chaney 2002:55). From the extraordinary proliferation of lifestyle television in the past decade to recent political

debates about the urgency to find a 'work/family balance', the everyday is no longer the background against which important public
issues are considered, it is itself the issue.

(Parkins and Craig 2006, p. 8)

As individuals adopt a more reflexive stance in the everyday, the
opportunities for 'utopian possibilities' within that space are increased.
In other words, as individuals begin to question established social practices and traditions (or, in the case of slowness, consumerism) there
are chances for the transformation of behaviour to align with political ideals such as those found in sustainability, environmentalist and
post-materialist movements (cf. Tomlinson 2007).

However, an increased presence of individual reflexive awareness is
only part of the picture. Indeed, if individuals have been adopting slow
practices through a cognitive reflexivity, what is it that they are critically engaging with? The answer lies for Parkins and Craig in the vices
and virtues of a globalised world culture. 'Contemporary forms and
practices of slow living,' they argue, 'arise from, and in response to
processes of globalisation' and not just 'immediate pressures of daily
life' (Parkins and Craig 2006, p. 9). Yet unlike that of anti-globalists,
their argument does not hinge upon the notion that global forces produce the 'dislocations and dissonances that make slow living seem an
appealing alternative' (Parkins and Craig 2006, p. 9). Rather, the processes of globalisation are treated in a sophisticated manner as almost
binary. On the one hand, there are the structural impacts of the phenomenon which involve a quickening of social, economic and cultural
life as technological advances increase the 'time–space compression',
leading us into a 'runaway world' (Giddens 2002). From this standpoint, slowness is a desire to return to the traditional as an escape from
the accelerated social world that globalisation has encouraged, produced
and institutionalised. It is a quaint form of living not too distinct from
the alternative movements of the 1960s and 1970s.

On the other hand, however, globalisation can actually also be seen
to unintentionally encourage the types of social attitudes that oppose
its fast persona. Once more tuning into Beck's (2006) conceptualisation
of cosmopolitanism, the authors suggest that an opening up of the
local to the global allows individuals to reflect upon their actions in
a wider sphere. 'Slow living' becomes not just a 'retreat to the local',
but is also part of a 'reconfiguring of local social relations and identities in new reflexive ways' (Parkins and Craig 2006, p. 11). They argue,
further – using Beck's (2006) position that cosmopolitanism involves an
internalisation, individually, of globalism – that the 'impulse towards

slow living' demonstrates reflexive engagement with broad global outlooks.

> Everyday experience is understood to have global implications and effects beyond the personal implications of a slower, more attentive approach to life. Indeed it could be said that attention is directed outward as well as inward in practices of slow living. The person who walks rather than drives may be cognizant of the environmental implications of fossil fuels and freeways as well as the pleasures to be derived from bodily exercise, for instance ... the slow subject may live a kind of 'ethical glocalism'.
>
> (Tomlinson 1999: 195–196; Parkins and Craig 2006, p. 11)

It is within the local, therefore, that the individual can enact a reconfiguration of the consumer ethic that embraces broader global concerns and other alternative political narratives.

Like Soper (2007) and to a lesser extent Tomlinson (2007), however, the Parkins and Craig (2006) project is not blind to the 'hedonistic' aspects of slow living. Pleasure, joy and a feeling of enchantment are integral to empowering slowness. Slowness is almost the antithesis to Weber's now famous prediction of a social world enveloped by an 'iron cage'. Following Jane Bennett's thoughts, the authors suggest that within slow living the 'cultivation of an enchanted sensibility' is a fundamental aspect of the embracing of alternative lifestyles or modes of consumption. The importance of sensuality and pleasure within their thesis is highlighted in an entire chapter designed to explore what they call 'situated pleasures', which professes that pleasure is 'firstly grounded in the body – in the physicality and affectivity of the incorporation of food – and secondly based on an attentiveness to the location of the body' (Parkins and Craig 2006, p. 87). Thus, while the political dimensions and ethical potential of slow living are a key characteristic of quasi-social movements like Slow Food, one cannot disregard the pleasurable and powerful emotions that reward the individual for their alternative approach to everyday lifestyle.

Reflections and departures

The above, albeit brief, introduction to the examination of the 'slow' provides some grounding for this volume of work; however, we depart somewhat from it. While advocates such as Parkins and Craig (2006) focus their attention on the political and ethical potentiality of a broad uptake of slow within contemporary society, they perhaps analyse and implicitly characterise slowness too narrowly. In *Slow Living* in particular, their work highlights mostly those movements that hold the title 'slow' and which are now well-established organisations with, interestingly, bureaucratic models of governance. Yet despite focussing on movements like Slow Food, Parkins and Craig (2006, p. 139) seem apprehensive of carving out a definitive characterisation of slowness:

> We have resisted delineating a set of practices that would constitute or define slow living, even as we have used a number of examples throughout (cooking, knitting, walking, gardening, cycling, reading, meditating – although, with the possible exception of meditating, all of these activities can also be done quickly!). Rather than defining slow living by its practices, then, we have proposed that slow living is a way of cultivating an ethical approach to the everyday. Thought of in this way, slow living becomes as much an attitude or disposition as an action, one that combines wonder and generosity.
>
> (Parkins and Craig 2006, p. 139)

Yet from this admission, we can still see that embedded in the notion of the slow person is a broader ethical concern or 'disposition' which embraces wider ecological or social concerns while also preaching private hedonistic enjoyment. In doing so, I would contest – as is demonstrated in this work – that slow living becomes tied inherently to a political ideal, or agenda, which seeks to challenge broader institutional practices and values.

It is my contention that not all manifestations of the 'slow' need be founded in a dialectic of ethical and personal interests. Rather, by focussing attention on the cultural aspects of the slow, we can broaden the defining features to include areas which at times appear apolitical. For instance, individuals who embrace the Amenity or Lifestyle Migration phenomenon have often been portrayed by analysts as less concerned with environmental issues and more focussed on a quest for slower, meaningful and more communal lifestyles (Ragusa 2010; Moss 2006; Osbaldiston 2011, 2012; Benson 2011). In other words, the emphasis in this movement is not (though admittedly, at times, it can be) centred on issues of ecological or broader post-materialist concerns. Rather, through a process of migration, individuals find solace from the stresses and strains of the city through rural or country living (cf. Benson 2011; see also Osbaldiston, this volume; Ragusa, this volume). Under a slow-living paradigm established by Parkins and Craig (2006), however, this phenomenon becomes a weak manifestation of the slow philosophy because it narrowly focusses on the re-enchantment of lifestyles and the self (such as in cycling – see Ryle and Soper, this volume). Consequently, this work is founded on a less stringent view of what slowness is and what it can or cannot be, departing somewhat from Parkins and Craig's (2006) theory of the slow. By emphasising it as a broad collective revaluation of meaning and action, whether or not this is ethically motivated by ecological or materialistic concerns, we can witness slowness within various pockets of everyday social activity. Again, this characterisation could be criticised as diluting the power within slow discourse to a mere transitory phenomenon. However, as this volume suggests, if we can envisage slowness as not just an organised response but a broad cultural reaction against speed, then the paradigm itself can be seen to have more influence than is at first recognised. People are reacting against 'fast capitalism' in a way which embraces meaningful or even authentic relations with environment, people and the self. Whether this has revolutionary potential or is simply another 'phase' of consumer capitalism is a question we will seek to answer in the chapters that follow and in the conclusion.

Overview of the book

As described above, the message of the chapters found in this book is that there has been a cultural shift toward slowness in the embodiment of activity in everyday life. Transformations have been from the significant, including the complete removal of individuals from the city to rurality, through to the minor, such as how one journeys to work daily. Slowness here does not simply encapsulate or encourage 'stillness' (Bissell and Fuller 2011, p. 13) but rather creates alternative spaces, times, socialities and experiences from the normalised everyday expectations of an advanced 'fast' capitalist society. While some contributors are sceptical of the intentions of those embracing the slow metaphor in lifestyles, especially Lindholm and Lie (Chapter 2), most describe slowness in terms of its potentiality to challenge the problems of contemporary life. For that reason, some of the chapters here are broad commentaries while others are specific descriptions of movements as they happen on the ground.

This volume reflects the many diverse traditions that are embraced in the social sciences and humanities. While most concentrate on the cultural, and this is the basis for their inclusion in the volume, some also engage with the movement at the political level. In the first chapter, Kim

Humphery offers a detailed exploration of the 'Time of Consumption'. Here, consumerism and consumer ethics are described in terms that are not simply associated with quickness, instantaneity and the fast. Rather, Humphery argues that we consume in a space that 'occupies numerous temporalities'. To talk of a politics and cultural transformation of consumption which embrace slowness need not require an actual measured change in how we consume time. For example, hyper-consumption, the type of practice that slow critiques, is not simply fast but also wasteful. Slowness attempts to revalorise the way in which we use time so that it is exercised 'well' and 'meaningfully'. The temporal question itself, especially in relation to clock-time, misses the point of performing the slow. We can indeed live our lives quickly, but also meaningfully. From this position, slow is not simply about slowing down our rushed existence. Slowness is a transformation of ethics around 'how' we consume time. Humphery's piece therefore provides a type of theoretical commentary and platform from which the remaining chapters emerge.

Demonstration of this is especially evident in Chapter 2. Here, Juliet Schor discusses the creation and expansion of alternative modes of fashion and consumption that are currently growing in importance in the USA and beyond. In particular in fashion, an industry where the turnover of goods within one's own wardrobe can be volatile and transient, Schor describes the new breed of 'young innovators' seeking to create a 'sharing economy'. In what she terms a 'connected consumption' movement, people have begun trading and exchanging social goods or commodities rather than buying new products in the market place. She explores this further, demonstrating how, through this activity, the lifespan of the use of goods is extended, which serves also to limit waste. Notably, therefore, not a post-materialist/consumer movement, the 'sharing economy' nonetheless produces a powerful critique of wasteful capitalism. While the numbers are too low for a prediction of the impact of 'sharing economies' on fast consumer capitalism, the growing popularity of 'connected consumption' illustrates another manifestation of slowness amidst a broader reaction against mainstream economic and social activities. This is significant also given the current economic crises of the USA and the Eurozone.

In Chapter 3, Charles Lindholm and Siv Lie explore the movement that arguably popularised the notion of 'slow' – Slow Food. Providing a thorough overview of the food revolution, Lindholm and Lie propose that at its heart is the question of authenticity and taste. Specifically, Slow Food opens up space for the individual through a collective to critique and subsequently protest against global food production and consumption. This is achieved, importantly, through seeking out 'authentic' local cuisine and tastes. Local traditions in food culture are important. Understanding tastes so that one can appreciate sensually the distinctiveness of high-quality foods is a long process of education and refinement. The problem associated with this, as Lindholm and Lie argue, is that these are subjective, constructed and often contestable even inside local communities. Who decides what is authentic? What does this then do for local cuisine that is deemed inauthentic? Is there room only for the middle classes at the table? These are certainly questions that cut to the heart of the entire book and which I return to later in the conclusion. Despite their tentative position on the ethics of Slow Food, Lindholm and Lie propose that through this movement other 'slow' narratives have emerged and grown in popularity – such as Slow Towns and Slow Travel. The trickling down of the slow 'ideal', whether it is embedded in a middle-class 'habitus' or not, could invoke changes for the good overall.

This is further demonstrated in Chapter 4, where I offer some notes on the slow in other transformations that occur through spatial negotiation. Looking predominantly into the manifestations of the slow in places, this chapter explores how objects and local amenity (environmental or cultural artefacts) can encourage contemplation, meaningfulness and a slowing down of usual activity. While the city is often viewed as the antithesis to 'slowness', it is shown here that it can also invoke both embodied and cognitive reflexivity through 'meaningful' narratives – especially through nostalgia. However, there is also often a strong desire to escape the city and the suburbs, manifested in the escapism of tourism and permanent migration. In this chapter, I explore Lifestyle Migration and the recent phenomenon of Slow Travel. Through these, people can be inspired by the romanticism of places far distinct from the city, which produces, as shown, changes in behaviour to slower forms. In the case especially of Slow Travel, the tourist intentionally journeys through locations in a less rushed and harried fashion in order to enjoy all the sensations that the land has to offer him or her – allowing for, it could be argued, more meaningful experience and a greater sense of self-authenticity. However, as Zukin (2008) argues and Benson (2011) demonstrates in her empirical work, who defines the authentic is a question worth asking. As gentrification projects around the world expand, we might question the ethics of some of the movements in question.

In keeping with the theme of spatial engagement, Chapter 5 examines a form of everyday travel and mobility that serves as an exemplar for the changing dynamic of lifestyle through slowness: the bicycle. Here,

Martin Ryle and Kate Soper interrogate the uptake of this more traditional form of transport in one of the busiest cities of the world, London.
The recent proliferation of bike travel is also to be seen in other countries including Australia, the USA and other parts of Europe. While Ryle
and Soper are cautious to attribute this rise to any ecological, political
or ethical motivation, they make the claim that the riding of bicycles
is evidence of a growth in alternative hedonistic practices (Soper 2007).
Through practices that enhance the experience of the everyday, in particular travel, macro environmental issues, including traffic pollution
and unsustainable practices, are challenged. Providing us with a brief
but intriguing history of the bicycle and an overview of its use across
the world, these authors present a stark case of how the everyday is
being challenged and altered by a slow paradigm – or in other words,
engaging in social practices that provide 'alternative' pleasures which
are ecologically sound and sustainable.

Chapter 6 continues the interrogation of slowness in place by investigating the specific Lifestyle Migration movement known as Treechange
in Australia. Angela Ragusa presents in this chapter a mixture of critical
social theory and empirical research to question the ethics of this new
form of 'slowness'. Although on the surface the phenomenon appears
to be motivated by a collection of individual and broad social needs,
Ragusa questions through interview data whether it is a new form
of 'conspicuous consumption' predominantly from the middle classes.
In what is a delightful, revealing and enlightening chapter, Ragusa is
able to show that despite initially seeking a transformation of self and
consumer ethics, many participating in this social trend fail to adopt
newer alternative practices of consumerism altogether. This conclusion
is discordant with popular rhetoric on the subject of Treechange or
Seachange in Australia and overseas (Osbaldiston 2012; Moss 2006) but
is comparable with recent works from Michaela Benson (2011). From
this perspective again, we begin to question whether slowness is a wider
social paradigm embraced by all, or whether it is a mere life project
entertained by the middle classes to develop a 'better life'. As is con-
cluded in my thoughts in Chapter 4, this question cuts to the heart of
understandings of gentrification and displacement through slow-based
movements like Treechange.

Moving away from the public or collective manifestations of the slow,
we turn in Chapter 7 to the very private sphere of sexual relations.
Psychoanalytical researcher and practitioner Barnaby Barratt offers in
this chapter a highly engaging theoretical piece on the transformative
potential of slow sex, or 'tantra'. Piecing together the development and

attraction of slowness in sexual intimacy, he argues that despite its lack of organisation or bureaucratic structure (such as in Slow Food), this form of 'slowness' can be viewed as a form of rejection of the commodified body. In short, slow sex (though admittedly not a widespread term as yet) presents back to the individual a type of social practice that offers authentic modes of enjoyment and pleasure distinct from the usual mainstream and potentially pornified sexual act. Importantly, the chapter delves into the manner in which this very private act has been challenged by the slow – not merely as a political act (though there is potential for the political within it) but rather as a form of mutual experiencing between partners that provokes meaning and authenticity. Sharing commonalities with the other sites of slowness explored in this book, this act of slow sex requires, fundamentally, taking time to explore physical and emotional sensations not found in mainstream sexual activities.

Most of the discussions located in the book operate outside the mainstream market place and consumerism. Even though Slow Food is based on consumption, it also emphasises production and support of local food culture. Yet slowness, as Parkins and Craig (2006) also suggest, can impact various facets of modern life. To demonstrate this further, Roberta Sassatelli provides in Chapter 8 a rigorous theoretical commentary on the commodity and its relationship to the slow. Her analysis, argued through the works of economist Tibor Scitovsky, reminds us of the potential for the consumer object to enable experiences that invoke creativity, learning and patience. Here, Sassatelli expertly picks through assumptions about consumer culture to present a case for the object as something which can encourage slower, meaningful engagement and which promotes a longer pleasurable experience through skill development and possible social interaction. For instance, the camera which requires some technical ability to utilise it to its full potential can indeed encourage a slower form of enjoyment, which adds to a broader critique of contemporary fast-paced, wasteful and ephemeral consumer culture. Unlike what critical theorists such as Fromm, Marcuse and Adorno contend, the object provides a pathway toward greater development of the self. It enables space for enjoyment, fulfilment and technical mastery, which requires patience, thoughtfulness and attention. These types of objects, unlike other consumer items which often lie dormant in the cupboard or garage, can invoke attitudes that resemble the slow despite their location in modern consumerism.

In my final departing remarks, I complete the volume by offering some summations on slowness and ask questions about its underlying logic. In particular, the inevitable question, posed with any new form of what appears as 'self-help' rhetoric, as to who exactly is participating in the movement is considered. Certainly, it is the hallmark of sociology and social theory to be sceptical about anything that appears tied to class, specifically the middle classes here. Yet, what this volume presents is a myriad of complex social theories and empirical examples that potentially answer this charge. While there is no doubt that slowness is predominantly enacted within the middle classes, can this always be treated with an air of discontent? As Tomlinson (2007, p. 159) suggests, the 'culture of speed' may well be in the long term unsustainable not only ecologically and economically but also individually. The chapters presented here provide an overview of the potentiality for 'slow' to 'disturb' the fascination with speed, while building momentum for cultural influence over institutional behaviour which is inherently tied to the middle classes.

References

Adam, B., 1995, *Timewatch: The Social Analysis of Time*, Polity Press, Cambridge.

Adorno, T. & Horkheimer, M., 1972[1944], *Dialectic of Enlightenment*, J. Cumming (trans.), Allen Lane, London.

Agger, B., 2004, *Speeding up Fast Capitalism: Cultures, Jobs, Families, Schools, Bodies*, Paradigm Publishers, Boulder.

Babauta, L., 2009, 'The 10 essential rules for slowing down and enjoying life more', viewed 19 January 2011, http://zenhabits.net/the-10-essential-rules-for-slowing-down-and-enjoying-life-more/

Bauman, Z., 2001, *The Individualized Society*, Polity Press, Cambridge.

Beck, U., 1992, *Risk Society: Towards a New Modernity*, M. Ritter (trans.), Sage, London.

———, 2006, *The Cosmopolitan Vision*, C. Cronin (trans.), Polity Press, Cambridge.

Benson, M., 2011, *The British in Rural France: Lifestyle Migration and the Ongoing Quest for a Better Way of Life*, Manchester University Press, Manchester.

Bissell, D. & Fuller, G. 2011, *Stillness in a Mobile World*, Taylor and Francis, New York.

Elgin, D., 1981, *Voluntary Simplicity: Toward a Way of Life That Is Outwardly Simple, Inwardly Rich*, William Morrow and Company, New York.

Etzioni, A., 2004, 'The post affluent society', *Review of Social Economy*, 62, no.3, 407–420.

Featherstone, M. 2007, *Consumer Culture and Postmodernism*, Sage, London.

Fromm, E., 1956, *The Sane Society*, Routledge & Kegan Paul, London.

Giddens, A., 1990, *The Consequences of Modernity*, Stanford University Press, Stanford.

———, 2002, *Runaway World: How Globalisation Is Reshaping Our Lives*, Profile, London.

Gorz, A., 1999, *Reclaiming Work: Beyond the Wage-based Society*, C. Turner (trans.), Polity Press, Cambridge.

Hamilton, C., 2004, *Growth Fetish*, Allen and Unwin, Sydney.

Hochschild, A., 1990, *The Second Shift*, Avon Books, New York.

——, 1997, *The Time Bind: When Work Becomes Home and Home Becomes Work*, Metropolitan Books, New York.

——, 2003, *The Managed Heart: Commercialization of Human Feeling*, University of California Press, Berkeley.

Honoré, C., 2004, *In Praise of Slowness: Challenging the Cult of Speed*, HarperOne, New York.

Lash, S. & Urry, J., 1987, *The End of Organised Capitalism*, Polity Press, Cambridge.

——, 1994, *Economies of Signs and Space*, Sage, London.

Lindholm, C. & Zúquete, J.P., 2010, *The Struggle for the World: Liberation Movements for the 21st Century*, Stanford University Press, Stanford.

Macnaughten, P. & Urry, J., 1998, *Contested Natures*, Sage, London.

Marcuse, H., 1976, *One Dimensional Man*, Abacus, London.

Moss, L.A.G. (ed.), 2006, *The Amenity Migrants: Seeking and Sustaining Mountains and Their Cultures*, CABI, Oxfordshire.

Osbaldiston, N., 2011, 'The authentic place in amenity migration discourse', *Space and Culture*, 14, no.2, 214–226.

——, 2012, *Seeking for Authenticity in Place, Culture and the Self: The Great Urban Escape*, Palgrave MacMillan, New York.

Parkins, W. & Craig, G., 2006, *Slow Living*, Berg, Oxford.

Possamai, A., 2005, *In Search of New Age Spiritualities*, Ashgate, Aldershot.

Ragusa, A., 2010, 'Seeking trees or escaping traffic: Socio-cultural factors and 'treechange' migration in Australia', in G.W. Luck, R. Black & D. Race (eds.), *Demographic Change in Rural Landscapes: What Does It Mean for Society and the Environment?*, Springer, London, pp. 71–99.

Ritzer, G., 2010, *Enchanting a Disenchanted World: Continuity and Change in the Cathedrals of Consumption*, (3rd ed), Pine Forge Press, Thousand Oaks.

Schor, J., 1993, *The Overworked American: The Unexpected Decline of Leisure*, Basic Books, New York

——, 1998a, 'Time, labour and consumption: Guest editor's introduction', *Time and Society*, 7, no.1, 119–127.

——, 1998b, *The Overspent American: Why We Want What We Don't Need*, Harper Perennial, New York.

——, 2000, 'The new politics of consumption', in J. Cohen & J. Rogers (eds.), *Do Americans Shop Too Much?* Beacon Press, Boston, pp. 3–33.

——, 2004, *Born to Buy: The Commercialized Child and the New Consumer Culture*, Scribner, New York.

——, 2010, *Plenitude: The New Economics of True Wealth*, Scribe, Carlton North, Victoria.

Sennett, R., 1998, *The Corrosion of Character: The Personal Consequences of Work in the New Capitalism*, Norton, New York.

Simmel, G., 1997[1903], The metropolis and mental life, M. Ritter (trans.), in D. Frisby & M. Featherstone (eds.), *Simmel on Culture*, Sage, London, pp. 174–186.

Soper, K., 2007, 'Rethinking the "good life": The citizenship dimension of consumer disaffection with consumerism', *Journal of Consumer Culture*, 7, no.2, 205–229.

Soper, K., Ryle, M. & Thomas, L., 2009, *The Politics and Pleasures of Consuming Differently*, Palgrave Macmillan, Bassingstoke.

Szerszynski, B., 2005, *Nature, Technology and the Sacred*, Blackwell, Malden.
Tomlinson, J., 2007, *The Culture of Speed: The Coming of Immediacy*, Sage, London.
Virilio, P., 1997, *Open Sky*, J. Rose (trans.), Verso, London.
Zukin, S., 2008, 'Consuming authenticity', *Cultural Studies*, 22, no.5, 724–748.

1
The Time of Consumption

Kim Humphery

Introduction

If there is one phrase that I most dread to hear, it's 'price check'. We all know this term by now; it is, in fact, definitive of the contemporary landscape of everyday shopping. We all know the routine as well. As the sound of this phrase floats in the supermarket air, having been sputtered into a public address system by some frazzled kid at the check-out, everyone in the queue slumps on one leg and breathes in frustration at the fact that we are going to have to wait. Meanwhile, the cost of the offending article is ever so slowly ascertained. This is not what computerised scanning was meant to be all about. Bar codes are supposed to put a bar on delay. But, of course, they don't; they bolster an efficiency of stock control with no promise of quick service. And in a world of fast consumption, a delay of any such kind becomes more and more intolerable. If it's not there in the shop or online; if it's not quickly purchasable or deliverable; it's not worth having. If the systems and technologies of consumption fail – and the queue moves too slowly – it's an excuse for consumer outrage.

That at least is the story so often told. Both in reality and in expectation, consumption in the affluent world apparently moves to a dizzy beat. Ours is, it would seem, a world of temporal velocity; a velocity in large part driven by the stuff we consume and the manner in which we consume it. For this reason, among others, a contemporary politics of 'slow living' has been both formative of and influenced by a re-energised critique of consumerism, particularly evident in the West. It is this critique, and the understanding of consumption as the thief of time, that I explore here.

In offering such an exploration, the first part of this chapter briefly surveys the field of anti-consumerist politics, particularly in relation to what contemporary critics, activists and a litany of theorists have had to say about the connection between temporality and commodity culture. In the second part I step back from this political and theoretical tradition in order to untangle and clarify the assumed connections between consumption and time. Analytically, this chapter seeks to be generative rather than merely critical; to reconstruct rather than dismiss an understanding of contemporary consumption as the vandal of a relaxed and contemplative life. Drawing on recent work in relation to social practice, it is suggested here that the doing of consumption and the doing of time are, of course, irrevocably overlapping, but that this relationship is not easily characterised through metaphors of speed. As some advocates of slow living have themselves observed, a vision of consumption as velocity threatens to relegate a politics of slow to a nostalgic critique of all that is ostensibly fast. In this context, the celebration of everything slow no doubt makes for a pithy and engaging branding of an alternative politics. Yet, this apparent alternative risks overlooking the subtleties and possibilities for change that are part-and-parcel of the very cosmopolitan world – including the practices of consumption – that it opposes.

The pace of anti-consumerism

Anti-consumerism as social critique, political activism and lifestyle change has undeniably enjoyed a big renaissance over the past decade or more, particularly in the consumer economies of the West. While there is a long tradition of academic and public intellectual critique of consumer culture, and a long history also of alternative living movements opposed to a commodification of everyday life, a renewed vigour and urgency has come to inflect debate about the ramifications and future of a globe geared to consumerism. This has been matched by an equally vigorous growth in political groupings and networks advocating responsible consumption. It has resulted also in the revitalisation of movements promoting various forms and degrees of simple or frugal living. Finally, as this book testifies, it has given rise to a renewed attention to the temporal imperatives, rhythms and pressures of consumer modernity. This too has translated into political and social action exemplified by the growth of 'decelerated living' movements of which Slow Food is perhaps the best known.[1]

This 'new politics of consumption', as Juliet Schor (2000) has dubbed it, is nothing if not diverse. The critical literature – mostly journalistic and accessible in style – now ranges from scholarly but highly readable contributions, such as Schor's *The Overspent American* (1998) or Robert H. Frank's *Luxury Fever* (1999), to a biting polemic on the Western 'affluenza' of never having enough stuff (see de Graaf et al. 2002; James 2007; Lawson 2009). What aligns these and many other such works is not so much a shared political line (although a social democratic liberalism pervades) but an opposition to wasteful, careless and status-driven consumption and a deep concern about what such consumerism is doing to nature, self and society.

The same target and concerns inform the activities of a range of groupings, networks and movements (of which there are now very many) that fall within the ambit of an anti-consumerist politics; from organisations such as Action Consommation in France or the Consumer Citizenship Network based in Norway, to the Centre for the New American dream in the USA or Adbusters in Canada. To these we could add many other political collectives and coalitions whose activities fade into a concern with issues of over-consumption and consumer culture; groups like Food Not Bombs, the International Society for Ecology and Culture or The Compact. Beyond the Western world, critique and activism in relation to the global consequences of Western consumerism and the global spread of consumer culture have been prominent in the writings of scholars and commentators such as Amartya Sen (1999), Martin Khor (2001) and Vandana Shiva (2005), and in the work of radical groups such as the Consumer's Association of Penang.[2]

The point to note here is that any identifiable new politics of consumption, any reinvigorated anti-consumerist sensibility, especially on a global level, evades identification as a stand-alone politics. Rather, as advocacy and activism, anti-consumerism arises out of and morphs constantly back into broader political concerns to do with environmental sustainability, global equity, democratic rights, social justice, existential equilibrium and the social and cultural 'health' of communities and nations.

What thus traverses the new politics of consumption, at least in its dominant Western manifestation, is a sense of the fourfold impact of consumerism and consumer culture. Environmental concerns are certainly primary, especially in terms of the impact of consumption on the depletion of resources and the production of consumer waste. Yet a contemporary anti-consumerism is not simply a politics of sustainability. The global inequities and the remaking of local economies wrought by the corporate globalisation of consumer capitalism animate the work of networks and movements oppositional to over-consumption just as forcefully as do environmental concerns.

Importantly also, it is the socio-cultural and personal ramifications of consumption that have occupied the work of many contemporary Western critics and inform the activities of alternative living movements in the affluent world. I have elsewhere observed the irony underlying a good deal of contemporary anti-consumerist polemics in which the environmental damage and the global injustice of high levels of Western consumption are resolutely acknowledged but most attention is then directed to the supposed impact of consumerism on the well-being of the *Western* individual and the moral state of the *Western* social fabric (Humphery 2010, p. 144).

Leaving aside this particular irony, and now bringing this discussion into clearer focus with the theme of this book, the new politics of consumption has tended unmistakeably to give renewed salience to certain abiding suppositions about the workings and consequences of a ubiquitous Western (and increasingly global) consumer culture. In both socio-cultural and existential terms, anti-consumerism connects a never satiated drive to consume, especially in affluent societies, to the dissolution of social and communal bonds and to the manufacture of a sense of self that is lost in a spendthrift and workaholic temporal maze of materialistic desire and status envy.

There's nothing especially out of the ordinary here. Public intellectuals and social movement activists have, after all, consistently and over many decades argued along these lines. So too, though through recourse to the conceptual armoury of mass modernities and postmodernities, have social and cultural theorists. In doing so, both the polemicists and the theorists draw on a common-sense logic of individualistic and acquisitive consumption as ultimately culturally destructive; a perspective that accords with how many Western citizens themselves feel about the 'consumer culture' in which they continue to live, despite economic downturn. Thus, while almost all consumption critics and activists now talk of the need for an environmentally sustainable mode of living, many also focus intently on how the consumerism driving the continued, if currently more muted, over-consumption of the affluent world undermines our sense of well-being and happiness; contributes to an ethos of overwork, haste and instantaneous gratification; underscores a bland, cultural homogenisation of life; and fragments communities and social relationships. This is a story of consumption that is both familiar and appealing to many. As such, it is not only meaningful in that it speaks of the felt reality of living in a consumerist society, but also politically useful in that it offers a narrative of destruction and the need for change that has motivated people to act – both individually and collectively – in opposition to a commodification of life.

This is why certain academic objections to the current anti-consumerist narrative of consumption as destruction, especially from those who insist that consumption is a complex activity, have little traction with consumption critics and activists outside the academy. Many of us working across disciplines such as sociology, geography, cultural studies and anthropology share in the political critique of consumerism. Yet we continue to insist that consumption and peoples' participation in it is not simply to be understood as mindless, meaningless and damaging. We might insist also that there is no simple connection to be made between contemporary affluent consumption and a supposed increase in rampantly materialistic and individualistic values, an apparent loss of caring communities or a straightforward temporal acceleration of everyday life.

But, so what? Right now, these interpretative nuances seem to detract from the need to raise the alarm; to demonstrate that a world geared – through good economic times and bad – to endlessly increasing levels of wasteful and unequally accessed consumption is not how we can or should live. The truth of the grand narrative – whether offered by polemicists, activists or theorists – of our consumption activity as highly damaging to nature, self and society remains far more readily accepted by those opposed to consumerism than a less morally cut-and-dry narrative that sees consumption as a material practice to be understood, not simply critiqued.

This kind of tension between what we might call an oppositional versus an interpretivist politics of consumption is well exemplified in relation to consumption and time. Alongside the central belief that contemporary consumption in the affluent world undermines the maintenance of lasting communities, consumerism has come for many to equal a loss of temporal sensibility and control. In fact, the new politics of consumption is very much a critique of the temporality of the consumer market place, not just of an obsession with stuff. Overwhelmingly, for anti-consumerist critics and activists, a culture of consumerism is essentially a culture of speed. As de Graaf et al. (2002, p. 39) insisted a decade ago, the consumer society creates a sense of 'time famine' driven by the acceleration of the (efficiency-oriented) pace of work and everyday life demanded by a consumer economy.

This point, one made also by Schor and others, has heavily informed the perspective of movements advocating downshifting and simple living. It has translated as well into an ancillary political movement through which American citizens have been urged to reclaim their time by refusing the pressure of increased working hours and the 'over-scheduling' of everyday life that arises as people attempt to juggle a plethora of work, social and consumption-oriented activities (de Graaf 2003). What has marked this North American discourse of contemporary anti-consumerism, particularly given the long tradition in the USA of transcendentalist frugality (and, indeed, of Puritanism), is a sense that consumption itself is merely a necessary activity that must be made subordinate to the 'real' pleasures to be derived from the non-material cultivation of the life of the mind and the emotions – and from the acceptance of our fundamental obligations to nature. All this is, in part, to be achieved through an awareness of time; through a re-awakening to its flow and through a concomitant reclaiming of considered action (Elgin 1993; Andrews 1998; Etzioni 2003).

A similar sensibility can, of course, be found elsewhere. For the now iconic and predominantly European-based Slow Food movement – arguably the major progenitor of a resurgent, late twentieth-century concern with consumption and time – a globalised consumer culture has been the chief harbinger of 'fast life'. As the chapters in this book document, the need to take purposeful control of the runaway speed of consumer modernity has from the outset informed the politics of slow. The Slow Food Manifesto (which has changed little since its adoption in 1989) is uncompromising in connecting the frenzied, industrialised consumption of the current era – emblematic of which is Fast Food – to a changed way of being; one enslaved to velocity (Petrini 2001). This perspective inflects the sister group CittaSlow, which extends the philosophy of Slow Food to the life of provincial towns. CittaSlow thus advocates for a return to a pre-globalisation governance and organisation of local communities that re-enlivens urban public space, connects townspeople to local, sustainable production and businesses, and emphasises a form of pleasurable living (including consumption) that is, above all, quiet and unrushed.[3]

This talk of pleasure – of 'quiet material pleasure', as the Slow Food manifesto puts it – unmistakeably tends to distinguish the advocacy of slow from that of the (predominantly US-based) promotion of downshifting and simple living. This contrast between the politics of slow and the politics of simplicity can no doubt be overemphasised (while it is equally clear that downshifting movements have taken hold in many countries beyond the USA). Nevertheless, a philosophy of slow does, in contrast with much talk of frugality, promote consumption as a continuing source of enjoyment and social connection. Rather than cast moral suspicion on the desire to consume, a politics of slow seeks to remake our consumer pleasures. Where simplicity and slowness thus intersect, and deeply so, is not in their approach to consumption *per se* but in their mutual critique of the manic, work-and-spend culture of consumer economies. That is, both the simple and the slow fundamentally reject the *pace* of consumer modernity.

It might be observed that few contemporary anti-consumerist arguments and perspectives are actually all that new. What is novel, however, is the particular sense of urgency with which we must now deal with consumption and its consequences in the face of both climate change and a clearly faltering global capitalism. The new politics of consumption is thus an of-the-moment redevelopment of long-held critical perspectives on consumerism. In this, it is a politics that rests easily with a now long tradition of social theoretical scholarship. This is especially so in relation to notions of fast consumption.

A vision of consumer modernity and its late or postmodern permutations as privileging a culture of speed is and remains one of the core assumptions underlying and shaping nineteenth- and twentieth-century social theory (not to mention successive literary and artistic movements). In his influential study of the experience of modernity, Marshall Berman bounced off and explored the evocative sentiment of the Mexican poet Octavio Paz, who insisted in the mid-1960s that modernity is 'cut off from the past and continually hurtling forward at such a dizzy pace that it cannot take root, that it merely survives from one day to the next...' (Berman 1983, p. 35) Consumption – or, more exactly, capitalist exchange – as a kind of motor of modernities has long been implicated (from Marx onward) in this hurtling forward. As the defining practice of contemporary economic and everyday life, consumption thus seemingly turns at the same rapid pace as 'modernity' itself.

This assumption has remained rock steady in the four decades separating the work of two of the pre-eminent Western theorists of consumption: Jean Baudrillard and Zygmunt Bauman. Prefiguring the edifice of postmodernity, Baudrillard by 1970 was insisting that 'We live by object time: by this I mean that we live at the pace of objects, live to the rhythm of their ceaseless succession' (1998, p. 25). For him, time occupies a privileged place in consumer society, not least because time itself – or rather abstract, measurable time – arises out of and has become one with commodity exchange. Time in 'primitive societies' (to use Baudrillard's term) does not in fact exist; it is simply the 'rhythm of repeated collective activities'. Time itself is thus invented *as* a commodity and *for* a commodity system. As such, it is earned (through work) and consumed (as the performance of leisure). Time in consumer society is never actually possessed as 'free' but is always experienced as 'constrained time' and always remains a 'functional mechanism'. As Baudrillard puts it, 'The time of consumption is that of production'; time is, quite simply, 'a rhythm of exchange' (1998, pp. 151–158).

Heralding the epoch of liquid (rather than post) modernity, Bauman too places consumption at the core of time. As he puts it, 'We can say that liquid modern consumerism is notable, more significantly than for anything else, for the (thus far unique) *renegotiation of the meaning of time*' (Bauman 2007, p. 32, his emphasis). What contemporary consumption – geared to a 'nowist' and 'hurried' culture – thus does is render life a series of perpetual presents. This is linked certainly to the desire to acquire and collect, but it is most pressingly connected with the imperative to constantly discard and replace (Bauman 2007, p. 36). The temporal gap between consumer desire and its satisfaction has thus become, in liquid modern times, a mere instant and, in the contemporary affluent world at least, consumerism becomes 'all about speed, excess and waste' (Bauman 2007, p. 8).

For both the contemporary anti-consumerist critic and the theorist, then, the issue is well and truly settled. To speak of consumerism and of consumer culture is to speak of the frenzy, instantaneity and shear velocity with which life must be lived in the consumer present.

Not so fast

I don't, here, want to spoil a good argument; it is undoubtedly the case that a consumer modernity in all its guises has fundamentally (and at times rapidly) altered the temporalities of life – especially in affluent nations. Our sensibility of being hurried and harried has a firm base in the temporal imperatives of the global production–consumption system. And yet, is contemporary consumption simply fast? Does consumption straightforwardly mirror the pace of the grand, amorphous force of 'speedernity'? To put it another way, is the fast–slow couplet an analytically good basis on which to question the temporalities of consumption and to forge an alternative? Frustratingly, the answer to these intertwined questions might be a qualified 'yes' and a firm 'no'.

It has clearly become difficult – at least in the context of anti-consumerist critique – to think of consumption outside the paradigm of speed. Like a spinning top on the surface of a table, consumption whirls frenetically toward a perilous edge. That consumerism is a dangerous and unsustainable logic is not in question, but liquid modern consumption is surely not a temporal singularity. To suggest that it is serves to close off a diverse understanding of and response to the time of consumption, the concrete rhythms of exchange (as thinkers like Baudrillard observed). The temporal paradox of contemporary consumption, particularly in the affluent world, is that it is both fast and slow, and everything in between. It is, in fact, *temporal juxtaposition* and *rhythmic variability* that characterise the cultures and practices of consumption. Recognising this is not simply an interpretative quibble: it is highly political, not least because it displaces the model of a bifurcated pace (the slow versus the fast) as the bedrock of understanding what a world of and beyond consumer culture is and could be like.

In the first place, dead time might well be at the core of the deadly fast. Even critics and theorists intent on mapping the frenzy of consumerism suggest that mania is not quite the full story – that underneath the tempest of exchange is cultural stasis or, worse still, the loss of time and rhythm itself. For many critics, the frenzy of consumption locks us into and disguises a comatose state. We both waste time consuming and have no time for thinking otherwise, thinking beyond our consumer desire. What thus seems fast actually takes us nowhere beyond a zombie-life as currently lived (Lasn 1999). In the realm of high theory, the time of consumption has long been linked – particularly with the advent of advanced information technologies – either to a postmodern implosion of the social (and with it the loss of all temporal and social rhythm) or to a late-capitalist shift from clock-time to temporal (and spatial) flows characterised by a disorienting and always unanchored instantaneity. This effectively precludes a grasp of 'human' time, since what is experienced as the temporal becomes increasingly abstracted from concrete social reality and is fundamentally emptied out by and through its relations with capital and commodity flows (Baudrillard 1983; Harvey 1990; Giddens 1990; Jameson 1991; Virilio 1986). Ironically, this suggests that in calling for a move beyond the temporality of consumerism, a politics of slow heralds a shift away from timelessness as much as from speedy time.

But all this is still to dwell in the realm of epochal shifts – from slow traditionality to fast modernity – and in the meta-level theoretical abstraction attending such visions. A contemporary politics of slow, and the assumption of fast life and frenzied consumption undergirding it, meets empirical rather than solely theoretical challenge in two key ways. The most straightforward contestation has involved the perennial issue of the 'leisure society'. Time-use data, routinely gathered for decades by government agencies and as part of various time-use studies for a century or more, do not straightforwardly indicate that affluent nations have experienced easily characterised shifts in the time individuals devoted to work and leisure. Indeed, time-use scholars point to a glaring irony: while many of us may well feel hurried and harried, time-use data suggest that, historically, Western populations have moved gradually toward enjoying more and more leisure time. This is a salient reminder of the dubiousness of terms such as 'time-famine'. Yet, the difficulty here is that such evidence courts a contestable dualism between work as constrained time and leisure as slow time. As we have noted above, leisure time is not simply a free space but has become increasingly commodified, and is now the busy temporal site into which a range of life activities are crammed. Equally, time-use data, while perhaps indicating a general population trend toward leisure, do not account for late twentieth-century rationalising shifts in the capitalist organisation of work. These shifts have wrought greater division between socio-economic cohorts and, in the context of an intensification of consumer culture, have pushed the professional middle classes in particular into generating income at the expense of attending to life beyond paid work.[4] It is thus no surprise, nor has it gone uncritiqued, that a central, underlying feature of the contemporary politics of consumption and lifestyle change is that it tends to speak to a particular social stratum (Maniates 2002; Humphery 2010; Littler 2009). This stratum is, nevertheless, one that is economically significant, politically connected and culturally influential.

Beyond the metrics of leisure, however, it is the renewed turn to consumption as social practice that, at least within the academy, has substantially challenged currently popular critical perceptions of the slow and the fast. This challenge has not come from a hostility toward the new politics of consumption but from an insistence that contemporary sensibilities of time – and the material practices that express these sensibilities – cannot be reduced to a notion of linear, historical transition from one temporal epoch to the next, nor to a view of social life as simply dominated by an ethos of acceleration. As Elizabeth Shove, Frank Trentmann and Richard Wilk (2009) insist, in introducing their recent collection of essays on consumption and time, traditional and modern temporal orders run in parallel with each other while natural and commercial temporal rhythms co-evolve and co-exist. This is to understand the social as made up of multiple periodicities or different temporal orders that are expressed in concrete social and material practices – that is, in everyday routines, habits and modes of action and in the socio-technical systems in which they are embedded. These practices speak not of a performance of a singular time but of different and overlapping rhythms and temporal flows. Moreover, the temporality of social practices is not simply shaped by external forces. Rather, the myriad of daily practices involved in working, resting, eating, cleaning, caring, socialising, shopping and so on are both enacted at different speeds and breathe life into the flow of time itself. Given that many of our daily social practices involve material and cultural consumption, this implies that our interaction with commodities is a central means by which we reproduce and transform given temporal regimes, routines and sensibilities. Consumption, in other words, is not the vehicle through which we are simply robbed of our time. As Shove, Trentmann and Wilk observe,

> This is an important shift in perspective in that it suggests that consumption – the arch-villain in critiques of hurriedness – contributes to the *making* of time, and is not simply a drain, a sink which takes time away from living.... [C]onsumption, broadly defined as a bundle of various practices and the use of things, constitutes an arena in which daily life is woven together... in ways that configure and reproduce its temporal texture.
>
> (Shove, Trentmann and Wilk 2009, p. 4)

For the purposes of this chapter, this is merely to insist, at the most basic level, that we consume in a manner that partakes of various temporalities. Thus seasonality continues to exist alongside the always available in terms of what we eat, window shopping (both physically and online) rivals the frenetic supermarket trip, holidays of lying on the beach compete with the organised whirlwind tour, the rapid take-away meal gives way to the leisurely dinner party and the quick Google for information remains matched with the reading of books and the slow flick of a magazine. These are all contemporary practices of consumption – and all are embroiled in resource use and the production of waste, the forging of sociality and identity, the utilisation of income and credit and the maintenance of local and global inequalities. But – and this is the key point – they are not all fast: they move at a variable pace.

On one level, this insistence on the temporal variability of social practice – including the contemporary practices of consumption – seems to positively glide past a politics of slow and to return us to the division between those who want to explore the detailed texture of material life and those for whom such ethnographic exploration evades the need to oppose a runaway world. The exploratory ethos is articulated well by Shove, Trentmann and Wilk (2009, p. 7) in arguing that 'The lives of objects and the lives of people intersect, but it is never possible to say one is simply driving the other.' Thus, when it comes to the contemporary practices of consumption, not only is agency dispersed but the progress of those practices is never simply known *a priori*. Rather, the nature and ramifications of a consumption practice – including its relation to the use and conception of time – unfolds through the practice itself. Consumption routines and regimes, from those connected with shopping, recreation or travelling to those embroiled in the household consumption of resources, are not merely solidified and always expressive of the one consumerist and hurried disposition toward commodities and commodified time. On the contrary, the routines of consumption are enacted in ways that both reproduce and disrupt given patterns of everyday life and culture.

Such a perspective seems a long way from the fundamentals of a politics of slow. This is, after all, a politics that rests for many of its advocates on an unwavering belief that the objects of the commodity world – and the culture of instanteneity in which they are encased – do in fact drive consciousness and action, including our sense and use of time. In this context, the insistence that people and objects merely intersect can be seen as politically timid. And, indeed it is: since an interpretative uncertainty is the very marker of attempting to locate possibilities for change in patterns of everyday action and agency, rather than in the adoption of overarching political certainties and projects by conscious minorities.

We should not overlook, however, the potential for a fruitful collision between the advocates of slow and the analysts of everyday routine, nor the fact that a politics of slow is not so easily characterised as merely obsessed with velocity. Wendy Parkins and Geoffrey Craig, for example, in their theoretically sophisticated exploration of slow living, rightly accept that 'the global everyday is not characterised by singular experiences of speed and geographical dislocation but by the negotiation of an increasingly complex co-existence of different temporalities and spatial contexts'. Slow living is thus 'a result of, and response to, the radically uneven and heterogeneous production of space and time in post-traditional societies' (Parkins and Craig 2006, p. 10). Interestingly, Dale Southerton, in drawing on theories of practice rather than on a politics of slow, makes a not dissimilar point in his comparative, qualitative study of daily life in the UK in 1937 and 2000. Life in both historical moments, he found, was felt to be harried and hurried, but the essential difference in 2000 was that such language was used more extensively, while 'the temporal rhythms of the contemporary period are characterised by the growing necessity for personal coordination of practices'. What he thus concludes is that 'Collective rhythms and routines of daily life remain [in 2000], only they are not "institutionally ordered" in the same way as they were in 1937' (2009, p. 62). In other words, just as we must, in the contemporary world, constantly sift through and select commodities, we must also constantly order the temporalities of everyday life.

Is there, then, a kind of theoretical middle-ground to be had in understanding the temporalities of contemporary consumer culture; one that admits of increasing velocity (as in a politics of slow) but rejects speed as a ubiquitous force? This is indeed the position adopted by Parkins and Craig when they insist that 'a temporality of speed dominates contemporary culture', but emphasise also the need to recognise the differential temporalities of modernity (2006, p. 42, their emphasis). There are certainly problems with this position, in that it appears to both adopt and then evade theories of a runaway world. But this is really no more problematic than a reduction of history to the unfolding of everyday practice, understood as an always indeterminant intersecting of bodies and things. Theoretical difficulties aside, what is being recognised by all concerned here is the temporal diversity, the differing pace, of everyday actions – including the actions of consumption. A politics of slow has in fact been instrumental in revalorising temporal diversity; a diversity always enacted through what we individually and collectively do as producers and consumers (among other things). On the other hand, what theories of practice enticingly suggest is that producing and consuming differently arises not simply from mindful and considered action – as theories of slow advocate – but from practice itself. Here, changing the way we consume is not about individual consciousness and conduct, though this remains of import, but about entrusting life to collectively held and nurtured routines, regimes and habits that work to lift us out of the need for permanent mindfulness and enable bodies, things, knowledge and values to move through time *well*.

Notes

1. The term anti-consumerism is used throughout this chapter to refer to an opposition to the dominant logic of over-consumption embedded in consumer capitalism. Over-consumption generally refers to the tendency to consume goods and services at a level over and above that which is necessary to maintain a reasonable standard of living and at a rate that is greater than can be sustained environmentally in terms of resource provision and the handling of waste. Importantly, the characteristic over-consumption of affluent nations must be contrasted with the underconsumption of economically impoverished populations. For an extended discussion of this, see my recent book, *Excess: Anti-Consumerism in the West* (Cambridge: Polity, 2010).

2. For more information about the various groups mentioned in this paragraph, see www.actionconsommation.org; www.hihm.no/concit/; www.newdream .org; www.adbusters.org; www.foodnotbombs.net; www.isec.org.uk; sfcompact.blogspot.com; www.cap.org.my/.
3. For more about Slow Food and Slow Cities, see www.slowfood.com and www .cittaslow.net.
4. For a useful brief discussion of this research, see Dale Southerton's 'Re-ordering Temporal Rhythms: Coordinating Daily Practices in the UK in 1937 and 2000', in Elizabeth Shove, Frank Trentmann and Richard Wilk (eds.) *Time, Consumption and Everyday Life: Practice, Materiality and Culture*, Berg, Oxford, pp. 49–50.

References

Andrews, C., 1998, *The Circle of Simplicity: Return to the Good Life*, Harper Perennial, New York.

Baudrillard, J., 1983, *Simulations*, Semiotext(e), New York.

——, 1998, *The Consumer Society: Myths and Structures*, Sage, London.

Bauman, Z., 2007, *Consuming Life*, Polity, Cambridge.

Berman, M., 1983, *All That Is Solid Melts into Air: The Experience of Modernity*, Verso, London.

de Graaf, J. (ed.), 2003, *Take Back Your Time: Fighting Overwork and Time Poverty in America*, Berrett-Koehler, San Francisco.

de Graaf, J., Wann, D. and Naylor, T. H., 2002, *Affluenza: The All-Consuming Epidemic*, Berrett-Koehler, San Francisco.

Elgin, D., 1993, *Voluntary Simplicity: Towards a Way of Life That Is Outwardly Simple, Inwardly Rich*, Harper, New York.

Etzioni, A., 2003, 'Introduction: voluntary simplicity: psychological implications, societal consequences', in D. Doherty and A. Etzioni (eds.) *Voluntary Simplicity: Responding to Consumer Culture*, Rowman & Littlefield, Oxford, pp. 1–25.

Frank, R. H., 1999, *Luxury Fever: Money and Happiness in an Era of Excess*, Princeton University Press, New Jersey.

Giddens, A., 1990, *The Consequences of Modernity*, Polity, Cambridge.

Harvey, D., 1990, *The Condition of Postmodernity: An Enquiry into the Origins of Cultural Change*, Blackwell, Oxford.

Humphery, K., 2010, *Excess: Anti-Consumerism in the West*, Polity, Cambridge.

James, O., 2007, *Affluenza*, Vermilion, London.

Jameson, F., 1991, *Postmodernism: Or the Cultural Logic of Late Capitalism*, Duke University Press, Durham.

Khor, M., 2001, *Rethinking Globalization: Critical Issues and Policy Choices*, Zed Books, London.

Lasn, K., 1999, *Culture Jam*, Eagle Books, New York.

Lawson, N., 2009, *All Consuming*, Penguin, London.

Littler, J., 2009, *Radical Consumption: Shopping for Change in Contemporary Culture*, Open University Press, Maidenhead.

Maniates, M., 2002, 'Individualization: plant a tree, buy a bike, save the world?', in T. Princen, M. Maniates and K. Conca (eds.) *Confronting Consumption*, MIT Press, Cambridge, pp. 43–66.

Parkins, W. and Craig, G., 2006, *Slow Living*, University of New South Wales Press, Sydney Press.

Petrini, C., 2001, *Slow Food: The Case for Taste*, Columbia University Press, New York.

Schor, J., 1998, *The Overspent American: Why We Want What We Don't Need*, Harper Perennial, New York.

———, 2000, 'The new politics of consumption', in J. Cohen and J. Rogers (eds.) *Do Americans Shop Too Much?* Beacon Press, Boston, pp. 3–33.

Sen, A., 1999, *Commodities and Capabilities*, Oxford University Press, New Delhi.

Shiva, V., 2005, *Earth Democracy: Justice Sustainability and Peace*, South End Press, Cambridge.

Southerton, D., 2009, Re-ordering temporal rhythms: coordinating daily practices in the UK in 1937 and 2000', in E. Shove, F. Trentmann and R. Wilk (eds.) *Time, Consumption and Everyday Life: Practice, Materiality and Culture*, Berg, Oxford, pp. 49–63.

Shove, Elizabeth, Trentmann, Frank and Wilk, Richard (eds.), 2009, *Time, Consumption and Everyday Life: Practice, Materiality and Culture*, Berg, Oxford, pp. 49–50

Virilio, P., 1986, *Speed and Politics*, semiotext(e), New York.

2

From Fast Fashion to Connected Consumption: Slowing Down the Spending Treadmill

Juliet B. Schor

The year 2011 was ecologically ominous. Record temperatures, extreme drought, virulent hurricanes and rapidly escalating food prices provided vivid evidence that climate change is upon us, that resource scarcities are intensifying and that humans have gone beyond safe planetary boundaries in our efforts to produce and consume. The science of ecology is complex, but the degradation now being visited on the earth can also be thought about in relatively simple terms. One of those is time. The rhythms of human impacts and natural systems are not in synch, and eco-degradation is the predictable result. Greenhouse gases are emitted too quickly for the earth's sinks (e.g. forests and oceans) to absorb them. Waste is generated too rapidly to break down and be re-incorporated into natural cycles. Maturing trees are cut down too soon and fishing stocks are depleted at too accelerated a rate. When the speed of production and consumption increases, nature does not adjust benignly: it roars back to re-establish its own temporal equilibrium (World Wildlife Fund 2010; Meadows, Meadows and Randers 1992; Wackernagel et al. 2002; Rockström et al. 2009).

The mismatch of the temporal rhythms of humans and nature is at the core of contemporary society and culture, particularly in the wealthy countries of the global North, but also in the global South. One way to understand development or economic growth is that it entails a speeding-up of economic and social life. More rapid growth is made possible by a faster cycling of raw materials, products, finance and even social meanings. Achieving an ecologically sustainable economy will require decelerating, on many levels. This chapter is about how that deceleration is beginning to happen in the consumer sphere. For it is only by matching humans' time scale to nature's that we can create an indefinitely reproducing (or sustainable) relationship with the planet. In the pages that follow, I detail how that balance careened badly out of synch, and how recent developments may be showing the way to a temporal rhythm that does not entail disaster for human and other living populations.

A problem with prices: the cheapening of apparel

The core of modern economic thinking is that prices are brilliant indicators of scarcity. They measure the relation between supply and demand across the many markets for goods and services. When supply is short, prices rise. When demand goes up, prices rise. Apparel is a fascinating case that reveals the dysfunction at the heart of the global economy. It's at the heart of the dangerous speed-up of recent decades, and its market price tells that story.

Throughout human history, apparel has been expensive. This has been true in most societies around the world for most of their histories. Producing a textile has traditionally required materials that are costly to produce, such as cotton, silk, linen and wool. Turning raw materials into cloth involves the time-intensive labour of spinning, knitting or weaving. This accounts for the fact that textiles were the most important commodity in the emergence of the modern global economy in the seventeenth and nineteenth centuries (Parthasarathi 2011). Decorative textiles and apparel were highly prized, required multiple skills to produce and commanded a nice price when offered for sale. Even everyday wear was relatively highly valued.

This basic economic reality resulted in a particular kind of social life for clothing (Appadurai 1986). Once fashioned, a garment would traditionally have a long life, which ranged over a variety of uses (Lemire 2005; Roche 1994). Consider the social trajectory of a garment originally slated for special occasion wear. Initially it would be worn relatively infrequently, at high-status events and functions. Over time it would appear at fewer of those and be donned more frequently for everyday outside use. As it began to wear out or develop blemishes it might be relegated to indoor, domestic wear. Eventually it would become unsuitable even for the most private settings, and so end its life as a textile rather than a garment. In that role it could be a household cloth, and eventually a rag or quilting square. Apparel might literally turn to dust in these cases, having had a long and productive social life.

Garments also moved across social classes during their lives. For example, in their classic account of the origins of the consumer revolution in the UK, McKendrick et al. (1982) noted that apparel was handed down from elite women to their servants. Recent historical contributions find that used clothing has traditionally been so valuable that it has served as a local or alternative currency in the extensive second-hand economies that have existed for centuries alongside markets in new goods. Beverly Lemire has found an 'overwhelming prominence of apparel as the primary article of exchange', second only to metals and precious stones (2005, p. 97). Only those goods that have, and hold, high value can serve as alternative currencies, and apparel has historically been the most important.

That history puts the present situation into stark relief. In the West, and the USA in particular, apparel has become perhaps the cheapest of the cheap commodities. New, branded, fashionable clothing can be acquired at strikingly low prices. In recent years, shirts can have been available for 99 cents. Free garments, particularly T-shirts, are ubiquitous. Used apparel can even be purchased by weight, rather than by the piece, at prices in the neighbourhood of $1–1.50 per pound. This makes clothing even cheaper by weight than many basic foodstuffs.

As a result, a surfeit of clothing has developed. Sale prices at mass retailers are eye-poppingly low. Internet searches reveal offerings of large lots of unused clothes, including by popular designers, at rock bottom prices. In the used clothing market, the excess is even greater. Supply moves out of households into a variety of outlets – the municipal waste stream, consignments shops and thrifts, and charitable organisations. The latter sell the top-quality and best-conditioned garments directly to consumers domestically, offload a high fraction to traders who export to the global South for re-sale, and sell what's left by the pound to shoddy mills that grind them up for upholstery. Through the 1990s and until the financial collapse of 2008, the supply of used garments was expanding rapidly. Goodwill and other charities could barely keep up with what was being supplied. By the end of the 1990s, my interviews with Goodwill officials revealed that they were only able to put a small fraction of what they collected into their stores. By the millennium, used clothing in the USA was so abundant that it became cumbersome even to give it away. The nation was awash in apparel. Its price was nearly zero or, in many cases, at that level.

What caused this shift to such low-priced clothing? Industry sources tout improvements in productivity, particularly in the distribution and inventory stage, and also in manufacture. And these have occurred. But they are only one of three major factors. The other two are far more noxious. One is the 'global sweatshop', a phenomenon that accelerated after 1980 as companies in the global North outsourced textile and apparel making to a series of low-wage countries. This history has been widely reported (Ross 1997; Ross 2004; Collins 2003; Shell 2009). By the millénnium, China was dominating those markets, but the previous decades had seen the appearance of a global sweatshop. Around the world, a female labour force was subjected to unspeakable exploitation and brutality, often working below subsistence wages for long hours. The Asian financial crisis of the late 1990s further eroded wages and working conditions, and reduced the price of both new and used clothing in the export markets (Schor 2000).

The final factor has been the failure to pay ecological costs. Textile and apparel production are resource intensive and ecologically degrading (Robins and Humphrey 2000; Schor 2000). But the impacts of toxic dyes, greenhouse gas emissions, water use and contamination, soil depletion and pesticide use are ignored. The manufacturers do not pay for what they do to local water supplies, worker and consumer health, farmland, atmosphere or climate. They pollute without accountability. Therefore they can afford to offer an artificially low price.

The fast-fashion model

Predictably, cheapness results in more purchases and a faster turnover of household clothing inventories. The average American consumer more than doubled his or her annual acquisition of clothing between 1991 and 2006, from 34.7 pieces of outer and underwear to 68. That's one new piece every 5.4 days (Schor 2010). Mass-market retailers offered prices that led to a culture of disposable fashion (Lee 2003). People bought more – much more. The industry shifted its operations onto a much shorter timeline (Abernathy et al. 1999), so that styles in the shops changed much more rapidly. On the consumer side, acquisition became indiscriminate, the period of usage became shorter, and discard more frequent. We don't have hard data on how long people keep clothing in their closets, or then garages or attics, but we do know that the cycle sped up, and rapidly. I call it the fast-fashion model.

The fashion cycle has a long sociological pedigree, beginning most famously with Georg Simmel, but Thorstein Veblen's account of consumption also incorporates fashion (Simmel 1957; Veblen 1899). More recent discussions include Crane (2001), Craik (1994) and the provocative account of Lipovetsky (2002), who sees fashion as central to

Western culture and democracy. Postmodern and other analyses of the growing importance of style and image also include the concept of fashion (Baudrillard 2001; Ewen 1988). Work on the aestheticisation of daily life, such as Mike Featherstone's widely cited work (1991) or Wolfgang Haug's concept of commodity aesthetics (1986), are also relevant. As everyday commodities become objects of aesthetic aspirations, they are drawn into a faster-moving aesthetic or fashion sensibility. Branding and advertising shape new symbolic meanings for goods, raising their social valuations. And so the cycle of purchase, diffusion and, eventually, discard accelerates.

This brings us back to the social life of clothes. A key point about recent apparel history is that the historic cascade of uses within a family or a social network (as in the case of elites passing on garments to their servants) has been disrupted. The rapid cycle of acquisition and discard associated with 68 purchases of new items a year meant that items were increasingly given or thrown away long before their useful or functional lives were over. Perfectly wearable garments began to be cast out of households. Even once-worn or brand-new clothing became a not insignificant portion of discards, as one could see from perusing the racks at thrift or consignment shops, yard sales or online vendors. The useful life of a piece of apparel was increasingly likely to diverge from its social life. Indeed, the scale at which this divergence was occurring suggested a mass 'social death' of these items, occurring alongside relatively greater stability in their functional or useful lives. (I say 'relative greater stability', because it is also true that for the bottom segment of the market, some garments did wear out more quickly because they were more cheaply tailored. On the other hand, a number of the newer synthetic materials, such as polyesters and microfibres, are more long-lasting than natural ones.) This disjuncture, between the useful and social lives of things, made apparel ripe for reform. But before we get to that story, we need to consider other commodities, and the spread of the fast-fashion model to many more items.

Beyond apparel: the expansion of fast-fashion

In the USA the apparel case is not unique. Looking at data on units purchased as well as the total volume of consumption (by weight), my research suggests that a fast-fashion dynamic has taken hold across a range of consumer goods. This is not a simple proposition to research – spending data are typically collected in units of monetary value. (Because of its historic importance and the long history of import controls, apparel is an exception in terms of readily available data on numbers of garments.) Dollar values do not reveal how many items are actually being purchased, and when prices change, monetary value represents a changing number of items. Only partial data on units are available, from measurements of imports. I have combined these with value data on domestic production to arrive at estimates of trends in purchasing for a variety of commodity categories. (This research is discussed in more detail in Schor 2010 and 2013, where data sources and methods are detailed. The years covered are from 1998 to 2007, the last year of growth before the financial collapse.) These data are collected in both weights and, where possible, units, the former being especially useful for measuring ecological impact, and the latter being most relevant to the fashion cycle.

My estimates indicate that from 1998 to 2005/7, the volume of imported consumption rose rapidly, both within individual categories and across manufacturing as a whole. Consider the case of furniture. During this period, IKEA, a low-cost producer specialising in up-to-date design, increased its presence in the US market considerably. Adding together 51 detailed categories of furniture (e.g. cotton mattresses, cellulose mattresses), I found that in 1998 there were 327.6 million pieces of furniture of all types imported into the USA. In 2005 the total was 651.3 million, representing a 99% increase. Domestic production also rose during this period.

A fashion cycle has also taken root in consumer electronics. According to my calculations, the number of imported cell phones rose from 14.2 million in 1998 to 177.2 million in 2005, a 12-fold rise. Laptops rose from 3.3 million to 23.8 million, a 7-fold expansion. But the increase has occurred not only in newer technologies. Ordinary household items, such as vacuum cleaners, more than doubled (67–188 million), ovens, toasters and coffeemakers rose from 76 million to 227 million. A subset of 10 small electronics categories for which I have calculated unit volumes increased from 715 million units in 1998 to 1.4 billion in 2005, a nearly 100% increase.

The consumption of ceramics doubled, although in this case the fast-fashion effect was joined by the remodelling boom to increase demand for bathroom fixtures and tiles. The weight of vehicles purchased increased by roughly 70%. Sales of knick-knacks, sporting goods, toys, jewellery, footwear and a variety of other manufactured goods also rose sharply. For the manufacturing sector as a whole, purchases far outstripped previous rates. Fashion was pervading the consumer sector as the rate of acquisition of items accelerated markedly.

From fast to slow spending: changing consumer attitudes and economic conditions

The financial collapse of 2007 and the subsequent economic downturn ended the dizzying pace of consumer purchasing that characterised the previous 10 years. As one might expect, the economic crash brought the fast-fashion model to a sudden halt. Although I have not extended my calculations of commodities by weight and units, there are considerable conventional economic data to suggest that the consumer treadmill slowed dramatically. In apparel, one category for which accessible data are available for 2007 and 2008, consumption declined in both those years. Units of footwear purchased also declined in 2007 and 2008 (American Apparel and Footwear Association 2009). Consumer credit, which had fuelled many purchases, dried up, as did consumers' appetite to take on liabilities. Saving increased markedly, to 5%, after its boom-year low of 1% (US Department of Commerce 2011).

The frequently cited index of consumer sentiment, which was at approximately 130 in 2007, fell to about 40 in late 2008 and has not recovered (and at the time of writing, mid-2011, it stood at 44.5%) (2007–2008 figures from Wikipedia (2011a); mid-2011 from the Conference Board (2011)). A central factor in consumers' grim outlook was that recovery failed to materialise. After the severe contraction of 2008–2009, stagnation plagued the economy, and the labour market in particular. By late 2011, four years after the original financial panic, more than 25 million Americans were either wholly or partly unemployed. The fraction of the population in employment fell to 58% (Bureau of Labour Statistics 2011), its lowest level since 1979, and a record 15% of Americans were receiving federal food stamp assistance (Cooke 2011). Economic growth was at a standstill, and the size of the economy, in comparison with its peak in 2007, was actually smaller. Under these conditions, attitudes toward consumption were bound to change.

One marker of that shift was the reversal in what had been, since the 1970s, a steady upward trend in consumer goods being regarded as necessities rather than luxuries. Once the recession hit, the fraction of the population telling pollsters that clothes dryers, microwaves, TVs, home air-conditioning and dishwashers were necessities dropped substantially (Morin and Taylor 2009). In other surveys, people expressed newfound enthusiasm for saving. Consumers articulated strong intentions to pay down debt, a determination that subsequently showed up in financial data. Researchers also found a new cultural attitude toward spending. One report described it as a shift from an orientation of me and mine toward a more communal sensibility. People expressed remorse about their prior freewheeling attitude to spending, in which they lived for the moment and without much thought for others. There was a turning-away from materialism, consumer excess and hedonism (Context-Based Research Group and Carton Donofrio Partners Inc. 2008).

In addition to the economic factors driving changes in consumption attitudes and patterns, concerns about ecological impacts began to intensify, driven largely by heightened attention to climate change. By the end of the 2000s, a Harris poll found that 53% of Americans reported that they had made changes in their lifestyle in order to make it more sustainable (Harris Interactive Poll 2008). Among that group, about half reported buying locally produced foods and/or goods. About the same fraction reported buying 'green' household products and energy-saving appliances. By mid-2009 only 13% of Americans had *not* engaged in any of a list of nine environmentally oriented behaviours, such as changing light bulbs, going paperless, installing low-flow showers and buying a more fuel-efficient vehicle (Harris Interactive Poll 2009). While attitudes toward climate change did begin to reverse at the end of the 2000s (Leiserowitz et al. 2011), the 'greening' of the consumer sector, at least on some dimensions, appeared to have become sufficiently entrenched among a sub-set of the population that its momentum continued. Particularly as mass-market brands introduced organic, eco- and non-toxic products, purchases of organic foods and beverages, cleaners, natural health and beauty aids, organic fibres and hybrid vehicles were all on a steeply rising curve.

The third factor leading to a shift from fast to slow consumption is generational. Generational theory is controversial, and I do not intend an uncritical adoption of it. However, the innovators and early adopters of slow consumption have been disproportionately young people (roughly those in the 18–35 age range, often termed the 'Millennial Generation'). This group is generally understood to be highly oriented to technology, and surveys show that they use digital technologies at a higher rate than previous generations. They are also heavily involved in social networking technology, which is a precursor to the sharing platforms of slow consumption described below. Their coming of age in the last decade is a currently unquantified, but likely important, dimension of the emergence of slow consumption (or what I have termed 'connected consumption').

Consumer innovations: connecting, reducing and saving

As the effects of economic stagnation rippled through the nation, a movement of young innovators attempted to transform the sphere of consumption. Their vision was centred on 'sharing' (rather than owning), re-using (rather than replacing) and optimising use of assets (rather than ignoring idle capacity). The movement they represented was originally dubbed the 'sharing' economy, and later came to be known as 'collaborative consumption', as the result of a popular book and website of that name. I call it 'connected consumption' to emphasise its social dimensions. All three terms refer to a wide and varied range of old, revamped and new practices whose central characteristics are the ability to save or make money, reduce ecological footprint and strengthen social ties. Not all of the practices have all three of these characteristics, but most do. And there is considerable scope for debate about the boundaries of the phenomenon. What is common to many of them, however, is that they slow down the cycle of acquisition and discard that characterises the fast-fashion model, as well as the speed at which energy and materials move through the economy. They are therefore appropriately seen as a form of 'slow spending'.

Collaborative Consumption Hub, which is collecting examples, claims that there are more than 1000 collaborative consumption initiatives operating around the world (Collaborative Consumption Hub n.d.). Our research has found that many of these are in the beta-stage, have not yet attracted users or are characterised by very low usage, so this is likely a gross overstatement. However, to our knowledge there is not yet a serious quantification of the size and extent of the phenomenon. Yet, there are still a considerable and growing number of functioning sites with significant participation across a range of different services. Indeed, by 2011, *Time* magazine had identified 'collaborative consumption' as one of its 10 ideas that will change the world. And a few months later, *Atlantic* magazine predicted that 'sharing is the inevitable next stage of the information revolution' (Gansky 2011). While the phenomenon is still in its early stages in many product and service categories, its combination of economic rationality, technological infrastructure and cultural appeal will likely lead it to grow significantly over the next decade (Schor 2010). If it does, it has the potential to reduce ecological footprint substantially in a number of key areas.

Connected consumption practices fall into four major categories – re-circulating goods, exchanging services, optimising use of assets and building social connections. Chronologically, the first innovation came with organisations devoted to the *re-circulation of goods*. eBay and Craig's List grew dramatically from their common 1995 origin year through the 2000s. They are both online sites for individuals to exchange used products and they are now for-profit entities. Both eventually moved beyond their beginnings to encompass a much wider range of offerings. The intensification of purchasing that occurred in the late 1990s and 2000s was undoubtedly key to their success because it led to a ready supply of items for sale. The growth of fast fashion was therefore crucial to the emergence of the connected consumption phenomenon: the large volumes and social excess of goods that fast fashion created led to the development of so-called secondary markets (i.e. those where goods are exchanged a second time). In addition, digital technology and sophisticated online software reduced what had traditionally been high transaction costs in these secondary markets. These transaction costs include the search time necessary to find buyers, given the relative absence of middle-men; buyers' need for good reputational information about sellers; and the relative shortage of cash which is more common among participants in secondary markets. So a combination of technological and economic changes facilitated the growth of connected consumption.

eBay and Craig's List are now enormous entities, and their example has been followed by many similar ventures. There are now dozens, if not hundreds, of internet sites that facilitate the exchange of used goods. They range from those that handle many products, to specialised sites for toys, apparel, books and DVDs. (There is even a site for exchanging used make-up.) Modes of exchange include two-way trades, gifting, sale and multiple-party exchanges.

Apparel has been an especially fertile area for secondary outlets on account of the history detailed above. Swapstyle is a cashless clothing exchange site that has been operating for more than six years and boasts more than 1 million items on offer and 40,000 participants. Registrants browse a worldwide inventory of fashion items and negotiate swaps with others on the site. The company's tagline is 'Open your worldwide wardrobe and start guilt free shopping.' Guilt here refers mainly to not overspending, but the company also prominently displays its green credentials. There are numerous other clothing-exchange sites that operate online, such as 99 Dresses, I-Ella, Rehashclothes and ThredUp, in addition to a growing number of local, face-to-face clothing exchange organisations and events.

But apparel does not exhaust the universe of what's available. An enormous range of commodities can be swapped, traded or purchased online using a variety of exchange formulae through general swap and exchange sites, such as swap, *Netcycler* (netcycler.co.uk) and *Bartercard* (bartercard.co.uk). Some facilitate two-way trades, such as the barter and swap sites. Freecycle emphasises the creation of a 'community' and operates with a gift model. There, people join a local community and all exchange is free. The expectation is that members both give and receive, and over time develop social bonds (Rademacher et al. 2007). Another variant of the exchange model is the sale of new, but home- or handmade, items. Etsy, which is a craft market place, is the largest and best known of these sites.

Another early innovator was Zipcar, founded by Robin Chase, a visionary entrepreneur with a strong sustainability motive. This was a membership organisation that placed vehicles in convenient locations in urban areas and rented them out for short periods. A central goal was to reduce urban car ownership. Over time, car sharing became very popular, particularly among young people, whose car ownership is lower than previous generations. Eventually the concept went mainstream. Major car rental companies began to offer hourly rentals. Zipcar expanded dramatically and recently began a partnership with Ford Motor Company. The rationale behind Zipcar represents the second major type of connected consumption – schemes for *optimising the use of durable goods or other economically productive assets.*

In a wealthy economy, individuals and households can afford to purchase durable goods that are used only intermittently, or to own assets, such as land, housing and other buildings, which are not operated to capacity. Examples include spare bedrooms, an unused garage or other storage space, unproductive lawns and square footage to spare in office environments. However, as joblessness rose and the economic prospects for the future dimmed, deploying unused assets for economic gain took on added appeal. A range of schemes for offering and benefitting from idle capacity began to emerge. Sharing or renting became increasingly popular.

After Zipcar, the concept spread quickly. The more conventional sharing schemes were focused on durable goods, such as lawn mowers, tools, expensive equipment for specialised uses and the like. In fact, some of them had histories that long antedated Zipcar, such as tool libraries, which were typically in low-income communities. These efforts tended to be small and local in order to facilitate the transfer and use of heavy items as well as to solve the problems of trust and credibility that arise with lending schemes. A number of neighbourhood sites attempted to replicate that functionality online, but with a local focus, by including durable goods sharing as one dimension of their efforts. These include *Share Some Sugar* (sharesomesugar.com), the Front Porch, Neigh*goods, *Hey, Neighbor* (http://heyneighbor.com) and *Neighborgoods* (http://neighborgoods.net/).

In 1999, Couchsurfing put together people with empty couches (or beds) who were willing to lend them to people looking for a cheap way to travel. Couchsurfing is a non-profit, B-corporation now operating on a large scale around the world. (It currently boasts about 45,000 weekly stays.) It aims to create 'a better world' through fostering new social experiences and connections. It led to AirBnB, which is a for-profit bed and breakfast in which people host travellers in their spare rooms, as well as Roomarama, Crashpadder and Tourboarder. Practices such as ratings, comments and feedback have helped to solve the problems of trust and reputation that are present in a context where people are opening their homes or lending expensive possessions to strangers. These sites devote considerable effort to gathering information from users and posting it in transparent ways.

Eventually the idea of renting out excess space was extended to empty garages, attics and parking spaces. Another variant is landsharing, which matches unused land with would-be gardeners who lack acreage. A related phenomenon is co-working, an arrangement through which unrelated individuals rent or share office space. Finally, Neighborhood Fruit identifies publically owned fruit trees and helps to transfer excess fruit from tree owners to others. In its peer-to-peer versions, these innovations get people cheap access to things and allow owners to earn modest amounts of money to supplement regular income streams.

The third major type of connected consumption involves *the exchange of services* rather than goods. Here the precursor is time banking, a practice whose origins as a formal institution date to the 1980s (there is some academic literature on time banks; see Cahn and Rowe (1992); Seyfang (2004); Collum et al. (2012); Dubois, Schor and Carfagna (2014)). Time banks are typically community-based non-profits whose members trade services on an egalitarian basis in which each member's time is equivalent in value to every other member's. Participants offer services such as baby-sitting, painting and massage, and earn 'time dollars' when they provide these to others. They can then use their dollars to receive services. Time banks explicitly aim to circumvent monetised market exchange and create more egalitarian relations. They are also useful in periods such as the present, when access to cash is constrained. There are now an estimated 53 time banks officially operating in the USA. They can also be found in 25 other countries (Wikipedia 2011b).

The impetus to innovate in the connected consumption space has led to a number of variants of time banking which introduce money or, in some cases, a convertible 'social currency' into the equation. Zaarly is a monetised site where people ask for services and others bid (in dollars) for the opportunity to supply them. Task Rabbit does something similar. Hub Culture is a social networking site for highly skilled management professionals in which advice, skill transmission and other services are offered and requested. Delivery is partly face to face, and the currency earned is called Ven, an online social currency with a dollar convertibility. The other major service-sharing category is in transportation, where there are a number of ride-sharing sites in operation. There are also now sites on which people offer 'authentic experiences', such as guided tours of local areas, help with apparel shopping and culinary tours.

A variant between goods and service provision involves the exchange of home-produced goods, such as food and crafts. Sites that facilitate this type of exchange include Mama Bake, Soup Sharing and EatWithMe. These also have as a main objective the *creation of more social connection and social experience*. This is a goal shared by many of the connected consumption groups, but it is also the key motivator for a number of the neighbourhood sites, such as those mentioned above (e.g. FrontPorch and Sharesomesugar). Facilitating peer-to-peer connection and avoiding financial institutions is also at the root of social lending sites, such as Kickstarter, Prosper, Zopa and the Lending Club, which allow people to go online, learn about initiatives that require financial investment and transfer money/invest in them. Finally, there are sites whose purpose is to help people build their own skills and capacities, such as Skillshare, which offers peer-to-peer workshops whose purpose is to democratise access to skill and knowledge and to supplant traditional educational institutions.

The transformative potential of connected consumption

As this brief summary suggests, the range of connected consumption initiatives is extensive. At least one of the motivations noted above characterises virtually all of them: they are economical, in the sense of being less expensive than conventional market-based alternatives. They also reduce eco- and carbon footprints, and they build social ties. In these respects they appear to be a positive social development. That view is represented in an uncritical, boosterish discourse that has arisen with the phenomenon. There are venture capital funds, magazines and careers devoted to 'the sharing economy' and 'collaborative consumption'. However, the diversity of activities under this rubric almost certainly means their long-term outcomes will be varied.

To what extent should we expect that connected consumption will lead to a truly new regime of consumption and production? Can it really slow us down? Some of these efforts, if they were to become large and entrenched, would have the potential of creating new economic relations and indeed a whole new sector that is more equal, more sustainable and more socially cohesive. On the other hand, others reproduce existing inequalities, foster high-impact consumer demand or are likely to converge to 'business as usual' if they are successful. The likelihood of going one way or another is determined by a range of factors, such as their basic construction, whether they are non-profit or for-profit and the nature of the service they provide.

While most of the for-profits also identify social goals as part of their mission, in some cases, as they grow and mature, they come to behave very similarly to existing businesses, and their transformative dimensions may be suppressed in deference to making money. Zipcar seems to be an example of this. Carbon footprint reduction was central to its original purpose; however, its partnership with Ford Motor Company involves offering sport utility vehicles to college students. Furthermore, its goal of putting cars on college campuses, where cars were rare, may end up increasing car use rather than reducing it. eBay has a mixed history. It started by selling used items but eventually included a large range of new products although in recent years it has been trying to emphasize its "green-ness." Similarly, sites such as Craig's List, which began as a non-profit, can convert to for-profit status, as it did. On the other hand, a number of the for-profit sites may be able to maintain their footprint reducing, social connection or other goals as they grow, particularly in cases where their service or product is itself low impact. ThredUp or Swapstyle come to mind. The differences and lines between the two are not hard and fast.

Another characteristic is whether the site uses money as a medium of exchange (versus goods, time or an invented currency, such as Ven). Those that create a new currency or trade in used goods have a much greater likelihood of fostering new economic relations. Time banks use an internal currency, measured time dollars or hours. In that way, they facilitate a new 'economy' in which all participants can deploy an equally distributed asset (their time) to secure access to needed services. This counteracts the highly unequal nature of the market economy and opens up opportunities for people whose labour market options are constrained. This is also a limiting feature of time banks, particularly in good economic times. If highly skilled professionals can sell their time on the market, they are unlikely to participate in trades with others whose market wage is low. (Trading plumbing services for babysitting on a one-to-one basis is not appealing to plumbers.) But trades among more equal partners can be attractive in a labour market where professionals are unable to work to their desired capacities. Other sites, such as Zaarly or TaskRabbit, operate within the dollar economy, and give people with excess time and inadequate cash a chance to sell their services to others with the reverse situation. TaskRabbit employs a group of people who carry out the tasks. It seems to differ little from an inexpensive concierge service and is likely to evolve into a conventional business if it is successful, but one in which 'rabbits' (the employees) lack secure hours, income streams and protections.

Given that connected consumption is so new, it is impossible to say how it will evolve. However, it is likely that it will grow, including in its more transformative forms, if the economy and especially the labour market remain weak. (The more conventional business models are also likely to achieve success, but because they serve wealthier markets for whom the internet reduces the temporal investment in consumption.) The need (or 'demand') for sharing comes from its capacity to foster economic activity among people with constrained earning power in the formal economy. On the one hand, it affords people access to free or low-cost goods and services. On the other hand, it opens up new ways for individuals to make money, particularly if they have excess time (as the underemployed do), or if they own assets that they can rent or share. I have argued elsewhere (Schor 2010) that we can expect long-term stagnation or at least lowered incomes for the majority over the next period in the USA. So far, this prediction is being borne out. The emergence of this sphere, therefore, helps to make possible a new kind of 'household economics', or what I have termed the 'plenitude' model. In this formulation, people work for limited hours in the formal labour market, earning cash. They acquire a much larger fraction of their consumer goods and services either by making and doing for themselves or via trades in informal economies, such as those of the connected consumption sector. In either case, the emergence of an informal, cash-constrained or even cash-free sector is likely to arise and thrive when the formal, cash-based economy fails to provide jobs and incomes. Economic need, rather than a commitment to sustainability, is likely to be the driving force behind this development, but lower footprints will result. A small-scale, local economy based on person-to-person service provision, the re-circulation of goods, the use of existing assets and dense social ties will wreak far less havoc on the planet than the dominant consumer sector currently does. Not all of the initiatives in the connected consumption sphere are obviously footprint reducing – couchsurfing may lead to more travel – but sleeping on the couch of an already-heated apartment generates less pollution than a stay in a large hotel. On balance, it's likely that the resulting mix of consumption activities and goods associated with the sharing economy will be more sustainable.

Acknowledgements

I would like to thank Abigail Letak, Luka Carfagna and Emilie Dubois for assistance.

References

Abernathy, F.H., Dunlop, J.T., Hammond, J.H. and Weil, D., 1999, *A Stitch in Time: Lean Retailing and the Transformation: Lessons from the Apparel and Textile Industries*, Oxford University Press, New York.

Appadurai, A. (ed.) 1986, *The Social Life of Things: Commodities in Cultural Perspective*, Cambridge University Press, Cambridge.

American Apparel and Footwear Association, 2009, *Trends: A Semi-Annual Compilation of Statistical Information on the U.S. Apparel and Footwear Industries*, Arlington, VA, viewed 5 September 2011, http://www.apparelandfootwear.org/Statistics.asp.

Baudrillard, J., 2001, *Selected Writings*, J. Mourrain (trans.), M. Poster (ed.), Stanford University Press, Stanford.

Bureau of Labor Statistics, 2011, *National Unemployment Rate*, viewed 4 September 2011, http://www.bls.gov/home.htm.

Cahn, E. and Rowe, J., 1992, *Time Dollars: The New Currency That Enables Americans to Turn Their Hidden Resource-Time-Into Personal Security and Community Renewal*, Rodale Press, Emmaus.

Collaborative Consumption Hub, n.d., *Snapshot of Examples*, viewed 2 September 2011, http://www.collaborativeconsumption.com/the-movement/snapshot-of-examples.php.

Collins, Jane L., 2003. *Threads: Gender, Labor and Power in the Global Apparel Industry*. University of Chicago Press, Chicago.

Collom, Edward et al 2012. *Equal Time, Equal Value: Community Currencies and Time Banking in the US*. Ashgate Publishing, Burlington, VT.

Context-Based Research Group and Carton Donofrio Partners, Inc., 2008, 'Grounding the American dream: A cultural study on the future of consumerism in a changing economy', *thegroundedconsumer.com*, viewed 5 September 2011, http://www.thegroundedconsumer.com/.

Cooke, K., 2011, 'USA becomes food stamp nation but is it sustainable?', *Reuters*, 22 August, viewed 5 September 2011, http://www.reuters.com/article/2011/08/22/us-usa-poverty-foodstamps-idUSTRE77L45Z20110822.

Craik, J., 1994, *The Face of Fashion: Cultural Studies in Fashion*, Routledge, New York.

Crane, D., 2001, *Fashion and Its Social Agendas: Class, Gender, and Identity in Clothing*, University of Chicago Press, Chicago.

Dubois, E., Schor, J. and Carfagna, L., 2014, "New Cultures of Connection in a Boston Timebank," in Juliet B. Schor and Craig J. Thompson, *Practicing Plenitude* (New Haven: Yale University Press), forthcoming.

Ewen, S., 1988, *All Consuming Images: The Politics of Style in Contemporary Culture*, Basic Books, New York.

Featherstone, M., 1991, *Consumer Culture and Postmodernism*, Sage, London.

Gansky, L., 2011, 'Do more, own less: a grand theory of the sharing economy', *The Atlantic*, 25 August, viewed 5 September 2011, http://www.theatlantic.com/business/archive/2011/08/do-more-own-less-a-grand-theory-of-the-sharing-economy/244141/.

Harris Interactive Poll, 2008, 'The environment...are we doing all we can?', *HarrisInteractive.com*, viewed 2 September 2011, http://www.harrisinteractive.com/Insights/HarrisVault.aspx?PID=917.

Harris Interactive Poll, 2009, 'How green are we? Putting our money (and our behaviour) where our mouth is', *HarrisInteractive.com*, viewed 2 September 2011, http://www.harrisinteractive.com/Insights/HarrisVault.aspx?PID=917.

Haug, W.F., 1986, *Critique of Commodity Aesthetics: Appearance, Sexuality, and Advertising in Capitalistic Society*, University of Minnesota Press, Minneapolis.

Lee, M., 2003, *Fashion Victim: Our Love–Hate Relationship with Dressing, Shopping, and the Cost of Style*, Broadway Books, New York.

Leiserowitz, A., Maibach, E. and Roser-Renouf, C., 2011, 'Climate change in the American mind', *Yale Project on Climate Change Communication*, Yale University, viewed 5 September 2011, http://environment.yale.edu/climate/files/CC_American_Mind.pdf.

Lemire, B., 2005, 'Shifting currency: the practice and economy of the secondhand trade, *c.* 1600–1850', in B. Lemire (ed.), *The Business of Everyday Life: Gender, Practice and Social Politics in England 1600–1900*, Manchester University Press, Manchester, pp. 82–109.

Lipovetsky, G., 2002, *The Empire of Fashion: Dressing Modern Democracy (New French thought series)*, Princeton University Press, Princeton.

McKendrick, N., Brewer, J. and Plumb, J.H., 1982, *The Birth of Consumer Society: The Commercialization of Eighteenth-Century England*, Europa, London.

Meadows, D.H., Meadows, D. and Randers, J., 1992, *Beyond the Limits: Confronting Global Collapse Envisioning a Sustainable Future*, Chelsea Green Junction, White River Junction.

Morin, R. and Taylor, P., 2009, *Luxury or Necessity? The Public Makes a U-turn*, Pew Research Centre, viewed 11 May 2009, http://pewresearch.org/pubs/1199/more-items-seen-as-luxury-not-necessity.

Parthasarathi, P., 2011, *Why Europe Grew Rich and Asia Did Not*, Cambridge University Press, Cambridge.

Rademacher, M.A., Nelson, M. and Paek H.J., 2007, 'Downshifting consumer= upshifting citizen?', *The ANNALS of the American Academy of Political and Social Science*, 611, no.1, 141–56.

Robins, N. and Humphrey, L., 2000, *Sustaining the Rag Trade: A Review of the Social and Environmental Trends in the UK Clothing Retail Sector and the Implications for Developing Country Producers*, International Institute for Environment and Development, London.

Roche, D., 1994, *The Culture of Clothing: Dress and Fashion in the Ancient Regime*. Cambridge University Press, New York.

Rockström, J., Steffan, W., Noone, K., Persson, A., Chapin, F.S., Lambin, E.F., Lenton, T.M., Scheffer, M., Folke, C., Schellnhuber, H.J., Nykvist, B., deWit, C.A., Hughes, T., van der Leeuw, S., Rodhe, H., Sorlin, S., Snyder, P.K., Costanza, R., Svedin, U., Falkenmark, M., Karlberg, L., Carrell, R.W., Fabry, V.J., Hansen, J., Walker, B., Liverman, D., Richardson, K., Crutzen, P. and Foley, J.A., 2009, 'A safe operating space for humanity', *Nature*, 461, 472–475.

Ross, A. (ed.), 1997, *No Sweat: Fashion, Free Trade, and the Rights of Garment Workers*, Verso, New York.

Ross, R.J.S., 2004, *Slaves to Fashion: Poverty and Abuse in the New Sweatshops*, University of Michigan Press, Ann Arbor.

Schor, J.B., 2000, 'Cleaning the closet', in J.B. Schor and E. Taylor (eds.), *Sustainable Planet: Solutions for the 21st Century*, Boston Press, Boston, pp. 45–60.

Schor, J.B., 2010, *Plenitude: The New Economics of True Wealth*, The Penguin Press, New York.

Schor, J.B. 2013. 'The Paradox of Materiality: Fashion, Marketing, and the Planetary Ecology', in M. McAllister and E. West (eds.), *Routledge Companion to Advertising and Promotional Culture*, Routledge, London.

Seyfang, G., 2004, 'Working outside the box: community currencies, time banks and social inclusion', *Journal of Social Policy*, 33, 49–71.

Shell, E.R., 2009, *Cheap: The High Cost of Discount Culture*, The Penguin Press, New York.

Simmel, G., 1957, 'On fashion', *American Journal of Sociology*, 62(6), 54–58.

The Conference Board, 2011, *Consumer Confidence Survey*, viewed 2 September 2011, http://www.conference-board.org/data/consumerconfidence.cfm.

United States Department of Commerce, 2011, *Personal Saving Rate*, viewed 5 September 2011, http://research.stlouisfed.org/fred2/data/PSAVERT.txt.

Veblen, T., 1899, *The Theory of the Leisure Class*, MacMillan, New York.

Wackernagel, M., Schulz, N.B., Deumling, D., Callejas Linares, A., Jenkins, M., Kapos, V., Monfreda, C., Loh, J., Myers, N., Norgaard, R. and Randers, J., 2002, 'Tracking the ecological overshoot of the human economy', *PNAS*, 99(14), 9266–9271.

Wikipedia, 2011a, *Consumer Confidence Index USA*, viewed 2 September 2011, http://en.wikipedia.org/wiki/File:ConsumerConfidenceIndexUSA.png.

Wikipedia, 2011b, *Time Banking*, viewed 5 September 2011, http://en.wikipedia.org/wiki/Time_banking.

World Wildlife Fund, 2010, *Living Planet Report*, World Wildlife Fund, Washington.

3
You Eat What You Are: Cultivated Taste and the Pursuit of Authenticity in the Slow Food Movement

Charles Lindholm and Siv B. Lie

Food, anxiety and belonging

Nowadays, finding and maintaining a secure identity can be a difficult task. Old certainties about the boundaries and content of the self and of the group have been eroded by the floods of people, goods and sinformation churned up in global capitalism's never-ending quest for profit. Cosmopolitan intellectuals and mobile elites may enjoy surfing the waves of the deluge, changing identities for amusement, but most others have fewer 'identity' resources and fear losing themselves in the waves (Harrison 1999). This fear is behind the rise of the identitarian social movements that prevail today (Touraine 1981, 2007; Melucci 1989).

To combat anomie, contemporary social movements often make use of a variety of symbolic indicators (flags, costumes, rituals, dances, poems, local argot and narratives of shared histories) to represent, inculcate and validate collective identities. One of the most effective of these symbols is 'authentic' food and drink. According to a standard definition, authenticity is defined as the ability to 'conform to an idealised representation of reality; that is, to a set of expectations regarding how such a thing ought to look, sound and feel' (Grazian 2003, pp. 10–11; see also Lindholm 2008). And, we can add, how it ought to taste. Like a regional dialect, the cultivation, preparation and consumption of authentic comestibles are culturally organised and historically constructed into distinctive regional and local traditions. Nostalgic memories of childhood, feelings of dependency and a sense of participation in the group can easily be awakened by the sight, smell and taste of beloved regional specialities.[1] As an embodied experience, the enjoyment of such a meal combines subjective pleasure with cultural practice and historical specificity, ratifying collective identity powerfully and immediately (Counihan and Van Esterik 1997; Seremetakis 1994; Sutton 2001). Thus, 'real Italians' affirm their national belonging by preparing and eating pasta.

Like all such symbolic correspondences, the relationship between pasta and the fragmented Italian identity is neither simple nor accidental, since pasta in Italy is manufactured in a seemingly infinite number of shapes, sizes, textures and consistencies, prepared with a huge range of sauces, and cooked and served in many different ways. Each combination is rigidly codified and reckoned to be characteristic of a region, locality and even family. At the same time, all are recognisable as pasta, and so as Italian, just as those who love to eat pasta are Italians, despite their many regional and local differences. As Castellanos and Bergstresser put it, 'the general concept, pasta, is shared nationally, while its specific forms allow for local identity to be represented' (2006, p. 190). Local variety is subsumed into national taste, which can then be contrasted to outsiders' inability to make pasta properly or to recognise the standards regulating variation. Equally complex symbolic correspondences have been documented in the elevation of retsina to the status of a national drink in Greece (Gefou-Madianou 1999), in the construction of a pan-Indian cuisine (Appadurai 1988) and in the intimate association of Champagne, *grand cru* wines and Camembert cheese with French identity (Guy 2003; Ulin 1995; Boisard 2003).

The power of food to define and unite groups is generally unremarked when life is lived within a relatively cohesive small-scale society, where there are only local comparisons to be made. Some people cook better than others; some people have specialities that they are known for and so on. But, when migrants face assimilation in a foreign country or a remote region within the nation, the consumption of 'traditional'[2] foods evokes an emotionally intense reminder of the lost homeland, while also serving as a marker of origin. For example, pasta first became Italian when Italian emigrants from different regions were lumped together by Americans as pasta eaters. This later played a large role in establishing a pan-Italian identity based on shared consumption patterns (Castellanos and Bergstresser 2006). In the USA, even the most integrated Americans nostalgically celebrate their ethnic heritages by preparing what they believe are authentic holiday dishes 'from the old country' – which in fact may not be distinguishable from the holiday foods eaten by their equally American neighbours to commemorate their own divergent roots (Waters 1990). Historical accuracy is far less important than the belief that the foods are traditional and representative.

Consumption takes on an equally heavy symbolic load in cases of internal stratification, where it can express resistance against the dominant group. For example, among some African Americans, collard greens, red beans, rice and chitlins (innards) are not just traditional foods; they symbolise the sufferings and triumphs of the race – the food of slaves that is now eaten and enjoyed as a point of pride. Similarly, by consuming poi and fish, native Hawaiians refuse the cuisine of American colonisers and assert their specific historical tastes (Linnekin 1983). Elsewhere, in a response to the arrival of national independence, Belizeans manufactured an indigenous cuisine of 'authentic Belizean dishes – Garnachas, Tamales, Rice and Beans, Stew Chicken, Fried Chicken' that reflects the hybrid character of the population. This new 'traditional' diet has replaced the former prestige foods of 'American Butterball turkey, Honey-Baked ham, Stove-Top stuffing, white-bread sandwiches filled with canned Armor Deviled Ham and Hellman's mayonnaise, potato salad and almost as an afterthought a small scoop of Belizean rice and beans' (Wilk 1999, p. 246; 2006, p. 166).

Yet, even as consumption has gained in symbolic importance in the modern world, asserting a collective identity by eating ancestral food has simultaneously become more complex and fraught. For example, immigrants have always been obliged to adapt to the food available in their new environments, but consumption practices in the homeland remained relatively constant. South Asian migrants in the USA might be reduced to eating Uncle Ben's rice at home, but at least they knew that Basmati rice remained the staple diet back in their natal villages. In the present-day global capitalist economy, such stability is no longer the case. American-based giants, such as McDonald's and Pizza Hut, appear on street corners from Algeria to Zambia, while Coke and Pepsi battle one another for the opportunity to quench thirsts worldwide. More and more the new generation in the homeland is just as likely to be eating a Big Mac as any traditional food (Ritzer 1998; Watson 1997). Even within the USA, national brands have crushed small-scale producers due to economies of scale, mass-market advertising and the demise of the mom and pop grocery store.

At the same time, the local has become global. For example, South Asians living in the USA can now purchase not only basmati rice but also flash-frozen dinners and savoury snacks imported daily from their own home regions. Their American neighbours can purchase these products as well and learn to enjoy them. As a result, while the food 'back home' has been polluted by foreign imports, the food exported 'from home' is no longer 'ours' but has become available to anyone, and liable to hybridisation or Creolisation in fusion cuisine. Globalisation deterritorialises local food, diluting it at one level, internationalising and diffusing it at another. Both trajectories can be sources of confusion about the stability of food-based sources of identity (Srinivas 2006).

More anxiety has been created by the rationalisation and bureaucratisation of food production. New and controversial technologies of genetic engineering, the propagation of hybrid crops, the extensive use of growth hormones and other chemicals, the development of industrialised techniques to produce meat, fruit and vegetables, and the breeding of highly specialised species, among other innovations, challenge taken-for-granted notions of the naturalness of what we eat and drink. All of this has led to a vastly heightened concern in the developed world with authenticity in the growing, producing and preparing of foods and to the rise of social movements dedicated to the purification of food production and the preservation of distinctive local cooking. In Europe, fears of genetic engineering, bureaucratic rationalisation of production and other 'EU horrors' have led to massive protests. Some of these are explicitly tied to nationalist ideologies that advocate the rejection not only of genetically engineered foods but also of mechanically produced foreign imports, such as McDonald's hamburgers and precooked TV dinners (Bové and Durfour 2002).

The organisation and ideology of revolutionary consumption

So far we have argued that the characteristic modern quest for identity is powerfully expressed via regionalised modes of eating and drinking. Yet, at the same time, the stability, purity and regional character of food and drink have been challenged by contemporary conditions of fluidity, capitalist expansion and the industrialisation of agriculture. In response, there has been a counter-impulse toward retention (or creation) of authentic national or ethnic cuisines, an increased emphasis on artisanal local farming and a return to traditional modes of food preparation. A major bearer of this oppositional message has been Slow Food. According to its ideology, concerted resistance to modern industrial agricultural practices and affirmation of traditional foodways will not only enable human beings 'to experience educated pleasure and to eat pleasurably' (Petrini 2007a, p. 55), but also result in a world community that 'singles out, highlights, and values difference' (Petrini 2001, p. 39) while being unified by a shared appreciation for ecologically sound, aesthetically satisfying food production, preparation and consumption. So, in contrast with national or regional invocation of cuisine as a symbolic expression of a particular collective identity, Slow Food seeks to establish a universal society based on 'educated pleasure'.

Using the method of archival ethnography based on a close reading of the movement's own public presentation of itself (Lindholm and Zúquete 2010), and relying as well on two years of ethnographic participant observation in Slow Food groups by Siv B. Lie (2008), the next few pages will outline the history, structure and value orientations of the global Slow Food organisation, which has served as an inspiration for many local efforts to support organic, sustainable food production. Here we will focus on the former (Slow Food capitalised) and less on the latter (slow food lower case), though we will remark on the proliferation of the Slow Food ideology in our conclusion. We will also point out some of the contradictions implicit in its ambitious mission.

The founder of Slow Food, Carlo Petrini, was born in 1949 to a family of socialist greengrocers in the impoverished provincial town of Bra in the Langhe Region of northern Italy. In 1981, disenchanted with the compromising politics and bureaucratic structure of the old left but repelled by the violence and extremism of the Italian radical parties, Petrini and some young members of ARCI (Associazione Ricreativa Culturale Italiana), the Italian national recreational association of the political left, formed the Free and Praiseworthy Association of the Friends of Barolo (later self-styled as the Arcigola or 'archgluttons'), with the aim of increasing awareness and consumption of local fine wine. Arcigola united a leftist ecological, anti-globalist agenda with the promotion of a healthy and egalitarian lifestyle based on the enjoyment of 'life's pleasures: good wine and food'. Their slogan, 'Barolo wine is democratic, or at least it can become so' (Petrini and Padovani 2005, pp. 4, 12), presaged the unique Slow Food combination of gustatory pleasure, social activism, the cultivation of tradition and pragmatic commerce.

Arcigola first gained widespread public recognition in 1986 when it protested the construction of a McDonald's near Rome's famous Spanish Steps by handing out bowls of penne pasta to illustrate the difference between the prefabricated and homogenised meals produced by a global conglomerate and the tasty particularity of authentic local food. At the

Second International Congress of Arcigola in 1991 in Perugia, Italy, Arcigola renamed itself Arcigola Slow Food. Later, as the movement gained international recognition, its name was shortened to Slow Food, with the snail as its logo.

Under Petrini's inspirational leadership, Slow Food grew rapidly into a worldwide phenomenon with over 100,000 official members in more than 100 countries, as well as attracting many unofficial followers. The dues-paying participants are loosely organised in voluntary groups called convivia (singular convivium). Their task, Petrini says, is to save 'historical and localized' producers, foster good taste, educate the public, and 'reconstruct the individual and collective heritage' by 'offering the world the hope of a future different from the polluted and tasteless one that the lords of the earth have programmed for all of us' (2001, pp. 69, 110).

An important tool in achieving this goal is the international biennial conference – entitled Terra Madre (Mother Earth) – which draws thousands of food 'co-producers' (Slow Food parlance for farmers, retailers and consumers) to Turin, where they 'explore important issues and share solutions to common challenges of producing food in a sustainable manner' (Weiner 2005, p. 27). By referring to all participants in the food chain as 'co-producers', Slow Food rhetorically transforms the distinct tasks of food production, distribution and consumption into acts of collective solidarity. As one activist says, Slow Food aims to be an 'earth democracy' that combines both a 'planetary consciousness and a local embeddedness' (quoted in Katz 2006, p. 129). At the same time, the gathering is sponsored by non-profit organisations, as well as by large corporations, whose logos are prominently displayed, confirming the organisation's emphasis on working profitably within the existing system, while still rhetorically opposing its excesses.

Occurring simultaneously with the Terra Madre gathering is the Salone del Gusto, a mammoth five-day celebration of regional food, cooking and eating. It too is corporately sponsored, and much attention is devoted to marketing properly manufactured produce. Since its inauguration in 1996, this commercial-cum-revolutionary festival has drawn thousands of enthusiasts who affirm the uniqueness of their own specific local 'Food Communities' while simultaneously celebrating their participation in the Slow Food collective and its ideals. This solidarity is increased as the Salone del Gusto participants mingle with the delegates from the Terra Madre conference. As a result, as Petrini explained in 2004, 'When you return to your villages... you will know that you are no longer alone.' Instead, you are 'brothers from all over the world' joined together in an 'international alliance of the Earth's caretakers' (2004).

Following its basic principle of providing an education in taste, Slow Food has established a University of Gastronomic Sciences in Italy. Outreach programmes on taste education in primary and secondary schools, and increased connections with college students and young people worldwide, promote a holistic 'eco-gastronomic' approach to food production, preparation and consumption. From the Slow Food perspective, gastronomy is a totalising discipline that entails a broad knowledge of botany, genetics, physics, chemistry, agriculture, zootechnics, agronomy, ecology, anthropology, sociology, geopolitics, political economies, trade, industry, cooking, physiology, medicine and epistemology, as all these subjects relate to food (Petrini 2007a, pp. 55–56). In another ambitious and potentially globally encompassing pedagogical effort, Slow Food initiated 'The Ark of Taste', which catalogues foods that are 'threatened by industrial standardisation, hygiene laws, the regulations of large-scale distribution and environmental damage' (Slow Food Foundation for Biodiversity n.d.). Locally organised 'Presidia' then strive to protect these endangered foods. The Presidia mission is to 'promote artisan products; to stabilize production techniques; to establish stringent production standards and, above all, to guarantee a viable future for traditional foods' (Slow Food Foundation for Biodiversity n.d.).

Slow Food promotes its 'defense of pleasure' through a remarkably effective communications and propaganda network that makes extensive use of the internet (*Slow Food*: www.slowfood.com). Its publishing house (Slow Editore) generates a variety of reports, studies, guidebooks, memoirs, surveys, newsletters and online material. Petrini and others in the movement have written books for both the mainstream and the alternative press. Each national association also has its own websites and blogs producing mountains of information about its activities, inviting response and participation at almost every point. Furthermore, Petrini urges all convivia to construct and strengthen their own local communities...beginning with widespread involvement with producers' communities, knocking on the door of local institutions to raise awareness, organizing markets, initiating small projects in the area, contributing to the international association's communication with news and issues to bring to the world's attention (2007b).

The hoped-for result, Petrini writes, is a 'communication strategy that makes it possible to "sell" the world a complex image combining history, landscape, wine, cuisine, and a style of welcome' (2001, p. 38).

Slow Food against fast food

The Slow Food manifesto, ratified by members from 15 countries in 1989, is admirably short (only 252 words) but extremely ambitious and polarising. It begins by stating that the nineteenth century 'first invented the machine and then took it as its life model'. The resulting passion for instrumental efficiency is evident in a universal devotion to the 'insidious virus' of speed, which 'has changed our way of being and threatens our environment and our landscapes'. But instead of calling for violent revolution, the Slow Food manifesto argues that the only solution to 'the contagion of the multitude who mistake frenzy for efficiency' is 'suitable doses of guaranteed sensual pleasure and slow, long-lasting enjoyment'. The way to find guaranteed virtuous pleasure is to 'rediscover the flavors and savors of regional cooking and banish the degrading effects of Fast Food' by 'developing taste rather than demeaning it' (Portinari 1989).

These words make it plain that Slow Food is not a mere attempt to provide a healthier alternative to fast food; it intends to be an aurora movement, a crusade to rescue humanity from the intrinsically wicked system that permeates and controls today's culture, politics, environment and economics (Lindholm and Zúquete 2010). What makes Slow Food unique is that its crusade is based in a belief in the salvationist power of pleasure, in particular gustatory pleasure. Ideally, the quest for 'slow, long-lasting enjoyment' will motivate the rank-and-file members of Slow Food to educate consumers, and to preserve endangered foods and authentic ways of life from destruction by the brutal forces of modernity. As Petrini writes, 'This age of globalization, the postindustrial age,' which 'the world system seems unlikely to tolerate for much longer' (2007a, pp. 17, 18) is 'dominated by hegemonic forces that are threatening to turn it into a desert' (2001, p. 58).

Symptoms of the problem include the introduction of 'a 'distinctively American' way of eating – the idea that food is something to be consumed as quickly, efficiently and inexpensively as possible' (Ritzer 1998, p. 8). Another symptom is the notion that 'by applying industrial techniques to agriculture it would be possible to solve the problems of hunger, profitability, the wholesomeness of food and the conservation of the environment' (Musso et al. 2005). This is 'a form of cultural annihilation that has affected the countryside of every part of the world, on a scale that is unprecedented in human history' (Petrini 2007a, p. 26). Although the Slow Food ideology allows some modern food growing and processing technology, and favours participation in a money economy, it adamantly rejects aspects of modern capitalism that promote wasteful practices and an unrealistic faith in continual expansion. Instead, what is required is a 'degrowth society' permitting 'the rediscovery of spontaneous giving and escaping the grip of purely commercial values. Deciding for degrowth corresponds to a triumph of quality over quantity' (Latouche 2007).

How this transformation is to be achieved is a question to which a number of solutions have been posited – some more practical than others. For example, in place of the heedless industrialisation and expansion of agriculture, Slow Food has promoted a long-term strategy supporting 'historical and localized' food production that will 'reconstruct the individual and collective heritage' (Petrini 2001, pp. 69, 110). The movement literature demands respect for traditional knowledge resting 'in the hands of humble people, of farmers, fishermen, [and] food producers' (Petrini 2007c). Official scientific knowledge[3] of biological engineering and industrialised food production is disparaged as a 'new ideology, which denies and conceals the complexity of the world and of the relations and interdependencies that characterise it, and also their value, tempting us to make the mistake of trying to analyse it in a linear manner, when this is not in fact possible' (Petrini 2007a, p. 18). The result is a 'demented drive toward a world of tomatoes that don't go bad and strawberries with salmon genes' and towards a 'wholesale loss of gastronomic and culinary knowledge that was once the basis of a correct – as well as enjoyable – use of agricultural resources' (Petrini 2001, pp. 26, 102). The blending of moral correctness and sensual enjoyment is characteristic of Slow Food rhetoric.

Slow Food maintains that industrialised fast food has not only destroyed traditional knowledge and upended the natural order but has also ruined the genuine communal spirit that was once realised in the venerable food traditions of the countryside. Without access to food grown, prepared and served in the original manner, people no longer experience firsthand the shared rituals of commensality, which fast food renders 'banal, functional or literal and increasingly reserved for the diversions of private life' (Seremetakis 1994, p. 37). Nor can individuals in a Fast Food culture ever be personally authentic, since they cannot participate in a rooted collective. From this perspective, regularly enjoying a McDonald's hamburger is not merely a lapse of taste; it is a fundamental betrayal of the self and the moral collective, and damning evidence of bad faith. 'When we pledge our dietary allegiance to a fast-food nation, there are also grave consequences to the health of our civil society and our national character. When we eat fast-food meals alone in our cars, we swallow the values and assumptions of the corporations that manufacture them' (A. Waters 2007, p. 13). Fast food and existential anomie go together, as do Slow Food and authenticity.

Pleasure and authenticity

In its endless quest for virtuous and fulfilling enjoyment, Slow Food does not favour a return to the rural world of yesterday when people ate the same things throughout their entire lives. Such a repetitious, tedious diet would destroy one's sense of taste, defined by Petrini as 'a restless creature that thrives on diversity, works retroactively to revive memories, and goes forward blindly, promising virtual pleasures' (2001, p. 71). Because habit is the enemy of pleasure, the ideal for the Slow Food initiate is to continually seek diversity. Petrini proclaims 'to eat a different kind of food in every street in the world is the best answer to fast food' (2001, p. 8).

However, for the ideal Slow Food gourmet only a certain type of variety will do if a newly discovered food is to be authentically pleasurable. In the first place, it ought to be made with the highest quality, certifiably purest ingredients, and cooked in a traditional, simple, unpretentious manner reflective of a unique terroir. The ideal of virtuous consumption also requires extensive knowledge of the varied historical, cultural and ecological background of local comestibles. As Petrini informs us, 'In order to learn how to find slow pleasure, one has to travel, read and taste, abandoning the temptation of entrenched isolation' (2001, p. 18).

Slow Food's battle to achieve an *authentic* diet and construct a global moral community is based on the assumption that edibles meeting the group's standards are intrinsically *good*: good in taste, good in moral value. Therefore, the conscious consumer's righteousness will necessarily be experientially validated and reinforced by immediate sensual pleasure. But, as we mentioned in our introduction, the relationship between pleasure, taste and morality is complicated by the fact that the enjoyment of food – even when it is traditionally prepared and organically grown – is learned and culturally specific, much like a regional dialect or language. Petrini illustrates this point by describing his own experience of tasting dried caterpillars offered to him by some women in Burkina Faso:

> Objectively speaking, I did not find anything that corresponded to my categories of 'good' ... to my personal taste, those insects are bad, but since they are important for that culture – they are part of the

tradition, they meet the criteria of naturalness, their consumption helps agriculture because they are parasites, and what is more they improve the diet of the *burkinabé* (who love them) – I *must* say that they are good.

(2007a, p. 107)

Or, as another Slow Food official put it,

What we are saying is that if there is a product that is the result of the history and culture of a people, that hasn't been studied in a laboratory by food engineers to formulate it to be accepted by a large number of people, then this product has taste.

(Lhéritier 2006)

From this perspective, the fundamental difference between a dried caterpillar and a McDonald's hamburger is the connection that the first has with local tradition while the second is manufactured and homogenous, without cultural specificity. Slow Food convivia conduct taste workshops 'so that people can understand why a certain taste is particular, so they can learn about it and appreciate it. But one has the right to not like something. What we're concerned about is the culinary culture of a social group' (Lhéritier 2006). Whether something tastes disgusting to a particular individual is irrelevant. What is crucial is that it is a part of an authentic food tradition, uncorrupted by industrialisation and the other evils of an anti-human modernity.

As Petrini's dried caterpillar anecdote illustrates, if food items meet traditional local standards for authenticity, then they are *fundamentally* good, though actual sensual enjoyment of them may well require considerable learning and practice. Conversely, the nostalgic pleasure of sucking on a favourite childhood sweet or the animal enjoyment of wolfing down a greasy hamburger is morally inferior to the cultivated, restrained and responsible pleasure felt by true eco-gastronomes, munching on caterpillars they have learned to appreciate by arduous training and an effort of will. Or, if that effort fails, the educated eco-gastronome still recognises that the preparation and consumption of dried caterpillars is worth preserving as an authentic aspect of traditional foodways in Burkina Faso. Ideally, then, Slow Food members are obliged to explore and protect traditional local cuisines worldwide, even if they still remain distasteful to those for whom they are not part of childhood experience.

According to its critics, the Slow Food stress on the moral importance of tradition and authenticity leads inevitably to romanticising and essentialising the foodways of traditional cultures (Leitch 2008). This attitude can cause the condemnation of some present-day local production practices for not meeting Slow Food standards. As one critic argues, for Petrini,

> certain traditional Italian foods...just aren't up to snuff. Herders spend the summers with their families instead of isolated in alpine huts. Farmers in the Abruzzi eat their own cured meat instead of selling it on the market. Sardinian peasants make second-rate cheese and need to improve their techniques. They have to be chivvied into producing high quality 'traditional' products...It is as much, if not more about the invention of culinary patrimony as it is about its preservation.
>
> (Laudan 2004, p. 140)

As this comment suggests, Slow Food's subordination of immediate sensual pleasure to a more ascetic and educated appreciation of authentic tradition (even if it consists of dried caterpillars) does not solve the problem of what is good, since authenticity is a cultural construction, prey to the vicissitudes of history (Bendix 1997). However, those who are striving to maintain stability in an anomic universe are unlikely to be convinced by such slippery relativism (Lindholm 2008). Instead, in the realm of food – as in other cultural realms – purportedly objective measures of authenticity abound: you can't get *real* barbecue outside the south; you haven't tried *real* paella until you've been to the Valencian coast; only *real* aquavit (a Norwegian potato-derived liquor) has journeyed twice over the equator to achieve its distinctive barrel-aged flavour; *real* champagne must be French, from the proper region; and so on.

By relying on authenticity as its marker for the really real, Slow Food glosses over the ever-changing socio-economic and historical construction of 'tradition'. Its heroic and polarising public rhetoric also ignores the tensions involved in Slow Food's dependence on business sponsorship for events like the Salone del Gusto and the Terra Madre celebration, as well as the fact that the Presidia could not exist without corporate support, and that authenticity is itself a marketable commodity. Many rank-and-file members recognise the disjuncture between *is* and *ought*, and privately accuse the leadership of wishful thinking at best, hypocrisy at worst. Yet many also recognise that such idealistic rhetoric, however impractical or ambitious its implications may be, is necessary to invigorate the movement and maintain its momentum.

Spontaneity and structure

If Slow Food has an intellectual problem reconciling idealised notions of authenticity with the realities of production and the culturally varied experiences of pleasure, it also has the practical difficulty of reconciling bureaucratic rationalisation with its own stated prioritisation of immediacy and enjoyment.[4] Organisationally, Slow Food is very complex. Its programmes are implemented by an impressive bureaucratic apparatus and a daunting profusion of statutes, articles and provisions that codify every aspect of the organisation's structure. The most recently ratified international statute is 45 articles long – a far cry from the terse original manifesto. However, to offset this bureaucratic efflorescence, Slow Food has also constituted itself as a decentralised and democratic 'horizontal' organisation, which gives the local convivia very considerable autonomy.

The inevitable tension between centralised structure and horizontal spontaneity is also eased through the cultivation of an atmosphere of informality and celebration, as actualised in the Salone del Gusto and in other mass meetings, where music, feasting and related pleasures make Slow Food's centralised structure and bureaucratic apparatus more palatable. As Petrini told his audience during his opening speech at the 2007 Slow Food International Congress,

> Being in an association means a rational project, but often pushed by non-rational impulses ... We must be joyful, happy, happy people! This is the only antidote to getting a big head; this is the only great ingredient for friendship. Craziness, happiness: this is at the basis of our joyful association!
>
> (Petrini 2007c)

In fact, from its beginnings, Slow Food has attempted to cultivate a light-hearted and lively approach to combating more serious issues. As one member stated,

> We are creating a kind of celebratory, inclusive activism – an activism based on enjoyment, pleasure, and the desire to create whole communities. We all eat. And we should all want to eat food that nourishes our bodies, our families, our communities, and our environments. Food is a catalyst for so many other issues, yet it is (or should be) a pleasurable activity.
>
> (Upton 2008)

According to Petrini, the Slow Food combination of nurtured craziness in service of a rational project 'creates an original and unusual social group that would be open, democratic, and uncontaminated by particular interests, and that would avoid making itself ridiculous with rites, protocols, and trappings' (2001, p. 12). The emphasis on structural horizontality and ritualised spontaneity also serves to undercut the most common criticism of Slow Food – that it 'is a grassroots movement of influential urban elites' (Veseth 2006, p. 201; for a statistical breakdown of official Slow Food membership, see Weiner 2005).

However, the struggle against elitism and pretension may be a losing battle. A convivium in Cambridge, Massachusetts, once spent an evening solemnly sampling 30 different kinds of salt, painstakingly marking scorecards to be compared and tabulated at the end of the exercise. Wealthy Slow Food members in Cape Town, South Africa, crushed grapes and ate a tasty organic picnic while underpaid workers toiled in the fields around them. As one friendly critic warns, 'the Presidia products, or even the simple discourse of Slow Food, can be utilised to bring a good conscience to an approach more closely resembling snobbism than social engagement' (Chabrol n.d.). In an effort to combat this accusation, Slow Food, at least in the USA, has become more explicitly involved in lobbying activities and has emphasised schemes such as school garden initiatives, nutrition programmes and outreach to poor communities. Many Slow Food members sincerely hope to 'do good' through such initiatives. Yet even the most democratic and participatory methods of programme design and implementation may appear to the recipients as charitable acts by wealthy gourmets, which serve mainly to ease donors' consciences, or even as patronising extensions of neocolonialism. As a result, those on the receiving end sometimes resist Slow Food involvement in the interest of self-empowerment.

There are many other criticisms of the Slow Food revolution. Some say it returns women to their traditional role as kitchen drudges (Belasco 1993 citing Meyer 1971), others complain that it transforms cheap local food into expensive international products (Laudan 2001), and that it cannot spread beyond its food-loving Italian base.[5] All of these critiques have a degree of merit. Nonetheless, the Slow Food message of opposition to the rush of modern life has spread far beyond the bounds of the original organisation. For example, from Italy to Korea, Cittaslow activists lobby for city planning that favours a slow-paced life (Zelmanov 2003; Pink 2008). Other slow associations include the Transition Movement (toward sustainable communities), the Car-free Movement, the Sloth Club and BeGood network in Japan, the Long Now Foundation in the USA, the European Society for the Deceleration of Time, Slow Travel, Slow Design, Slow Money, Slow Schooling, Slow Housing cooperatives, speeders anonymous, Slow Music, superslow weightlifting, slow therapies (e.g. reiki healing, chi kung and yoga) and even a slow sex movement.

Some enthusiasts even imagine that the basic philosophy of Slow Life can reverse the present direction (and pace) of history:

> Fast is busy, controlling, aggressive, hurried, analytical, stressed, superficial, impatient, active, quantity-over-quality. Slow is the opposite: calm, careful, receptive, still, intuitive, unhurried, patient, reflective, quality-over-quantity. It is about making real and meaningful connections – with people, culture, work, food, everything... The big question now is when the individual will become the collective. When will the many personal acts of deceleration occurring across the world reach critical mass? When will the Slow movement turn into a Slow revolution?
>
> (Honoré 2004, pp. 14–15, 279; see also Andrews 2006)

To this, Petrini gives a cautious reply: 'We are not trying to change the world anymore, just to save it' (2001, p. 86). Nonetheless, the dreams of Slow Food are very grand. In its own self-description, implementing its programme will lead to greater pleasure, deeper knowledge and shared social responsibility for the environment. Most importantly, a Slow revolution will expand and soften human sympathies. As Petrini puts it, 'we catch barely a glimpse of the fundamental concept that ought to underlie all these projects: that of "feeling good" with oneself and with others' (2001, p. 73). That this pronouncement sounds remarkably like an advertisement for self-help therapy does not lessen its appeal.

Conclusion

Slow Food has been and will probably continue to be an important social movement, not only in itself but also in its wide sphere of influence. Sparked by the charisma of its leader, it has successfully managed to tread the delicate balance between structure and spontaneity that plagues all social movements. Savvy marketing and an inclusive ethic of pleasure soften its often apocalyptic, revolutionary rhetoric, making it simultaneously radical and welcoming, transformative yet market friendly. Linking the pleasures of the palate with the authenticity of local tradition, while stressing the need to learn the virtues of other cuisines worldwide, has allowed it to expand beyond the limits of nation, race and religion (although it still remains very much based in Italy). Slow Food hedonism is also a highly moralistic enterprise. At the very least, pursuing authentic food is thought to lead to a shared concern for protecting the environment and tradition, as well as personal empowerment, greater knowledge and increased social responsibility. At best, it will change the world, eradicating exploitation, pollution and alienation.

The core of the Slow Food ideology is the premise that authenticity is required for true enjoyment. If comestibles are authentic – that is, properly grown, prepared and served – they are *ipso facto* more pleasurable to consume than those that are inauthentic. This value orientation assumes that morally good pleasure is the ultimate basis for judging value, not just of food but universally. Unfortunately, the capacity for judging and experiencing authentic and virtuous pleasure is not easily won. As noted, Slow Food consumers are freed from the bonds of cultural conditioning only by a never-ending education of the senses, which allows them to determine what is genuine in the world around them. This postulate requires glossing over the contingent nature of authenticity, as well as assuming that proper pleasure is based an ascetic devotion to the serious study of the infinite varieties of taste.

As a social movement that relies on an ethic of pleasure as the source of commitment, Slow Food is, in many senses, a realisation of what Alasdair MacIntyre (1981) termed the dominant morality of modernity: emotivism – that is, the utilitarian assumption that only personal preferences can determine virtue. As he argues, this value orientation eliminates the possibility of developing a substantive morality, while also fostering conformity (since preference is rarely unambiguous, and so leads to anxious perusal of the preferences of others for reassurance). To its credit, Slow Food has attempted to offset these possibilities by proclaiming that authenticity and tradition provide *objective* sources of virtuous enjoyment. Believers then must search the world for gustatory pleasures that are *proven* to be authentic. But who decides the reliability of such proofs is left in the air. This move escapes the trap of solipsism but falls into another: reification.

Notes

1. The power of these cultural practices cannot be overestimated. For example, in the early fifteenth century, Norse colonists in Greenland starved to death because they refused to eat the fish that swarmed in the waters around their settlements (Diamond 2004).

2. We will forgo the use of scare quotes after the first instance, assuming that our readers take for granted the contingency of words like 'tradition', 'authenticity' and 'culture'.
3. Slow Food posits 'traditional' knowledge against 'official' scientific knowledge, associating the latter with corporation- and government-sanctioned knowledge produced and disseminated with little regard for local, historically grounded food-production practices. See Pollan (2007) for a discussion of 'nutritionism' (the 'official' scientific ideology of nutrition) and its relationship with 'culturally' determined foodways.
4. 'It is the tension between spontaneity and structure that gives a social movement its peculiar flavor' (Freeman and Johnson 1999, p. 2).
5. Convening the 2007 International Slow Food Congress in Puebla, Mexico, was an attempt to expand membership into the global South.

References

Andrews, C., 2006, *Slow Is Beautiful: New Visions of Community, Leisure and Joie de Vivre*, New Society Publishers, Gabriola Island, BC.

Appadurai, A., 1988, 'How to make a national cuisine: Cookbooks in contemporary India', *Comparative Study of Society and History*, 30(1), 3–24.

Belasco, W.J., 1993, *Appetite for Change: How the Counterculture Took on the Food Industry*, Cornell University Press, Ithaca.

Bendix, R., 1997, *In Search of Authenticity: The Formation of Folklore Studies*, University of Wisconsin Press, Madison.

Boisard, P., 2003, *Camembert: A National Myth*, University of California Press, Berkeley.

Bové, J. and Durfour, F., 2002, *The World Is Not For Sale: Farmers Against Junk Food*, Verso, London.

Castellanos, E. and Bergstresser, S.M., 2006, 'Food fights at the EU table: the gastronomic assertion of Italian distinctiveness', *European Studies: An Interdisciplinary Series in European Culture, History and Politics*, 22(1), 179–202.

Chabrol, D., n.d., 'Slow Food, un mouvement qui crée le chemin en marchant...' unpublished article.

Counihan, C. and Van Esterik, P. (eds.), 1997, *Food and Culture: A Reader*, Routledge, New York.

Diamond, J., 2004, *Collapse: How Societies Choose to Fail or Succeed*, Viking, New York.

Freeman, J. and Johnson, V.L., 1999, 'Introduction', in J. Freeman and V.L. Johnson (eds.), *Waves of Protest*, Rowman and Littlefield, Lanham, pp. 1–6.

Gefou-Madianou, D., 1999, 'Cultural polyphony and identity formation: Negotiating tradition in Attica', *American Ethnologist*, 26(3), 412–439.

Grazian, D., 2003, *Blue Chicago: The Search for Authenticity in Urban Blues Clubs*, University of Chicago Press, Chicago.

Guy, K.M., 2003, *When Champagne Became French: Wine and the Making of a National Identity*, Johns Hopkins University Press, Baltimore.

Harrison, S., 1999, 'Identity as a scarce resource', *Social Anthropology*, 7, 239–251.

Honoré, C., 2004, *In Praise of Slowness: How a Worldwide Movement Is Challenging the Cult of Speed*, Harper, San Francisco.

Katz, S., 2006, *The Revolution Will Not Be Microwaved: Inside America's Underground Food Movements*, Chelsea Green Publishing, White River Junction.

Latouche, S., 2007, 'The wisdom of the snail', *Sloweek*, viewed 22 March, http://www.slowfood.com/sloweb/eng/dettaglio.lasso?cod=3E6E345B07dcf2516CxiI 344F097.

Laudan, R., 2001, 'A plea for culinary modernism: why we should love new, fast, processed food', *Gastronomica*, 1(1), 36–44.

———, 2004, 'Slow Food: the French Terroir strategy, and culinary modernism', *Food, Culture and Society*, 7, 133–144.

Leitch, A., 2008, 'Slow Food and the politics of pork fat', in C. Counihan (ed.), *Food and Culture: A Reader*, Routledge, New York, pp. 381–399.

Lhéritier, J., 2006, 'Personal interview', *Tours*, France, 24 November.

Lie, S.B., 2008, *GastroRevolution: The Age of Slow Food*, Undergraduate Honors Thesis, University Professors Program, Boston University.

Lindholm, C., 2008, *Culture and Authenticity*, Blackwell Publishing, Oxford.

Lindholm, C. and Zúquete, J.P., 2010, *The Struggle for the World: Liberation Movements for the 21st Century*, Stanford University Press, Stanford.

Linnekin, J., 1983, 'Defining tradition: variations on Hawaiian identity', *American Ethnologist*, 10(2), 241–252.

MacIntyre, A., 1981, *After Virtue: A Study in Moral Theory*, Duckworth, London.

Mayer, J., 1971, 'Foreword', in M. F Jacobson (ed.), *Eater's Digest: The Consumer's Factbook of Food Additives*, Doubleday, Garden City.

Melucci, A., 1989, 'New perspectives on social movements: an interview with Alberto Melucci', in J. Keane and P. Mier (eds.), *Nomads of the Present: Social Movements and Individual Needs in Contemporary Society*, Temple University Press, Philadelphia, pp. 180–232.

Musso, V., Abbona, A. and Nano, P., 2005, '4th Slow Food International Congress', *Slow Food International*, viewed 5 November, http://press.slowfood.com/press/eng/leggi.lasso?cod=527&ln=en.

Petrini, C., 2001, *Slow Food: The Case for Taste*, W. McCuaig (trans.), Columbia University Press, New York.

———, 2004, 'Address to the Salone Del Gusto', *National Public Radio Morning Edition*, 7 November.

———, 2007a, *Slow Food Nation: Why Our Food Should Be Good, Clean and Fair*, C. Furlan and J. Hunt (trans.) Rizzoli, New York.

——— 2007b, 'Taking back life', *Slow Food Deutschland*, http://www.slowfood.de/w/files/wir_ueber_uns/taking_back_life_petrini.pdf.

———, 2007c, Speech delivered at the Slow Food International Congress in Puebla, Mexico, 9 November, transcription by S.B. Lie.

Petrini, C. and Padovani, G., 2005, *Slow Food Revolution: A New Culture for Eating and Living*, F, Rizzoli, New York.

Pink, S., 2008, 'Re-thinking contemporary activism: from community to emplaced sociality', *Ethnos: Journal of Anthropology*, June, 73(2), 163–188.

Pollan, M., 2007, 'Unhappy meals', *The New York Times*, viewed 28 January, http://www.michaelpollan.com/article.php?id=87.

Portinari, F., 1989, 'The Slow Food Manifesto,' *Slow Food*, viewed 6 December 2012, http://www.slowfood.com/about_us/eng/manifesto.lasso.

Ritzer, G., 1998, *The McDonaldizatiion Thesis: Explorations and Extensions*, Sage, New York.

Seremetakis, C.N., 1994, 'The memory of the senses, part II: Still acts', in C.N. Seremetakis (ed.), *The Senses Still: Perception and Memory in the Material Culture of Modernity*, Westview, Boulder, pp. 23–44.

Slow Food Foundation for Biodiversity, n.d., http://www.slowfoodfoundation.com.

Srinivas, T., 2006, ' "As mother made it": the cosmopolitan Indian family, "authentic" food and the construction of a cultural utopia', *International Journal of Family Sociology*, 32(2), 191–221.

Sutton, D.A., 2001, *Remembrance of Repasts: An Anthropology of Food and Memory*, Berg, New York.

Touraine, A., 1981, *The Voice and the Eye: An Analysis of Social movements*, A. Duff (trans.), Cambridge University Press, New York.

Touraine, A., 2007, *A New Paradigm for Understanding Today's World*, Polity Press, Cambridge.

Ulin, R.C., 1995, 'Invention and representation as cultural capital: Southwest French winegrowing history', *American Anthropologist*, 97(3), 519–527.

Upton, C. 2008, personal email correspondence with S.B. Lie, 18 March.

Veseth, M., 2006, *Globaloney: Unraveling the Myths of Globalization*, Rowman and Littlefield, Lanham.

Waters, A., 2007, 'Preface', in C. Petrini (ed.), *Slow Food Nation: Why our Food should be Good, Clean and Fair*, Rizzoli, New York.

Waters, M., 1990, *Ethnic Options: Choosing Identities in America*, University of California Press, Berkeley.

Watson, J.L. (ed.), 1997, *Golden Arches East: McDonald's in East Asia*, Stanford University Press, Stanford.

Weiner, S., 2005, *The Slow Food Companion*, Slow Food Editore, Bra, Italy.

Wilk, R., 1999, ' "Real Belizean food": building local identity in the transnational Caribbean', *American Anthropologist*, 101(2), 244–255.

—— 2006, *Home Cooking in the Global Village: Caribbean Food from Buccaneers to Ecotourists*, Oxford University Press, New York.

Zelmanov, E., 2003, 'Preaching a slow approach', *Mother Jones*, viewed 5 May, http://www.motherjones.com/news/featurex/2003/05/we_406_01.html.

4
Consuming Space Slowly: Reflections on Authenticity, Place and the Self

Nick Osbaldiston

Introduction

Slow living may not necessarily be limited to particular places, but there are, nonetheless, certain kinds of spaces that best facilitate slow living and the value of these arises from a consideration of their contexts in the deterritorialised global culture in which we live (Parkins and Craig 2006, p. 63).

Throughout the academic debates that engage in slow culture, there is a recurring theme of time. Indeed, throughout this volume, time is a prominent feature of analysis not just in relation to the clock or calendar. There is a need to consider time further in relation to all modes of temporality as well, including aging, natural rhythms and other 'times' which contribute to slow movements (cf. Adam 1990, 1995). It might be that in the future, theoretical engagement with slowness could embrace a 'timescape' project which encapsulates a range of temporalities that coalesce to create the potentiality of slow living (Adam 1998). For instance, nostalgia or at least a collective version of it (Davis 1979) could be seen as an important motivator to return back to the 'good ol' days before society became hyper-consumerist.

In this chapter, however, I want to posit that important in the development of slow culture is the problem of spatial relations. Certainly the subject of place/space has been high on the agenda of those seeking to understand amenity-led migration or Lifestyle Migration for some time (see Benson and O'Reilly 2009; Benson 2011; Moss 2006; Ragusa 2010, this volume; Osbaldiston 2011, 2012). However, none of these assessments of this migratory phenomenon seeks to link the movement back to slow narratives (the exception being Osbaldiston 2012).

Furthermore, the negotiation of space within the everyday has been limited in relation to slowness. Kate Soper's (2007) 'Alternative Hedonism' discourse is an exception in that it provides some important insight in relation to how people engage with space differently, which can have political implications long term, specifically under the banner of sustainability.

Parkins and Craig (2006) have also entertained the notion of place/space in their work on slow living. Specifically they consider two areas where spatial relations encourage slowness. One area is in the home where it is 'possible to mobilize a positive potential in domestic space in the conceptualizing of the spatial contexts of slow living' (Parkins and Craig 2006, p. 65). They argue that

> [t]he home is an important site in slow living because it can represent a demarcated sphere of existence that can facilitate a particular quality of time. That is, the home can represent a relatively fixed site in the flux of everyday experience and in this sense it is a space that can enable the kind of care and attentiveness that we have posited as central to slow living.
>
> (Parkins and Craig 2006, p. 65)

Certainly the home plays an important role in the representation of the self but also in the development of meaning in an individual's life (see Woodward 2007). The arrangement of the home and the markers of identity found in material objects are potentially important sites for analysis in the binary division between work and private life. What activities occur within the confines of the home are also of great interest. Quality time with children and partners acts to counter the influence of the 'pressures of speed' found in the everyday (Parkins and Craig 2006, p. 64; for more on 'quality time', see Hochschild (1997)). From this perspective, the home becomes the 'haven in the heartless world' (Lasch 1979), a place where the family is a refuge and 'where the wounds of life find their consolation' (Davy 1925, cited in Lamanna 2004, p. 15).

However, the relatively mundane setting in the home is not the only space where slowness can be initiated. Parkins and Craig (2006) finalise their analyses of space and slow living by exploring Cittaslow or Slow Cities. The movement, which follows closely after the fundamental tenets of Slow Food, seeks to reconnect townships back to a more authentic identity. Important in this, as Parkins and Craig (2006, p. 83) propose, is not just an 'aesthetic of rural', though vital, but a shaping of the townships' aesthetic towards a rich and meaningful sense of place. Subsequently, the vices of the metropolis are actively avoided through planning mechanisms and policies that seek to limit vehicular traffic and instantaneous consumption (e.g. of fast foods) while promoting alternative activities, such as food markets (which tie back to a collective identity through food consumption of local traditional cuisine and local produce) and community events. While the notion of an authentic community derived through nostalgia for times forgotten is quite obviously socially constructed, Parkins and Craig (2006) remind us that this can have a very real impact on individual identity. Thus, while notions of rurality important to the movement can be criticised for being dependent upon a 'middle-class' version of what is 'real' (see Murdoch and Day 1998; Pahl 2005), Parkins and Craig (2006, p. 85) are quick to remind us that the Cittaslow movement remains a powerful narrative against the tide of fast-paced globalisation that often dislocates and displaces local traditions and communities, having a detrimental impact therefore on the individual.

> Our point here is that the mindful consciousness that we position as central to slow living generates an awareness of the specificity of place, and more particularly a material relationship to the land, as well as an attentiveness to those who coexist in the same territory and who collectively give their territory identity and value. This is *not based upon a bourgeois, romantic valorization of either rural life* or small, sophisticated towns in exotic locales, but is rather based upon a belief that in the contexts of our fast, deterritorialised, modern lives, we need to retain an ethical and political disposition that is grounded in awareness of our fundamental relationship to the specificity of place, the land, its produce and each other.
>
> (Parkins and Craig 2006, p. 85, italics added)

Others through ethnography tell a story of Cittaslow that is engaging and important. Pink (2007), for instance, demonstrates how the towns embrace different sensations compared with the city, while Miele (2008, p. 148) empirically shows how Cittaslow places use 'Slow Food technologies for performing boundaries between slow and fast'. In each instance, the binary between city and the homogenous influence of globalisation and the 'slow town' is demonstrated as having a heavy influence on the everyday experience of those within the townships.

By concentrating on Cittaslow and the home, however, Parkins and Craig (2006) limit their discussion of place in the context of slowness.

A host of social behaviours embedded in the 'slow' philosophy are seen not just through movements such as lifestyle or amenity migration but also within everyday life (Soper 2007). Once this debate is opened up beyond the political as well, the expansive influence of the slow narrative on spatial practices becomes apparent. Further, by doing so the darker side to slow living also begins to emerge. Surprisingly, Parkins and Craig (2006) neglect any reading of slow culture through critical theorists like Bourdieu. Such notions are central tenets to theses from Karen O'Reilly and Michaela Benson (see below). Furthermore, as Simmel (1997[1895], p. 220) once fatalistically declared, 'the power of capitalism extends itself to ideas as well'.

This chapter, however, is not fatalistic. It does not argue that all slow movements are necessarily doomed to neither fall victim to hyper-consumerist tendencies nor lose their inherent 'alternative hedonist' qualities (Soper 2007). Rather, it seeks to engage with differing spatial practices under the guise of slowness and thus present a reading of place that is different from those of Parkins and Craig (2006). While these two authors advance a case for slowness and space/place that is coherent and highly engaging, they are unnecessarily dependent on analysing organised social movements, like Cittaslow, in their works. In this chapter, I wish to explore the cultural conditions that encourage a range of slow activities through both the everyday and the more exotic ritualistic escapes. In both instances, the role of the city is predominant. As Parkins and Craig (2006) note in particular, the metropolis creates the spatial possibilities for the embracing of slow lifestyles. While they do not explicitly characterise the city as profane or degrading on the self, there is a hint that they consider it as the primary seat for a homogeneity which is developed through globalisation. Yet, the city also encourages a cosmopolitan self which opens up the individual to possibilities beyond the urban environment. So while the metropolis is dotted with 'homogenized "non-places" ', we must also be fully aware of the potential that global city culture has to produce a sense of oneness with the world (Parkins and Craig 2006, p. 71; see also Kendall, Skrbis and Woodward 2008; Beck 1992, 2006).

In what follows, however, the city is described as a site for highly mundane activities but also one which can, in Durkheimian language, suffer a decline in status towards the 'profane' (Smith 1999; Osbaldiston 2012). While some engage with alternate activities in the city with a quasi-adventure type of attitude (Simmel 1997[1910]), others find themselves in a push–pull situation where the lifestyles of the city and the promises of the rural/coastal life encourage a ritualistic escape into 'sacred places' (Smith 1999). Lifestyle or Amenity Migration (Benson and O'Reilly 2009; Benson 2011, forthcoming; Moss 2006; Osbaldiston 2011; Ragusa 2010; Hoey 2010) is one such manifestation of this dilemma. It has become a worldwide phenomenon and subsequently deserves some consideration in the analysis of the slow (see Parkins and Craig 2006, p. 67 for a brief reading of this phenomenon). However, not all 'escapes' from the city are permanent. Overseas tourism, for instance, bears witness to another form of escapism – the temporary journey from the mundane to the extraordinary. Under the guise of the slow paradigm, 'slow tourism' has developed as an alternative mode of touring other places (Lumsdon and McGrath 2011; Dickinson, Lumsdon and Robbins 2010). At the foundations of slow tourism, the slow tourist is the antithesis of the postmodern subject who treats the tourist moment as a fleeting experience or game rather than as an opportunity for self-fulfilment and authenticity (Rojek 1993; Urry 2002, 2011; Craik 1997). Slowness, as Parkins and Craig (2006) describe, however, seeks for moments of meaning, contemplation and care. While there are inherent political narratives embedded in slow travel (such as environmental concerns), the underlying cultural narrative is one which promotes a quest for the authentic, or potentially seeks out the sacred for the enhancement of the self (Cohen 1979; Smith 1999; Shields 1992).

A mundane city?

Before examining these engagements with space in detail, though, it is first important that we discuss the role of the city in modern life. Parkins and Craig (2006), as mentioned earlier, view the city through the paradigm of cosmopolitanism; or rather the potential for cosmopolitan identity to be formed individually. Yet alongside this is a homogenisation of place and the proliferation of spaces that are meaningless or 'placeless' (Relph 1976). In other words, the indistinguishable features of a metropolitan shopping mall, including the countless fast-food, retail and other outlets, create a landscape that is bland. The impact of their increased presence in the city strips away a sense of connectivity with place for individual identities. Such ideas have permeated through sociology and geography since modernisation. As Simmel (1997[1903]) proposes in his famous 'Metropolis and mental life' essay, the city has long been regarded as overwhelming and inhibiting. The design of the cities, for the classical sociologist, is such that it encourages a flat and dull attitude towards things (objects) and inculcates distrust and disdain towards other people deemed strangers. The latter point is evident in the disposition which 'small-town people' have towards urbanites who are considered 'cold and heartless' (Simmel 1997[1903], p. 179). These ideas permeate discourses and narratives of the country/city dialectic in Lifestyle Migration, or Seachange as it is referred to in Australia (Osbaldiston 2012; Ragusa 2010; Dowling 2004).

However, it would be a mistake to suggest that Simmel (1997[1903]) is entirely pessimistic about the cultural conditions of the modern city. The growth of a money economy and the expansiveness of population sizes means individuals are freed from a 'village' type of sociality where everyone knows everyone, and also personal business. The opportunity for one to be 'hidden' within the masses is more possible in an advanced metropolitan environment. However, it is in later essays, in particular his small examination of 'The adventure', that we can see optimism from Simmel. Here, specifically, he appears to perceive that within the very mundane flows of everyday life there are opportunities for escape (cf. Frisby 1992). On this issue he writes:

> An adventure is certainly part of our existence, directly contiguous with other parts which precede and follow it; at the same time, however, in its deeper meaning, it occurs outside the usual continuity of this life. Nevertheless, it is distinct from all that is accidental and alien, merely touching life's outer shell... Because of its place in our psychic life, a remembered adventure tends to take on the quality of a dream... The more 'adventurous' an adventure, that is, the more fully it realizes its idea, the more 'dreamlike' it becomes in our memory.
>
> (Simmel 1997[1910], p. 222)

Adventure seeking is therefore a form of experiencing that can emerge in the everyday. For Simmel (1997[1910]) the content is meaningless to the analyst; rather it is the interpretation of events for the individual which deems it as an extraordinary adventure or not. Thus, adventuring can be as simple as taking alternative routes to work through to mutual gazing or flirting on the train.

In relation to a slow narrative, we can begin to see how the desire to engage in alternative spatial practices appears as a type of 'adventuring'. As a symbol of homogeneity and mundane sociality, the city and the everyday work that occurs within it are transcended momentarily through various behaviours. Cycling, for instance (see Ryle and Soper, this volume), enables the individual to experience enjoyable sensations, such as the wind blowing on one's face, that are largely 'denied' in the usual experiences of vehicular and public transport (cf. Soper 2007). Going to food markets allows the consumer to embrace and experience local cuisine and culture, which binds the individual's sense of identity to a 'sense of place' (Parkins and Craig 2006). Even the ability to meet with friends to have lunch in a park, where sociality and meaningful conversation (which Simmel also felt escaped the rational cage of modernity) are enjoyed, could be considered as an alternative practice to the everyday.

These notions are reminiscent, certainly, of the 'alternative hedonism' theories produced by Kate Soper (2007). She argues that through consumption practices, including that of consuming space, individuals' own pursuit of hedonistic pleasure, combined with a wider concern for issues like pollution and environmental degradation, can result in a broad uptake of activities that are conducive to a sustainable future. She writes:

> Under this impulse, the individual acts with an eye to the collective impact of aggregated individual acts of affluent consumption for consumers themselves, and takes measures to avoid contributing to it. It is, for example, a decision to cycle or walk whenever possible in order not to add to the pollution, noise and congestion of car use. The hedonist aspect, however, of this shift in consumption practice does not reside exclusively in the desire to avoid or limit the unpleasurable by-products of collective affluence, but also in the sensual pleasures of consuming differently (Levett 2003, pp. 60–61). There are intrinsic pleasures to be had in walking or cycling which the car driver will not be experiencing.
>
> (Soper 2008, p. 572)

She suggests (2008, p. 572), though, that these 'alternative' means of consumption must at times be encouraged though local/state 'policies' that actively aim to reduce car traffic and enhance the bicycle and walking experience. Planning initiatives of this type recur across metropolitan environments in which more traditional forms of transport, such as walking and bike riding, are encouraged and spaces for them constructed. My point of matching Soper's (2007, 2008) work to Simmel's here, however, is concerned less with the political and more with a cultural condition in the city which creates a desire for extraordinary sensations. Adventuring, whether it be through modes of transport or farmer's markets on a Saturday morning, taps into a collective disaffection with the offering of sensual pleasures found in the everyday, fast, homogenous and habitual consumer capitalist life. Not all spaces in the city, however, are meaningless. There are areas which can encourage a 'slow' mindset, if we consider slowness to mean 'mindfulness', 'care' and 'attention' (see introductory chapter). It is important to reflect on these in order to locate the city symbolically as not simply another 'cathedral of consumption' (Ritzer 2010) but also a place with culturally meaningful spaces. These can include sites that encourage reflection on 'charismatic' pasts. Terlouw (2011, p. 339), for instance, suggests that

> The here and now of everyday life is the domain of established regimes. To legitimize their ordinary rule, established regimes try to link up with distant charisma. This is one of the ways in which both traditional and bureaucratic regimes seek support from their population. They can legitimize their rule by linking their national narrative with the charisma embodied in special iconic places. Space is frequently used to construct linkages with the pure charisma of other times.

Monuments to past charismatic authority including monarchs and religious leaders reinforce for Terlouw (2011, p. 341) the legitimacy of present regimes. These include legitimating bureaucratic structures that have overcome old traditional forms of charismatic authority. The charismatic space in this case serves to identify that the present 'regime will perform even better' than its predecessors (Terlouw 2011, p. 341). How this relates to slowness, however, is less clear. I propose, though, that in certain spaces within the city the individual is called to reflect and meditate on symbols rather than just walk effortlessly past them without any reflexive prowess.

In neo-Durkheimian language, these sorts of area are those that not only allow people to reflect upon past traditions and perhaps feel some 'collective nostalgia' (Davis 1979) for times forgotten, but also enforce change on the body which results in shifts in micro-behaviour because of the force of broader cultural narratives. Described as 'sacred places', Phil Smith (1999, p. 19) suggests that

> nearing the sacred place a penumbra of solemnity imposes itself on human behaviour, inviting, for example, the hushed tones, the straightened back, silent footsteps, slow breathing which in turn invoke physiological changes and direct memory towards the sacred and away from the mundane, liminal and profane.

From war memorials to churches and through to sites of national significance (e.g. the Bastille or the World Trade Centre Memorial), these sites carry a cultural force which imposes itself upon the individual, but not as a form of discipline (cf. Foucault 1991[1975]). Rather, as Durkheim (1995[1912]) derived from his study of religion, they draw people in through collective values and mythologies or cultural narratives, and encourage contemplation, meaning and, potentially, slowness.

In relation to the slow paradigm, these sorts of space which are not hidden within the city can induce feelings of collective effervescence but mainly invoke a feeling of the sacred within the individual. This contrasts the proposal that the city is embedded in speed, consumerism and meaninglessness. From this perspective, cities are not simply monolithic consumer capitalist spaces that rely on re-enchantment through spectacle and/or simulations (Ritzer 2010; Baudrillard 1994); rather, cities are replete with those forms of place which create opportunities for engagement with sacred things that can enhance an 'authentic self'. Unlike a 'cosmopolitan' identity which can result in 'cosmopolitan' individuals (Parkins and Craig 2006, p. 4), the city with its various sacred places has for some time owned the cultural artifacts that encourage 'care, attention and mindfulness', which are central to the slow culture.

Escaping the city

The metropolis therefore cannot be seen as merely devoid of distinctiveness and cultural importance. However, these ideas are slightly discordant with the understanding of 'slowness' that is developed by Parkins and Craig (2006). Rather than seeing slowness in those social movements that embrace the logic of Carlo Petrini's 'slow food', slow culture has developed into a narrative that motivates a number of 'alternative' approaches to the everyday. The negotiation of space or the consumption of spaces that enhance the authentic self are examples of this.

However, for a growing set of disgruntled and disaffected individuals living within the confines of suburbia or the urban, city life imposes a level of stress and unhappiness that creates a desire to escape. It is clear that the city and its associated infrastructure and day-to-day activities, promotes habitual and ordinary behaviour. Most important, as Simmel (1997[1910]) shows in his essay on the adventure, are the interlocking moments of life that are accentuated by work. The city is for many people a place for work rather than play, and for a growing set of disgruntled individuals it is now becoming the profane. For instance, one participant in a study conducted in 2006 complains that

> I was sick of the city, and it was dirty and people are sort of always angry and stuff like that...yeah, and it was a stressful place and I wanted somewhere that was more peaceful
>
> (Osbaldiston 2006, pp. 49–50)

Another participant in the same study says that they

> got sick of the traffic. I got sick of the fake lifestyle really, you know no community mindedness everybody is so solitary...encapsulated in their own sort of space and just seem to be about achieving money and not caring about the planet.
>
> (Osbaldiston 2006, p. 50)

For these individuals and thousands like them, the city has a profound influence on their daily lives, in a somewhat degrading manner. Stress, pollution, anger, traffic, congestion, overcrowding and speed are all problems of which these individuals finally get tired (see Osbaldiston 2006, 2012; Ragusa 2010, this volume; Dowling 2004).

Unlike sacred places, which invoke micro-bodily changes through meaningful and deeply subjective narratives and themes, the city leaves such a negative impression on these people that it becomes the 'profane place' (Smith 1999). For neo-Durkheimian Smith (1999, p. 19), this type of 'place' has an influence on the individual as profound as the sacred:

> These narratives see human actions as polluting to the moral fabric of society and degrading to human spiritual values. Like sacred places, those which are profane are often founded upon narratives of violence...Profane places are more often, but not always – the locus of subsequent, equally ritualistic (to the sacred) attempts at destruction and obliteration...marked out by taboos and what Durkheim called 'rituals of avoidance'.
>
> (Smith 1999, p. 19)

Within the city, there are several instances of once perceived profane places receiving significant rejuvenation to create new, sometimes chic, housing and other development. Inner-city suburbia and old factory districts are often turned into boutique-style living, attracting those from within the middle classes who seek a new 'style' of alternative living. Acknowledging this, we can also begin to question who defines the authentic here and who decides when the profane requires 'bulldozing', as Zukin (2008) reminds us.

For a growing group of individuals, however, the city has become a symbol of the profane. Not only are the objective surrounds considered an impediment to self-actualisation (Simmel (1997[1903]) but the speed of the city and the velocity of contemporary life creates a need to 'slow' down and find more balance to living. This realisation encourages the individual to seek out alternative lifestyles, usually found outside the city and suburbs, called Lifestyle Migration, Amenity Migration or Seachange. These disgruntled urbanites seek a life more conducive to a sense of well-being and self-actualisation which they believe can be found in the rural or coastal lifestyles. Towns selected by these urban refugees are often underpinned by broad and romantic narratives which suggest that the place is the answer to life's ills. In particular, there are three major facets of regional living which attract the lifestyle migrant: the natural world, a nostalgia for the past and the notion of community (see Osbaldiston 2011, 2012; Moss 2006). In each instance the binary interplay between the country and the perceived profane qualities of the city is stark. The country is conceived of as clean, pure, untouched, sociable, warm, friendly, creative and, most importantly, slow. Areas like Canmore in Alberta, Canada, the Town of Golden in British Columbia, Jackson Hole in Wyoming, Tasmania in Australia, parts of rural France and the English countryside have all in recent years encountered unprecedented population growth, to which these slow seekers contribute significantly (Mitchell 2005; Osbaldiston 2012; Ragusa 2010; Burnley and Murphy 2004; Benson 2011). Importantly, like the sacred places above, these areas are perceived to offer sensations that are lacking in the metropolis and a natural environment that promotes slower, more meaningful lifestyles. The 'distinctiveness' of the landscape is also often considered as iconic to a national identity. For instance, Robinson and Stark (2006, p. 120) illustrate that Canadians, in particular Albertans, often describe their state through imagery of 'rolling foothills, forests without end and glacier-capped mountain playgrounds'. In Australia, iconic beaches and dusty outback landscapes sit deep in the collective imagination of Australiana, revealed specifically in film and literature (see Booth 2001; Drewe 1993). Classics such as Lawson's *The Drover's Wife* or Patterson's *The Man from Snowy River* serve to sacralise a particular type of landscape into the collective narrative of Australia. For those seeking refuge from the city, it is these types of narrative, alongside the general appeal of slower living, which reconnect the individual to a collective identity, promoting self-authenticity and, potentially, distinction (see below).

It may be said, however, that this particular adoption of 'slowness' is not particularly new. The city has, since the development of industrial modernity, been construed in some circles as 'profane'-like, while the countryside lifestyle was seen to be unpolluted. Macnaughten and Urry (1998, p. 175) reveal, for instance, that in industrialised England

> the countryside came increasingly to be desired because of its visual qualities mediated through the representation of space via the notion of landscape ... the industrial town was seen as thoroughly polluted, as unnaturally invading all the human orifices.

Country life was lauded as 'significant' and a symbol of true 'Englishness' (Macnaughten and Urry 1998, p. 180). Their landscapes were 'unspoiled' by modernisation and a proper mode of engagement which involved thoughtful, quiet and unobtrusive practices was established. In places like the Lake District, these practices, which involve quiet walking, yachting and various other forms of 'romantic' negotiation of the landscape, are still in fashion today (Macnaughten and Urry 1998, p. 187). However, escaping the city was seen as more than just an escape from a horribly polluted city environment; it also became a sign of good taste for the bourgeois and a symbol of proper living. This reality raises new questions of motivation among today's lifestyle migrants (see discussion below). In particular, who defines what is authentic and the impact that this has on local dynamics and cultural form are important considerations.

However, this aside, there are other historical examples of those who sought out the simplicity of the good life in the country prior to the emergence of the lifestyle migration phenomenon. For instance, Thoreau's (2008[1854]) sojourn to Walden reflects a similar ideal to today's amenity-led migrants. He writes:

> I went to the woods because I wished to live deliberately, to front only the essential facts of life, and see if I could not learn what it had to teach, and not, when I came to die, discover that I had not lived ... I wanted to live deep and suck out all the marrow of life, to live so sturdily and Spartan-like as to put to rout all that was not life, to cut a broad swath and shave close, to drive life into a corner, and reduce it to its lowest terms.
>
> (Thoreau 2008[1854], p. 45)

The logic of Thoreau's thoughts here is that within the city, the ability to achieve what he desired most of all, which we could surmise was a type of self-authenticity, was impossible. The country, on the other hand, and it's simple and slow tempo encourage feelings of solitude, peace and contemplativeness. The disjuncture between the city and the country here is reminiscent of Raymond Williams' (1973) famous claim that the two places are embedded in a slow/fast rhetoric. Those living in the country were considered old-fashioned or 'traditional', whereas the city was conceived of as progressive and advanced (Williams 1973). From a broad perspective, this is essentially what Lifestyle Migration is founded on (see e.g. Benson 2011). This view designates the country lifestyle as simple and community focused – a step back in time. Most importantly, however, it is symbolically distant from a city that is forever advancing, progressing and accelerating, but which also inhibits the self in its development. In short, the contemporary escape from the city can be seen as a manifestation of a long historical binary opposition between the sacred countryside and the profane and unnatural cityscape.

Lifestyle Migration from this angle can again be seen as an 'alternative' method of consuming places slowly. In this instance, it is a more drastic measure wherein the individual employs a significant ritualistic avoidance strategy and immerses themselves into a culture and landscape which are far removed from the city. Once the individual is immersed into a space that is surrounded by a pristine natural world and a small-town country atmosphere, the opportunities to 'slow down' are abundant. As Smith (1999) considers in the 'sacred place', these new surroundings promote a change in behaviour and subsequently in identity. This is precisely what they seek through their urban escape. It is via their new location that lifestyle migrants find a 'congruence' between their own values and beliefs, thus providing a feeling of affirmation and authenticity (Vannini and Burgess 2009, p. 104). Like 'alternative hedonism', however, there are critical questions about who can actually engage with this slow form of living. The premise, though, is that by consuming different or alternative places that are considered more authentic, individuals can find more meaning in their life and can find slow havens. This conceptual framework is found not only within this dramatic movement but also within other manifestations of slowness (including Slow Food; see Lindholm and Lie, this volume).

Discovering new places slowly

Another growing social trend is the adoption of a form of tourism under the banner of the slow. Called simply 'Slow Travel' or 'Slow Tourism', this apparently new modality of travel seeks to overcome the rushed nature of the postmodern tourist by allowing them to become immersed in the local culture, cuisine and landscapes. Unlike Urry's (2002, p. 92) 'three-minute' tourist, those engaging in slow travel experiences spend lengthy amounts of time in accommodation that is often self-catering (Footprint Choices 2012). This means essentially that the traveller is not just 'staying' at their destination but 'living' there (Footprint Choices 2012, para.5). This includes being able to enter into local settings and immersing oneself in the cultural life that is found within it. Such a view also encourages a flaneuristic type of engagement with place where the individual becomes part of the social life though their wanderings and slow engagement with the social. Rather than speeding in hire cars to 'must-see' destinations and other speedier modes of transportation, the slow traveller experiences sensations that other tourists miss in their harried and often stressful journeyings. Speakman (2005, cited in Lumsdon and McGrath 2011, p. 269) discusses this point further:

> Contrary to the seductive automobile advertisements, quality of experience is not about speed. The real pleasure of travelling on barge or cruise boat along a waterway lies in travelling at a gentle pace through a slowly changing landscape. Walking and cycling are forms of tourism transport that offer so much more than the car in terms of perceiving the environment in far greater detail, and allowing other senses to share in that perception – experience the sounds, the touch, even the taste and the smell of the natural world and cultural landscape. In transport for tourism terms, therefore slow is beautiful.

Once again the emphasis in this statement is on the alternative sensations that one can experience through a slow form of experiencing place. Thus tourism is less about the 'gaze' that Urry (2002) famously argued for and more about the holistic experience of a new place, a new culture and subsequently a distinction from fake tourism.

Conceptualising this evolving form of tourism has been limited in the academic sphere. One of the few illustrations can be found in Lumsdon and McGrath's (2011, p. 276, italics added) work, which suggests that slow travel can be thought of in the following way:

> Slow travel is a sociocultural phenomenon, focusing on holiday-making but also on day leisure visits, where use of *personal time is appreciated differently*. Slowness is valued, and the journey is integral

to the whole experience. The mode of transport and the activities undertaken at a destination *enhance the richness of the experience through slowness*. Whilst the journey is the thing and can be the destination in its own right, *the experience of locality counts for much*, as does reduced duration or distance of travel.

The emphasis here is again on the individual consuming differently for their own sensual delight. However, websites dedicated to advocating slow tourism are keen to identify other ethical reasons for enjoying an alternative approach to travel. This includes 'voluntourism', where people can utilise their skills and resources to assist less advantaged communities through welfare groups and non-government agencies (Footprint Choices 2011). *Voluntourism* (voluntourism.org 2012), a website designed to assist those considering the option, portrays the opportunity to combine volunteer work with the tourist experience as allowing the individual to interact with a destination in ways that exceed 'expectation'.

Like 'alternative hedonism' or 'slow food', the political potential of slow tourism is described by Lumsden and McGrath (2011, p. 277) as a way for tourism to be 'reconfigured to offer an enhanced experience and reduced environmental impact'. In another exploration of the topic, Dickinson, Lumsdon and Robbins (2010, p. 295) suggest that in the future, in the case of a 'low-carbon' transition, the ability of slow tourism to become a tool for a more sustainable outcome should be taken seriously. Certainly, in an age when climate change mitigation and the debates within it weigh heavily on fossil-fuel-dependent industries, this suggestion has merit. Like the consumption of alternative food practices that identify with concerns for sustainability (Parkins and Craig 2006), or even of other products, such as fashion (see Schor, this volume), which recognises the finitude of resources, slow travel can adopt those narratives that seek to lessen the footprint of travel upon the world.

However, conceptualising slow travel further for the purposes of this chapter need not go too far beyond the Durkheimian language presented by Smith (1999) and others. Simply put, slow travel engages a narrative that views the tourist experience as 'sacred'. This subject – the sacred – has been the focus of important pieces of research on previous tourism (Cohen 1979; MacCannell 1973; Rojek 1993). However, rather than treating the experience as a pilgrimage similar to the rituals found in Durkheim's *Elementary Forms of Religious Life*, I wish to suggest that the tourist experience through the 'mindfulness' of slow travel encourages a rendering of these 'new' places as sacred. As Smith (1999) locates in his typology of sacred places, these new locales are treated with high esteem and, like the sacred places found in the city, encourage a different perception and behaviour that is distinct from the profane city/urban life. Thus, unlike a narrative that suggests that tourism is simply for rest and recovery from a stressful and alienating world (Cohen 1979), slow tourism embraces a paradigm that suggests that this consuming place enables a sense of self-authenticity or self-actualisation. It is only through experiencing place slowly that this is made possible, however. Again, unlike Urry's (2002) conceptualisation of the tourist who consumes predominantly with their eyes, the slow tourist seeks to discover newness by embracing all of the sensations that are on offer. By engaging fully with the local culture, space, natural wonder and everyday life, the individual immerses themselves into new and distinct tastes, smells, sounds and sights. Admittedly this is only a brief theoretical discussion of what is a burgeoning social practice. More thought will need to be applied in the future to how we might conceptualise it not only within the broader slow cultural narrative but also within the expansive and well-founded tourism literature.

Whose authenticity is it anyway?

The thread tying what is essentially a messy reading of slowness and place in this chapter is the notion of authenticity or, rather, self-authenticity, which has re-emerged in importance during the past few years (Lindholm 2008; Lindolm and Zúquete 2010; Vannini and Burgess 2009). The argument which has been implicit throughout has been that authenticity is a driving force behind the re-negotiation of spatial practices through slowness. Embedded in the theory that the slow is equated with other narratives, such as 'care', 'mindfulness' and 'contemplation', is a desire for self-authenticity by engaging with authentic objects and surrounds. Such notions are built upon Simmel's own principles for cultivation that are found in his theories of culture (cf. Nedelmann 1991). Here, objective culture is subjectified for the development of the self or, in the case of this chapter, the actualisation of the 'authentic' or genuine self. However, as Simmel (1997[1912], p. 73) recounts in his essay 'The tragedy of culture', this process has been significantly disturbed through modernisation. He writes:

> There thus emerges the typical problematic condition of modern humanity: the feeling of *being surrounded by an immense number of*

cultural elements, which are not meaningless, but not profoundly mean-
ingful to the individual either; elements which have a certain crushing
quality as a mass because an individual cannot inwardly assimilate
every individual thing, *but cannot simply reject it either, since it belongs*
potentially, as it were, to the sphere of his or her cultural development.

As suggested earlier in the discussion on the city, objective culture has
outgrown the capacity for the self to subjectify it for self-development.
Perception becomes deadened and cultural life blasé. Of course, such
metaphysical commentary derived from Kantian discourse should be
treated with some scepticism. Elsewhere in relation to Lifestyle Migration or Seachange, I have argued that these theoretical notions should
not be considered as 'real' but in fact as 'social constructs' which appear
to guide behaviour today (Osbaldiston 2012). In other words, individuals recognise that in order to self-actualise, they need to embrace an
alternative mode of living that engages with slower or more even modes
of objective culture. Negotiating space and place under the paradigm of
the slow is to do so with an eye towards experiencing something which
enchants the senses rather than deadens them.

However, in analysing cultural life, we cannot be naïve to the problems of authenticity. In particular, the ability for the narrative of
authenticity to distinguish, separate or gentrify is a side effect of the
slow phenomenon that needs to be considered (Benson and O'Reilly
2009; Zukin 2008). For instance, in response to Soper's (2008) proposition for more investment in 'alternative hedonism', both theoretically
and politically, urban sociologist Sharon Zukin (2008, p. 728) reflects
that 'we can only see spaces as authentic from outside them'. In her
assessment of Soho, for instance, this critical perspective takes on more
empirical shape:

When consumption spaces manipulate authenticity for new residents' needs, they enable them – not so innocently – to stake their
own claim to the neighborhood. But as SoHo shows, alternative consumption sites legitimise the area as a commercial attraction. The
neighborhood becomes a target of wealthy consumers, chain stores,
and real estate developers – an emporium for tourists and shoppers.
When commercial rents rise above what experimental outposts of
difference can afford to pay, they shut down or migrate to less expensive areas. (Unlike some small, specialised retail stores, they depend
on face-to-face experience, so they cannot just move their business to
the Internet.) Artists and hipsters are well aware of the significant role

their tastes play in this process. But it is not the presence of artists that sets the process of displacement in motion: it is the presence of their taste for authenticity in the product mix, store design, and intangible ambiance of restaurants, boutiques, and gourmet stores.

From here we can question the notion of authenticity which is derived from outside (see above) and then imposed upon spaces by outsiders. Zukin (2008, p. 745) concludes by arguing that despite the work of authenticity which occurs in places that are selected for rejuvenation (or gentrification) by the middle or creative classes, such as Soho, 'the norm of alternative consumption becomes a means of excluding others from their space'. This includes racial as well as social class distinction.

This notion of how taste operates as a mode of class distinction is developed in relation to lifestyle migration in the work of Benson (2011; see also Benson 2009, forthcoming) on British residents in rural France. Their imaginings of the area, which drive the decision to migrate and also their expectations and experiences of life at their destination, are encapsulated within the notion of the rural idyll, a cultural construction of rurality through which the French countryside is appropriated. As Benson argues, the migration to this rural destination can be read, in Bourdieusian terms, as a 'desire for difference' (2009); driven by the pursuit of distinction, it makes apparent the intra-class processes that go on within the British middle classes.

Authenticity is central to these processes of distinction. The image of the rural idyll mobilised by Benson's respondents focuses on the authentic life that is uniquely available at their destination which through migration they desire to become part of. Their practices and actions reveal the self-conscious performance of this better way of life, as they seek authentication from their middle-class peers. Increasingly, notions of what constitutes authentic living in rural France become increasingly individualised and nuanced. While the general tropes of rurality remain central, individual migrants present their own understandings of how this authentic life can and should be led. The pursuit of a better way of life that lay at the core of their migration is a persistent feature of their post-migration lives, as the genteel struggles over their class position continue (Benson 2011, forthcoming).

Conclusion

This chapter has sought to explore the notion of slowness within space/place. Unlike the work of Parkins and Craig (2006), it has to avoid discussing the culture of the slow through only explicitly named 'slow' movements. Rather, as discussed earlier, there are several key sites where alternative modes of consuming space fall under the umbrella of what is a loose definition of what constitutes the 'slow' (see Introduction). Indeed, in the everyday, as Soper (2008) has shown, there are many instances where the same principles of care and mindfulness that attend to movements like slow food are embraced by individuals seeking escape from the everyday or the rationalised world. In particular, the city not only causes some to seek ritualistic escape through Lifestyle Migration but also encourages alternative modes of experiencing space. Whether it is through bicycle riding, walking, taking ferries or simply through enjoyment of friends during lunch breaks in the park, there is a sense that the everyday can be transcended through spatial practice – a moment of adventuring in an otherwise seamless day (Simmel 1997[1910]).

In the latter half of the chapter, the notion of sacrality was introduced to the debate through Smith (1999). Here, using Lifestyle Migration and Slow Tourism as examples, it was argued that under the paradigm of authenticity, individuals seek out sites for their own personal actualisation which can be considered as the 'sacred experience'. However, as the chapter concludes, the notion of authenticity can be contested critically. Benson's (2011) work alongside other thinkers, especially Zukin (2008, 2010), opens up space for this critique. Who decides what is authentic? Who decides what is sacred? How does this decision impose itself upon local spaces and cultural conditions? What impact does this have on equity? Who is excluded? Such questions need not remain the focus of spatial analysis. For instance, in the discussion of Slow Food, the critical argument of who is invited to the table and who is excluded is worth debating. In particular, cuisine that is at times quite expensive ultimately denies entry to the lower classes. Further, it is evident that authenticity is a contested issue, and who decides what is authentic is open (see Lindholm and Lie, this volume). There is no room to expound upon this idea here, though.

For the middle classes, however, the quest for the authentic remains a real pursuit. The side effects are something to debate among analysts of space and culture. While slowness has emerged as a political narrative worthy of consideration for a sustainable future, this chapter shows that there is a powerful cultural theme which needs to be acknowledged. Not all consumers of slowness do so with a broader ecological focus alongside their own personal desires. Lifestyle migrants, slow travellers, bicycle riders, walkers and other proponents of spatial consumption can at times be centred solely on individual 'hedonist' desires for alternatives to the mundane. Simmel (1997[1910]) shows us that this is not new. Rather, we have been seeking enchantment for a disenchanted world since modernity. Slowness potentially emerges as another manifestation of this. However, as quoted earlier, Simmel's (1997[1895]) powerful critique that capitalism subsumes ideas as well as objects gives us caution to be too optimistic on this latest counter to rapid modernisation.

Acknowledgement

I would like to acknowledge the assistance of Dr Michaela Benson of York University for her assistance in the compiling of thoughts and ideas for this chapter.

References

Adam, B., 1990, *Time and Social Theory*, Temple University Press, Philadelphia.

——, 1995, *Timewatch: The Social Analysis of Time*, Polity Press, Cambridge.

——, 1998, *Timescapes of Modernity: The Environment and Invisible Hazards*, Routledge, New York.

Baudrillard, J., 1994, *Simulacra and Simulation*, S. F. Glaser (trans.), University of Michigan Press, Michigan.

Beck, U., 1992, *Risk Society: Towards a New Modernity*, M. Ritter (trans.), SAGE, London.

—— 2006, *The Cosmopolitan Vision*, C. Cronin (trans.), Polity Press, Cambridge.

Benson, M., 2009, 'A desire for difference: British lifestyle migration to southwest France', in M. C. Benson and K. O'Reilly (eds.), *Lifestyle Migration: Expectations, Aspirations and Experiences*, Ashgate, Farnham, pp. 121–136.

Benson, M., 2011, *The British in Rural France: Lifestyle Migration and the Ongoing Quest for a Better Way of Life*, Manchester University Press, Manchester.

Benson, M., forthcoming, 'Living the 'Real' dream in La France Profonde: Lifestyle migrants and the ongoing quest for the authentic', *Anthropological Quarterly*.

Benson, M. and O'Reilly, K., 2009, *Lifestyle Migration and the Ongoing Quest for a Better Way of Life*, Manchester University Press, Manchester.

Booth, D., 2001, *Australian Beach Cultures: The History of Sun, Sand and Surf*, Frank Cass & Co, London.

Burnley, I. and Murphy, P., 2004, *Sea Change: Movement from Metropolitan to Arcadian Australia*, UNSW Press, Sydney.

Cohen, E. H., 1979, 'A phenomenology of tourist experiences', *Sociology*, 13, 179–201.

Craik, J., 1997, 'The culture of tourism', in C. Rojek and J. Urry (eds.), *Touring Cultures: Transformations of Travel and Theory*, Routledge, London, pp. 113–136.

Davis, F., 1979, *Yearning for Yesterday: A Sociology of Nostalgia*, Free Press, New York.

Dickinson, J. E., Lumsdon, L. and Robbins, D. K., 2010, 'Slow travel: Issues for tourism and climate change', *Journal of Sustainable Tourism*, 19(3), 281–300.

Dowling, C., 2004, *Seachange: Australians in Pursuit of the Good Life*, Exisle, Sydney.

Drewe, R., 1993, *The Penguin Book of the Beach*, Penguin Books, Melbourne.

Durkheim, E., 1995[1912], *Elementary Forms of Religious Life*, K. E. Fields (trans.), The Free Press, New York.

Footprint Choices, 2012, 'What is slow travel?', *Slow Movement*, viewed 23 February 2012, http://www.slowmovement.com/slow_travel.php.

Foucault, M., 1991[1975], *Discipline and Punish*, A. Sheridan (trans.), Penguin Books, London.

Frisby, D., 1992, *Simmel and Since: Essays on Georg Simmel's Social Theory*, Routledge, London.

Hochschild, A., 1997, *The Time Bind: When Work Becomes Home and Home Becomes Work*, Metropolitan Books, New York.

Hoey, B., 2010, 'Personhood in place: Personal and local character for sustainable narrative of self', *City and Society*, 22(2), 237–261.

Kendall, G., Skrbis, Z. and Woodward, I., 2008, *The Sociology of Cosmopolitanism*, Palgrave Macmillan, Bassingstoke.

Lamanna, M., 2004, 'Decentering Durkheim: his writings on the family', in *Proceedings of the American Sociological Association Conference 2004*, San Francisco, viewed 14 August 2009, http://www.allacademic.com/meta/p108541_index.html.

Lasch, C., 1979, *Haven in a Heartless World: The Family Besieged*, Basic Books, New York.

Lindholm, C., 2008, *Culture and Authenticity*, Blackwell, Malden.

Lindholm, C. and Zúquete, J. P., 2010, *The Struggle for the World: Liberation Movements for the 21st Century*, Stanford University Press, Stanford.

Lumsdon, L. M. and McGrath, P., 2011, 'Developing a conceptual framework for slow travel: a grounded theory approach', *Journal of Sustainable Tourism*, 19(3), 265–279.

MacCannell, D., 1973, 'Staged authenticity: arrangements of social space in tourist settings', *American Journal of Sociology*, 79, 589–603.

Macnaughten, P. and Urry, J., 1998, *Contested Natures*, Sage, London.

Miele, M., 2008, 'Cittaslow: producing slowness against the fast life', *Space and Polity*, 12(1), 135–156.

Mitchell, C. J. A., 2005, 'Population growth and external commuting to Canada's rural and small town municipalities', *Canadian Journal of Regional Science*, 20, 15–34.

Moss, L. A. G. (ed.), 2006, *The Amenity Migrants: Seeking and Sustaining Mountains and Their Cultures*, CABI, Oxfordshire.

Murdoch, J. and Day, G., 1998, 'Middle class mobility, rural communities and the politics of exclusion', in P. Boyle and L. Halfacree (eds.), *Migration into Rural Areas*, Wiley, Chichester, pp. 186–199.

Nedelmann, B., 1991, 'Individualisation, exaggeration and paralysation: Simmel's three problems of culture', *Theory, Culture and Society*, 8(3), 169–193.

Osbaldiston, N., 2006, *Risk and Seachange: Discourses of Risk-Taking and Individualisation within a Contemporary Australian Phenomenon*, BSocSci (Hons) thesis, Queensland University of Technology, Brisbane.

————, 2011, 'The authentic place in amenity migration discourse', *Space and Culture*, 14(2), 214–226.

————, 2012, *Seeking for Authenticity in Place, Culture and the Self: The Great Urban Escape*, Palgrave MacMillan, New York.

Pahl, R., 2005, Are all communities communities in the mind?', *Sociological Review Monograph*, 53, 621–640.

Parkins, W. and Craig, G., 2006, *Slow Living*, Berg, Oxford.

Pink, S., 2007, 'Sensing cittaslow: slow living and the constitution of the sensory city', *Sense and Society*, 2(1), 59–77.

Ragusa, A., 2010, 'Seeking trees or escaping traffic: socio-cultural factors and 'treechange' migration in Australia', in G. W. Luck, R. Black and D. Race (eds.), *Demographic Change in Rural Landscapes: What Does It Mean for Society and the Environment?*, Springer, London, pp. 71–99.

Relph, E. C., 1976, *Place and Placelessness*, Pion, London.

Ritzer, G. 2010. *Enchanting a Disenchanted World: Continuity and Change in the Cathedrals of Consumption*, Sage, Thousand Oaks, California.

Robinson, B. and Stark, C., 2006, 'Alberta's amenity rush', in L. A. G. Moss (ed.), *The Amenity Migrants: Seeking and Sustaining Mountains and Their Cultures*, CABI, Oxfordshire, pp. 120–134.

Rojek, C., 1993, *Ways of Escape: Modern Transformations in Leisure and Travel*, Palgrave Macmillan, Bassingstoke.

Shields, R., 1992, *Places on the Margin: Alternative Geographies of Modernity*, Routledge, London.

Simmel, G., 1997[1895], 'The alpine journey', S. Whimster (trans.), in D. Frisby and M. Featherstone (eds.), *Simmel on Culture: Selected Writings*, Sage, London, 174–186.

————, 1997[1903], 'The metropolis and Mental Life', M. Ritter (trans.), in D. Frisby and M. Featherstone (eds.), *Simmel on Culture*, Sage, London, pp. 174–186.

————, 1997[1910], 'The adventure', K. Wolff (trans.), in D. Frisby and M. Featherstone (eds.), *Simmel on Culture: Selected Writings*, Sage, London, pp. 221–232.

————,1997[1912], 'The concept and tragedy of culture', M. Ritter and D. Frisby (trans.), in D. Frisby and M. Featherstone (eds.) *Simmel on Culture: Selected Writings*, Sage, London, pp. 120–130

Smith, P., 1999, 'The elementary forms of place and their transformations: a Durkheimian model', *Qualitative Sociology*, 22(1), 13–36.

Soper, K., 2007, 'Rethinking the 'good life': the citizenship dimension of consumer disaffection with consumerism', *Journal of Consumer Culture*, 7(2), 205–229.

————, 2008, 'Alternative hedonism, cultural theory and the role of aesthetic revisioning', *Cultural Studies*, 22(5), 567–587.

Terlouw, K., 2011, 'Charisma and space', *Studies in Ethnicity and Nationalism*, 10(3), 335–348.

Thoreau, H. D., 2008[1854], *Walden and on the Duty of Civil Disobedience*, viewed 15 January 2009, http://www.gutenberg.org/etext/205.

Urry, J., 2002, *The Tourist Gaze* (2nd edn), Sage, London.

————, 2011, *The Tourist Gaze 3.0*, Sage, Los Angeles.

Vannini, P. and Burgess, S., 2009, 'Authenticity as motivation and aesthetic experience', in P. Vannini and J. P. Williams (eds.), *Authenticity in Culture, Self and Society*, Ashgate Publishing, Burlington, pp. 103–120.
Voluntourism, 2012, 'Welcome potential VolunTourists', viewed 23 February 2012, http://www.voluntourism.org/travelers.htm.
Williams, R., 1973, *The Country and the City*, Chatto and Windus, London.
Woodward, I., 2007, *Understanding Material Culture*, Sage, London.
Zukin, S., 2008, 'Consuming authenticity', *Cultural Studies*, 22(5), 724–748.
———, 2010, *Naked City: The Death and Life of Authentic Urban Places*, Oxford University Press, Oxford.

5

Alternative Hedonism: The World by Bicycle

Martin Ryle and Kate Soper

Introduction

Our subject is speed in perhaps the commonest use and meaning of the word: speed as the pace at which we move across the earth. Our especial focus is on the bicycle, a machine both slow and fast, as it is still – in some places increasingly – ridden in the countries of the rich world. We draw above all on our knowledge and experience of England and Britain, but refer also to the USA, and to the northern European nations where cycling holds a significant place in the culture and ecology of urban transport.

Our discussion begins with some more general critical reflections on the place of speed in contemporary work and consumption, and it is framed throughout by ideas and values associated with the concept of alternative hedonism. We have discussed and illustrated this concept elsewhere (Soper 2006, 2007a, 2007b, 2008, 2009; Ryle 2009). Its central tenet is that while in the near future human societies will undoubtedly have to observe stringent constraints on their recently profligate use of energy and raw materials, the necessary transition can be grasped as an opportunity to 'advance beyond a mode of life that is not just unsustainable but also in many respects unpleasurable and self-denying' (Soper 2009, p. 3). Such a perspective enjoins us to be alert to the pleasures destroyed, pre-empted and threatened by hegemonic forms of development.

The bicycle prompts alternative hedonist reflection, and celebration, because it has persisted across more than a century of innovation in which motorised vehicles have come to dominate most transport systems in the world. It is politically important because its continued use often signifies resistance to one-dimensional narratives of progress. Its practical utility, its cheapness and its environmental virtues are reason enough for its survival. But beyond these everyday motivations, bicycle riders in over-developed nations since the 1960s have sometimes nurtured a sense – a pleasurable sense – of defying or transgressing dominant norms of convenience, of visible status and of speed. Bicycle counter-culture has given semi-formal expression to these oppositional motives. Now, as mainstream political economy struggles to come to terms with the 'limits to growth' – above all in the domain of energy – that the green movement was already speaking of 30 years ago (Ryle 1988, pp. 1–6), the bicycle seems less a residual element of a vanishing life-world than a prefiguration of what is to come.

The pains of speed

Consumer culture glorifies speed, and it has developed in tandem with the provision of the means for human beings to communicate and to travel at an ever-faster pace. The bid to do things faster, and thus reduce time spent on any given activity, is at the heart of the consumerist dynamic, whether it be a matter of information technology or of physical transport. The ideas of 'progress' and 'development' have become more or less synonymous with those of saving time or speeding up, to the point where it is now almost impossible to travel long distances except by air, and where it would be thought bizarre for research and development teams and industrial designers to promote product innovations on the grounds that they allowed their users to proceed at a more relaxed pace. The tacit assumption in this association of human advancement with increased speed is that the faster we travel and communicate, the more exciting life will become, and the fuller and richer our experience will be. This assumption needs challenging from a number of differing but mutually reinforcing perspectives.

Speed is, of course, convenient and it can be thrilling. Yet we should be aware of the relative aspect of such a judgement. A pace of 15 miles per hour was regarded as exhilaratingly rapid by the young Charles Dickens, who in *The Pickwick Papers* (1836) describes a horse-drawn chaise rushing past fields, trees and hedges 'with the velocity of a whirlwind' (Dickens n.d., pp. 125–126). Today, car-drivers see a 20 mile per hour limit as restrictively slow. There is no doubt that we have come to tolerate, expect and often enjoy ever-faster modes of transport, but the implications of this are complex and need to be reviewed dialectically. On the one hand, this relativity may be seized upon by the advocates of faster travel: attempts to slow us down, they may say, no more 'naturally' correspond to human needs than do endeavours to go ever faster (though it can hardly be denied that there are, in any case, absolute limits on the speeds at which drivers can operate safely). On the other hand, our historical adaptability can be said to prove how easily we might come to enjoy much lower speeds as quite exhilarating enough. To acknowledge the fluidity of tastes and preferences is to reject any claim that 'progress' can only mean going faster along the path we are on today.

A similar dialectic is at work in our accelerating capacity to produce and disseminate information, and in the speeding-up and depersonalisation of communications that have been its most salient cultural and social consequences. Thanks to the ever-increasing power of computers, engineering calculations that would have taken a year or more in the 1940s are now completed in fifteen minutes (Bunting 2004, p. 45). There is no doubt that we have very quickly adapted to – and become extraordinarily dependent upon – this rapid processing of information and the billions of electronic exchanges it allows on a daily basis. But at the same time, information overload is a major contributor to stress at work. Email is indeed very rapid, but for precisely that reason it results in unmanageable inboxes. It invites careless and imprecise writing, and it can generate confusing and convoluted spirals of correspondence that test patience and take plenty of time in the end to sort out (Bunting 2004, pp. 42–45). In general, we may admit that the subsumption of virtually all clerical and administrative work to the protocols and rhythms of the computer and the screen has certainly speeded things up; but it has also multiplied incessantly the volume of routine tasks. Mental and intellectual labour tends to grow ever-more quasi-automatic, de-skilled and alienated: those who work at a desk – more and more of us, in the over-developed world – now find our minds and bodies becoming appendages of technical systems at a rate and to an extent barely envisaged in Harry Braverman's classic and prescient study (1974). Far from allowing us to escape, the latest incarnations of the machine imprison us more securely in the 'iron cage' of which Weber wrote, and intensify the long process by which, since the inauguration of capitalist industry, time has become (as E. P. Thompson pointed out in a celebrated article) an objective force imprisoning workers rather than a milieu in which they live their lives (Weber 1984[1930], pp. 181–182; Thompson 1967).

In the market place, increased telemediation and internet ordering have blurred the boundaries between work and consumption. For workers, it has created the anomic new culture of the call centre; for customers, it has resulted in increasing time spent, often very frustratingly, in telephone queues (Huws 2003, pp. 42–60). Rapid innovation and the constant manufacture of new consumer 'needs' is facilitated by information technology at all levels and in every sphere of production and distribution, fuelling the 'work and spend' culture; but in this general sense too, the advantages that speed possesses in terms of prevailing economic rationality entail destructive consequences: resource attrition and environmental degradation are also accelerated. In the domain of e-goods themselves, the disposal of electronic waste resulting from product innovation and obsolescence poses a growing problem, causing pollution and ill-health in those areas (parts of China in particular) that recycle e-waste from the USA and elsewhere (*Science Daily* 2007; Greenpeace 2005). In all of these ways, what can be presented as the gains of going faster appear, from another perspective, as costs and losses.

The demand for speed is relative in another sense, since how fast we want – or 'need' – to travel and communicate is a function of other aspects of our overall lifestyle and pattern of consumption. Affluent modern lives involve a structure of interconnected modes of consumption, each of which is integral to the whole and reliant upon it. For that very reason, shifts in one area will have knock-on effects in others. The greater speeds at which both shoppers and goods can now travel are an instance of how this interplay works itself out in everyday life. The proliferation of 'clonetowns', each with its moribund high street and busy 24/7 out-of-town hypermarket, is the negative outcome of current preferences for speed and convenience: were more people to shop on foot or by bike or bus rather than in their cars, that would help the survival and might encourage the renaissance of high-street shops. The speed with which air-freighting brings perishable goods to supermarket shelves from distant countries and continents is the 'positive' aspect of a globalisation of food supply that has many deleterious consequences: campaigners argue that reducing 'food miles' instead of exploiting the supposed advantages of speed would bring many benefits for consumers, local economies and the environment (Seyfang 2009).

Environmental damage, above all carbon dioxide emissions, is the most evident cost paid for speedy transport. In the threats and discourses of climate change and 'peak oil', contemporary affluent societies confront and half-acknowledge the fact that rather than speeding up, or even going on at today's pace, we are going to have to slow down. Based on present trends, air flight will contribute to more than half of the UK's share of greenhouse gases by 2050. When in 2003 the UK government committed itself to a 60% reduction in emissions, expert opinion over-whelmingly agreed that continued expansion of flying at present rates would make it impossible for such a target to be met; and this was clearly recognised in the House of Commons Environmental Audit Commit-tee report of March 2004 (for further information, see 'The case against airport expansion' at Pledge Against Airport Expansion (n.d.)). The envi-ronmentalists who were protesting at that time against the construction of the new Terminal 5 at London Heathrow are unlikely to have taken much comfort from the plans to collect run-off rainwater to flush the toilets (as reported in the *Guardian* of 29 September 2005).

The Queen opened the new terminal building in March 2008. However, the additional runway that was until recently also planned for Heathrow is now not to be built. There are signs that for journeys of moderate length within Europe, travellers are turning in growing numbers to the railways (Parode n.d.). The admirable website run by 'the man from seat 61', which for several years provided British trav-ellers with advice on inland and continental train travel on a voluntary basis, now operates as a small commercial enterprise with links to rail ticket sales-points. High-speed trains cause their own kinds of dam-age to the environment, and at speeds that can exceed 200 kilometres per hour they are hardly going slowly. However, to take a train rather than a plane not only signals a willingness to spend slightly – or considerably – longer getting to one's destination but also involves a different relation to the space through which one travels. Fields and hedges, rivers and hills, villages and towns, even if they flash past 'with the velocity of a whirlwind', offer images of nature and cul-ture that restore something of the visual and existential delight long associated with travel. What we glimpse reminds us that to speed along is to miss something, and this might entice us to go slower next time.

As with the aeroplane, the speed of travel by car is in its own terms an undeniable advantage. Speed and convenience, elusive though they become once traffic volumes approach the capacity of road systems, account for the continued spread of car culture across the globe, even as its unsustainability (like that of flying) grows more evident each year. Here, too, the evident kinds of damage that the car does to the local and global environment have to be acknowledged as the corollary of these benefits. And again, we can move another critique, in the spirit of alternative hedonism, highlighting the pleasures that drivers forego, and may come to forget, if they jump in the car every time they want to go anywhere. For the car, at least as much as the train, insulates us from the world we travel in, reducing to a single dimension our engagement with the landscapes that roll or flash by beyond the glass, as Alexander Wilson argued in the first chapter of *The Culture of Nature* (1991). Walking and cycling offer, by contrast, a synaesthetic rather than merely voyeuristic experience.

We turn shortly to the pleasures of the bicycle. A highly sophisticated and efficient machine that has nonetheless been central to utopian critiques of machine culture, the bicycle is also poised intriguingly between slowness and speed. Most cyclists will have found themselves going a good deal more quickly than Pickwick's headlong carriage. Indeed, a cyclist in the late nineteenth century might have travelled more rapidly along the roads than any human had travelled before. If we acknowledge that the sensation of speed has its own special delights (see Solomon 2009), we can salute the bicycle for providing the joy of harmless speed – even if it is a speed that many would call slowness.

There is at any rate no doubt about the harms that accompany the benefits of the fast car. It is above all the sheer speed of road traffic that brings many lives to a premature and horrible end. In Britain alone, more than 6,000 pedestrians – nearly half of them children – were killed or seriously injured in 2009 by cars or lorries. The total casualties among pedal cyclists that year numbered 17,064, of whom 104 were killed and 2,606 seriously injured (Department of Transport 2010). Jan Hancock recently surveyed evidence showing that vehicle emissions are the major source of toxic air pollutants in industrial societies (Hancock 2007). This included a United Nations report into the health effects of vehicle exhaust in France, Austria and Switzerland (which found emissions responsible for 21,000 deaths annually, more than the deaths caused in traffic accidents, and for 300,000 extra cases of bronchitis in children and 15,000 additional hospital admissions for heart disease); and a British government report of 1998, which found that 24,000 deaths were hastened by the effects of three toxic pollutants.

Road traffic also kills communities, since parents' fear of accidents makes streets no-go areas for their children. Where once children were free to play with friends right outside their homes, forgetting their cares in the moonlit ludic time-space so evocatively summoned in the nursery rhyme, 'Girls and boys come out to play...', today, whether in the country or in the city, they are seldom released from either the nervy surveillance of their elders, on the one hand, or the dangers posed by adults driving motorised vehicles, on the other hand. They are all too often vulnerably exposed to traffic, or else confined indoors, or stuck in cars themselves. And it is not only children who suffer. For most of human history, as the Living Streets campaign points out, streets accommodated a diverse range of human activity: they were the place for socialising, markets, public meetings, entertainment and demonstrations. But 'the only right enshrined in the Highways Act is to "pass and re-pass along the highway" and it's a sign of the times that most words we use to describe stopping in the street should have negative connotations – "loitering", "lingering", "hanging about" ... Living Streets need nooks and corners, benches and walls where people can pause and pass the time' (Living Streets Manifesto n.d.). In many town and city centres, pseudo-public shopping malls offer a rare opportunity to get away from traffic; but here, putatively 'disreputable' non-shoppers are under surveillance, and security guards may ask them to move on if they linger. Little or no seating is supplied in these retail clone-zones lest people take advantage of it and sit down (Worpole 1991, pp. 141–142).

Wherever urban space is organised around the expedition of the car rather than the slower-paced walker and cyclist, streets become traffic corridors, cutting swathes through local communities:

> Roads are classified and designed with one overwhelming factor in mind: how much traffic they carry. This ... ignores the fact that in many streets – particularly local high streets – there are far more people on foot than in vehicles. Roads and side turnings are widened and pavements narrowed to speed up the traffic. Barriers are erected to stop people crossing where they want. The lighting and street signs are designed for people travelling at speed in vehicles. The result: an unfair, ugly and intimidating environment for people on foot.
>
> (Living Streets Manifesto n.d., para.6)

New attitudes and policies are belatedly gaining ground here and there in Britain – for example, Brighton and Hove Council, where the Greens form the largest group, plans to reduce the speed limit from 30 to 20 miles per hour in residential areas (*Brighton Argus*, 13 June 2011). But this is a very modest, not to say feeble, step toward restoring the lost amenities of the street, especially if we note that in the Netherlands far more ambitious projects to restore the '*Woonerf*' (living street) were being realised 25 years ago (Ryle 1988, pp. 71–72).

Since fast transport destroys the lives and habitat of living beings other than ourselves, it also threatens the pleasure we take in an abundant and flourishing wildlife and a greener environment. Car users, insulated from the environmental impact of speed, are also rendered insensitive to it. Anyone who walks or cycles on country roads that are heavily used by cars will be altogether more aware of the many small birds killed on the wing, the mangled pheasant and rabbit flesh, the fly-blown fox or badger decaying in the ditch. They will also see tell-tale signs of painful moments for drivers and their passengers: the tyre marks streaking the tarmac; the verges littered with debris of cracked mirror, fragments of red Perspex or plastic bumper; the odd shoe or motorbike boot.

Speed and slowness: Vélorutionary perspectives

The Montreal cyclists who in the mid-1970s formed an advocacy group known as Le Monde à Bicyclette ('The World by Bicycle') also referred to themselves as 'vélo-Quixotes' and 'vélorutionaries'. The Provo anarchists of Amsterdam, who in a famous 'happening' of 1965 left 50 white-painted bicycles around the city for anyone to use as they needed (urging the municipal authorities to follow suit and provide 20,000 free bikes annually), proclaimed that 'the white bicycle is a symbol of simplicity and cleanness in contrast to the vanity and foulness of the authoritarian car. In other words, 'A bike is something, but almost nothing!' (Furness 2010, pp. 63, 55–57; Stansill and Mairowitz 1971, pp. 26–27). The counter-culture of bicycle activism, like the wider green movement that was also emerging in the late 1960s and 1970s, drew on the arguments being developed by thinkers such as André Gorz, Ivan Illich and E. F. Schumacher (Gorz 1973; Illich 1973, 1974; Schumacher 1973; see also Gorz 1985). As part of their critique of waste, pollution and the growth economy, these movements sought to imagine another way of living that would be preferable not just environmentally but also in terms of pleasure and conviviality. The bicycle – easy and enjoyable to ride for anyone blessed with fair health, readily equipped to carry shopping or tools or books, silent, non-polluting, and outstandingly efficient in its conversion of renewable muscular energy into forward motion – provides a practical alternative for most of the short solo trips that so many city-dwellers prefer to make by car.

Long before the high tide of the counter-culture, the bicycle already signified social as well as mechanical innovation. In its earliest years, cycling was associated with the emancipation of women in both Britain and the USA. England's socialist Clarion Cycling Club was founded in 1894 (Furness 2010, pp. 20–26, 34–35; Eastoe 2010, pp. 19–22;

Watson and Gray 1978, pp. 133–137). Yet the bike emerged from a classic nineteenth-century matrix of technical inventiveness and entrepreneurial flair. It went on to survive the entire twentieth century in a form barely changed from the near-perfection reached in the 1880s (Penn 2010, pp. 26–27). And while this surprising persistence upsets the usual narratives of progress and obsolescence, it confirms that the bike embodies as well as queering machine culture, with its new appetite and new capacity for speed. The cyclist's velocity is a correspondingly paradoxical affair. The bicycle can be presented as a fast machine and its rider as wholly caught up in a vortex of effort, as in the Italian Futurist Umberto Boccioni's 'Dynamism of a Cyclist' (1913) (Watson and Gray 1978, p. 17). But such an image traduces the hedonistic essence of cycling, which involves the pleasures of slowness at least as much as those of speed: strolling and dawdling are terms that well befit the gentle progress a cyclist may choose to make, and free-wheeling (a word that the English language owes to the bike), when it does not mean going slowly, is a uniquely lazy mode of going fast.

Let us develop this theme by considering the interaction between organic and mechanical rhythms. Here, too, the bicycle both mirrors and subverts the general condition of bodies caught up in machine assemblages.

In cycling, the relationship between body and machine is symbiotic. Riders are subject to rhythms that they themself create and sustain. Pedalling, they impart them to the bike, which translates them into its own forward movement; but these rhythms comply in the last instance to the cyclist's will. This is why the first riders, manufacturers and advertisers often sought to convey the pleasures of bicycle riding in images of bird-like flight and centaur-like celerity, which suggest an extension of human powers within a new, integral and still-organic being. The first bicycle patented by the pioneering manufacturer James Starley was called the Ariel (Penn 2010, p. 138). An American journalist wrote in 1897: 'The wheel and the rider are one, as the centaur and his horse-body were one, and when the flight begins it is an intensely personal affair' (Furness 2010, p. 23).

In other contexts, however, most often associated with the labour process, mind and body must keep pace with heteronomous rhythms determined or mediated by the capacities and requirements of machines. Examples we all know of include the assembly line, the garment sweatshop and the supermarket check-out. The last of these is discussed by Braverman as an epitome of newly emerging work-disciplines, for 'computerized semi-automatic checkout systems' were already in common use in the USA in the mid-1970s (Braverman 1974, p. 371). A celebrated fictitious example is the machine which in Charlie Chaplin's *Modern Times* (1936) presents to the hapless factory-worker's mouth a corn-cob on a spindle, apparently revolving 'with the velocity of a whirlwind': here mechanical speed is intended to shorten the time in which the worker will consume his lunch, and to pre-empt the danger that he might loiter or linger over it. The machine-driven rhythms of the work place bid to cross the border into the dwindling territory of 'free time'.

In one dimension – at one extreme, we would say – the bicycle has proved conspicuously adaptable to that culture of compulsory mechanical speed. Cycle-racing epitomises the development, from the later nineteenth century onwards, of newly codified and commercialised sports to be watched by a 'working population [which] had itself become disciplined and attuned to the rigours of a clock- and machine-dominated life' (Walvin 1978, p. 87). Governed by the stop-watch's relentlessly uniform rhythm, the race apes the 'productivity' in which human faculties are objectified, to their possible jeopardy, as a means to an end. The end is self-chosen, but to quit is to fail, so riders, as if they must obey rather than control their machines, press on through the pain barrier – often fortified, if that is the word, by the injection of all but undetectable state-of-the-art drugs. 'Long-distance cycle-racing has been the most consistently drug-soaked sport of the twentieth century,' claims one expert (Gleaves 2010, p. 206; see Belliotti 2010).

Professional cycle-racing is a small world, but its ethos is influential beyond those boundaries. A toughly competitive spirit, in which cycling is synonymous with riding fast and hard, informs an extraordinarily large proportion of the contributions to a recent collection of essays entitled *Cycling: Philosophy for Everyone* by Ilundáin-Agurruza and Austin (2010). The same spirit governs the many sketches in Paul Fournel's *Need for the Bike* that celebrate close-to-the-limit physical exertion, invoking as heroes the *coureurs* of the gruelling long-distance stage-races. Fournel (2010) is associated with Oulipo, the French avant-garde writers' collective whose best-known member was Georges Perec. *Need for the Bike* is a celebration of cycling rather than racing, and at times eloquently captures the synaesthetic delights of riding the beautiful, quiet roads of rural France, but it constantly lauds the speed-rivalry whose darker potential is anatomised in Perec's novel *W or the Memory of Childhood* (1975). In the fictional world delineated by Perec, ruthless athletic competition is the basis of a fascistic social order. Italian Futurism offers a historical example of the link between speed-worship and fascism (Marinetti 1909; cf. Virilio 1977, 2003). When the bike is fetishised as a speed-machine, cycling becomes not the antithesis but the very sign of turbo-culture's conquest of mind and body: flesh is imagined as steel, rather than vice versa.

The newly completed Olympic Velodrome in east London (London 2012 n.d.) is an impressive temple to the self-imposed discipline of speed. Sustainable forests provided the wood and the ventilation is entirely natural. After the Games, a mountain bike course and road-cycle circuit will be added, along with bike hire and workshop facilities. The velodrome web page makes the claim that all this will be 'helping to make London the cycling capital of the world'. London's other pretensions to bike-friendliness include the recent inauguration of an on-street cycle-hire scheme. For everyday riders, however, the city remains notably – scandalously – inhospitable and dangerous compared with other northern European capitals, such as Copenhagen and Berlin (Ryle 2011). On 16 April 2011, launching a campaign to highlight these dangers, the *Independent* pictured on its front page 20 riders recently killed in collisions with cars, trucks and buses. Little wonder that transport researchers John Pucher and Ralph Buehler (cit. Furness 2010, pp. 3–4) reported that in 2007, England, along with Australia and the USA, had the lowest rate of cycling in the world.

There is an intelligible but contradictory relation, beyond the disingenuous hyperbole, between what London's velodrome represents and what it is like to ride in the nearby streets. The bike as a means of everyday transport, ridden slower or faster as you prefer, and whether you are thin or plump, old or young, fit or rather unfit, has nothing whatever to do with one-dimensional ideologies of speed, output and performance. But cycling as a sport, a quest for victory and a test of endurance conforms with the governing imperative to go faster and produce more, and the velodrome seems a fitting cathedral to the gods worshipped in the finance houses of nearby Docklands.

The study just cited found that just 1% of the English, Australian and American populations cycled regularly as a way of getting around. These are societies in which neo-liberalism seems to have sealed a definitive triumph. In England (more so than in Scotland or Wales), once-powerful egalitarian and social-democratic traditions have long been in eclipse, if they are not quite extinguished. Very notably higher rates of cycling were recorded in other European countries that might be seen as having stronger environmental, civic and social-democratic cultures: 27% in the Netherlands, 18% in Denmark (both nations with population densities, and climates, rather similar to England's); 10% or thereabouts in Germany and Scandinavia.

Positive and negative feedback loops are in play here. In the Netherlands, pressure from bike activists in the 1960s and 1970s, interacting with established national cycling traditions and organisations, encouraged planners to sustain and develop networks of safe cycle-routes, even though bicycle use was dipping, there as everywhere, as car ownership rose in the long post-1950 consumer boom (Eastoe 2010, p. 27; Furness 2010, pp. 57–59). The resulting excellent provision of safe routes in town and country means that lots of people ride. In such conditions the bicycle is not associated with 'athleticism or a specific cycling identity', but has become 'a practical, mundane and universal feature of everyday urban life – a technological embodiment of environmentalism' (Furness 2010, p. 59). In that setting, cycling can represent hedonistic values that include slowness and conviviality. We will turn in our conclusion to what this might imply for the future.

Where it is poorly provided for, cycling remains marginal and sub-cultural, a strongly marked activity and identity. Despite corporate-sponsored events like 'Team Green Bike Week', which represent it as newly fashionable (*London Evening Standard*, 22 June 2011), the bicycle in Britain is barely emerging from the near-oblivion into which it has sunk since the early 1950s when there were 12 million regular cyclists there (Eastoe 2010, p. 27). Cyclists here almost inevitably adopt oppositional and somewhat aggressive mental stances, since taking to the roads means accepting not only risks but often a deal of abuse from the drivers of cars, vans and trucks. Partly as a consequence, some cyclists in British (and no doubt US) cities ride rudely and in the wrong places, ignoring the rights and needs of pedestrians as well as infringing on the privileges of the car. Particular bike sub-cultures – couriers, off-road trail-bikers, some radical 'biketivists' – have codes and practices that may strike outsiders as unduly combative. A regime of reciprocal hostility begins to prevail, and the further development of dedicated bike routes becomes a matter of contention. In this dystopian dialectic, the hegemony of the car threatens to perpetuate itself because too little, too late has been done to tame it hitherto.

Adversity may keep the flame of radicalism burning brighter in these less congenial neo-liberal settings. But the price paid includes tension, a quicker heartbeat and a certain clenching of the spirit as of the body: speed rather than calm. Cyclists lose much of the enjoyment riding should bring, and cycling seems to signify not the pleasures of a different future but the pains of striving against an uncongenial present. As Brecht wrote in 'An die Nachgeborenen' ('To those born later'):

Hatred, even of meanness
Contorts the features.
Anger, even against injustice
Makes the voice hoarse. Oh, we
Who wanted to prepare the ground for friendliness
Could not ourselves be friendly.

(1976, p. 320)

A landscape which no longer exists?

Where it is completely normal to bicycle – in Lund in Sweden, for example, which we were visiting just before we began writing this chapter – most people who ride bikes are not cyclists. Cycling there has little to do with the emphasis on style, fashion and hi-tech consumerism which is found in some bicycle sub-cultures in Britain, Australia and the USA: most riders wear no lycra. The same goes for nearby Copenhagen (you can take your bike there from Lund across the Øresund by train), where cyclists on busier roads very rarely have to share space with motor traffic, and where as you mount a flight of steps to cross a canal you may find a little ramp running alongside so you can push your bike smoothly over rather than having to bump it along or shoulder it. Much of the Danish countryside, like that of Germany, Sweden and the Netherlands, has been made amenable to safe riding, too (the Danish tourist board website has a link on its home page to information about cycle-touring in the country; see VisitDenmark: visitdenmark.com). Cycling for pleasure, like urban commuting by bike, is for whoever fancies it.

All this bespeaks a sustained engagement with local environmental amenity and an imaginative conception of the pleasures that an enlightened administration can encourage. These differences matter greatly for cyclists, provoking envy and frustration among those of us who take to Britain's much less bike-friendly roads. However, cycling, of course, does not constitute anything like a total alternative. It may signal toward 'simplicity and cleanness' – toward the modes of voluntary self-restraint and the slower forms of pleasure of a society no longer based on ever-growing consumption – but precisely in those social democracies which have been most imaginative in their embrace of the benefits it can confer, it proves for the time being altogether compatible with the motor car and with consumer capitalism. In that larger picture, the differences between more and less bike-friendly societies in the over-developed world may seem insignificant compared with their similarities: the pace of traffic, and of life, is determined everywhere by a rate of energy consumption as addictive as it is unsustainable, and even where it has regained some of the ground lost to the car since the start of the post-war consumer boom, the bicycle is a marginal irrelevance. To be sure, nobody can know whether the bicycle is prefigurative or merely residual, to revert to our opening distinction. For the moment, we can only emphasise that it represents utopia as well as critique. Wherever people ride it, it remains an emblem of another way of being; more than an emblem, for cycling enacts what it represents. At once utilitarian and ecstatic, it unsettles those distinctions between labour and pleasure which the present order polices and requires. In its intimate symbiosis with the rider's body, this machine which makes no noise and burns no fuel can redress and reverse the mechanical colonisation of soma and psyche that Herbert Marcuse wrote of in *One-Dimensional Man*:

> In this society, not all the time spent on and with mechanism is labor time (i.e. unpleasurable but necessary toil), and not all the energy saved by the machine is labor power. Mechanization has also 'saved' libido, the energy of the Life Instincts – that is, has barred it from previous modes of realization. This is the kernel of truth in the romantic contrast between the modern traveler and the wandering poet or artisan, between assembly line and handicraft, [... between] the sailboat and the outboard motor, etc. True, this romantic pre-technical world was permeated with misery, toil and filth, and these in turn were the background to all pleasure and joy. Still, there was a 'landscape,' a medium of libidinal experience which no longer exists... With its disappearance [...], a whole dimension of human activity and passivity has been de-eroticized. The environment from which the individual could obtain pleasure ... has been rigidly reduced.
>
> (Marcuse 2010[1964], p. 76)

Cyclists, especially when they ride slowly, are keeping open the roads that lead into this landscape, hoping to preserve it as part of the world.

References

Belliotti, R. A., 2010, 'Out of control: the pirate and performance-enhancing drugs', in J. Ilundáin-Agurruza and M. W. Austin (eds.), *Cycling: Philosophy for Everyone*, Wiley-Blackwell, Chichester, pp. 200–213.

Braverman, H., 1974, *Labor and Monopoly Capital: The Degradation of Work in the Twentieth Century*, Monthly Press, New York.

Brecht, B., 1976, *Poems*, J. Willett and R. Manheim (eds.), Eyre Methuen, London.

Bunting, M., 2004, *Willing Slaves: How the Overwork Culture Is Ruling Our Lives*, Harper Collins, London.

Department of Transport, 2010, 'Reported road casualties in Great Britain: 2010 annual report', Department of Transport, viewed 29 June 2011, http://assets .dft.gov.uk/statistics/releases/road-accidents-and-safety-annual-report-2010/ rrcgb2010-01.pdf.

Dickens, C., n.d., *The Pickwick Papers*, Collins, London and Glasgow.

Eastoe, J., 2010, *Britain by Bike*, Batsford, London.

Fournel, P., 2010, *Need for the Bike*, A. Stoekl (trans.), University of Nebraska Press, Lincoln.

Furness, Z., 2010, *One Less Car: Bicycling and the Politics of Automobility*, Temple University Press, Philadelphia.

Gleaves, J., 2010, 'What to do once they're caught', in J. Ilundáin-Agurruza and M. W. Austin (eds.), *Cycling: Philosophy for Everyone*, Wiley-Blackwell, Chichester, pp. 188–199.

Gorz, A., 1973, 'The social ideology of the Motorcar', *Le Sauvage*, September–October, http://www.web.net/~lukmar/gorz.pdf.

———, 1985, *Paths to Paradise*, M. Imrie (trans.), Pluto, London.

Greenpeace, 2005, 'Toxic technology contaminates e-waste recycling yards in China and India', 17 August, viewed 21 June 2011, http://www.greenpeace.org/ international/en/press/releases/toxic-technology-contaminates/.

Hancock, J., 2007, 'Contradictions in Feinberg's formulation of the Harm Principle: toxic pollution as a right to harm others', *Capitalism, Nature, Socialism*, 18(2), 91–104.

Huws, U., 2003, *The Making of a Cybertariat: Virtual Work in a Real World*, Merlin Press, London.

Illich, I., 1973, *Tools for Conviviality*, Harper and Row, New York.

——— 1974, *Energy and Equity*, Harper and Row, New York.

Ilundáin-Agurruza, J. and Austin, M. W. (eds.), 2010, *Cycling: Philosophy for Everyone*, Wiley-Blackwell, Chichester.

Living Streets, n.d., 'Living streets manifesto', *Hackney Council*, London, viewed 26 February 2011, http://apps.hackney.gov.uk/servapps/Reports/s_ ViewRptDoc.aspx?id=1080.

London, 2012, 'Velodrome', viewed 22 June 2011, http://www.london2012.com/ velodrome.

Marcuse, H., 2010 (1964), *One-Dimensional Man*, Routledge, London.

Marinetti, F. T., 1909, 'Manifeste du futurisme', *Le Figaro* (Paris), 20 February.

Parode, N., n.d., 'Train travel 101: is train travel right for you?', *Senior Travel*, viewed 29 June 2011, http://seniortravel.about.com/od/transportationoptions/ qt/TrainTravel101.htm.

Penn, R., 2010, *It's All About the Bike: The Pursuit of Happiness on Two Wheels*, Particular Books (Penguin), London.

Perec, G., 1975, *W or the Memory of Childhood*, D. Bellos (trans.), Harvill Press, London.

Pledge Against Airport Expansion, n.d., 'The case against airport expansion', *Airport Pledge*, viewed 29 June 2011, http://www.airportpledge.org.uk/case_ against_expansion.php.

Ryle, M., 1988, *Ecology and Socialism*, Radius (Random House), London.

————, 2009, 'The past, the future and the Golden Age: some contemporary versions of pastoral', in K. Soper, M. Ryle and L. Thomas (eds.), *The Politics and Pleasures of Consuming Differently*, Palgrave Macmillan, Basingstoke, pp. 43–58.

————, 2011, 'Vélorutionary?', *Radical Philosophy*, July–August, 2–5.

Schumacher, E. F., 1973, *Small Is Beautiful: A Study of Economics as if People Mattered*, Harper and Row, New York.

Science Daily, 2007, 'Recycling of e-waste in China may expose mothers, infants to high dioxin levels', 22 October, viewed 29 June 2011, http://www.sciencedaily.com/releases/2007/10/071022094520.htm.

Seyfang, G., 2009, 'Growing sustainable consumption communities: the case of local organic food networks', in K. Soper, M. Ryle and L. Thomas (eds.), *The Politics and Pleasures of Consuming Differently*, Palgrave Macmillan, Basingstoke, pp. 188–205.

Solomon, J., 2009, 'Happiness and the consumption of mobility', in K. Soper, M. Ryle and L. Thomas (eds.), *The Politics and Pleasures of Consuming Differently*, Palgrave Macmillan, Basingstoke, pp. 157–170.

Soper, K., 2006, 'Conceptualizing needs in the context of consumer politics', *Journal of Consumer Policy*, 29(4), 355–372.

————, 2007a, 'Re-thinking the "good life": the citizenship dimension of consumer disaffection with consumerism', *Journal of Consumer Culture*, 7(2), 205–229.

————, 2007b, ' "Alternative Hedonism" and the Citizen-Consumer', in K. Soper and F. Trentmann (eds.), *Citizenship and Consumption*, Palgrave Macmillan, Basingstoke, pp. 191–205.

————, 2008, 'Alternative Hedonism, cultural theory and the role of aesthetic revisioning', *Cultural Studies*, 22(5), 567–587.

————, 2009, 'Introduction: the mainstreaming of counter-consumerist concern', in K. Soper, M. Ryle and L. Thomas (eds.), *The Politics and Pleasures of Consuming Differently*, Palgrave Macmillan, Basingstoke, pp. 1–21.

Stansill, P. and Mairowitz, D. Z., 1971, *By Any Means Necessary: Outlaw Manifestos and Ephemera*, Penguin, Harmondsworth.

Thompson, E. P., 1967, 'Time, work-discipline and industrial capitalism', *Past and Present*, 38, 56–97.

Virilio, P., 1977, *Speed and Politics: An Essay on Dromology*, Semiotexte, New York.

————, 2003, *Art and Fear*, J. Rose (trans.), Continuum, London.

Walvin, J., 1978, *Leisure and Society 1830–1950*, Longman, London.

Watson, R. and Gray, M., 1978. *The Penguin Book of the Bicycle*, Penguin, Harmondsworth.

Weber, M., 1984(1930), *The Protestant Ethic and the Spirit of Capitalism*, Talcott Parsons (trans.), Unwin Hyman, London.

Wilson, A., 1991, *The Culture of Nature: The Making of the North American Landscape from Disney to the Exxon Valdez*, Blackwell, Oxford.

Worpole, K., 1991, 'The age of leisure', in J. Corner and S. Harvey (eds.), *Enterprise and Heritage: Crosscurrents of National Culture*, Routledge, London, pp. 135–150.

6
Downshifting or Conspicuous Consumption? A Sociological Examination of Treechange as a Manifestation of Slow Culture

Angela T. Ragusa

Introduction and contextualisation

> *In the early years of the twenty-first century, everything and everyone is under pressure to go faster.*
>
> (Honoré 2004, p. 3)

At least since the Industrial Revolution, 'progress' in Western societies has frequently been equated with speed. Examples abound in advanced industrial and post-industrial societies, with capitalists and consumers developing a taste for fast food and desiring increasingly faster machines. In an historical nanosecond, computers made typewriters obsolete and Henry Ford's automobiles fostered the creation of Grand Prix winners. Today, optical networks permit even faster telecommunication, turning the vast majority of our planet into a so-called 'global village' where modern perils and advances now reach even the remotest locations. Modern technology has permitted nearly every corner to be electronically mapped, and hence accessible, thanks to imagery provided by Google Earth (earth.google.com).

Changes in technology have spurred changes in pursuits, both work and leisure. Many in our postmodern society are preoccupied around the clock with blogging, tweeting, instant messaging and SMS-ing. In our post-industrial society, it is often the technologically willing and/or able who lead trends. Critical social commentators, such as Freeman (2009, p. 194), ask us to question linear notions of progress, 'to step back from the frenzy and the flurry of the now – the now we have created and the now we have to slowly remove ourselves'. His (2009) recounting of a man with newly acquired broadband access spending night and day downloading music until the practice, the leisure pursuit of listening to music, was replaced by the process of monitoring its obtainment. Listening was supplanted by round-the-clock downloading, giving cause for reflection. When is 'fast' too fast? When does convenient become stifling, or choice seem paralysing?

Advanced civilisation may be characterised as a society plugged in and logged on. Social interactions in the twenty-first century are mediated by digital technologies to an unprecedented degree (Ragusa 2010). The information economy has blurred the boundaries between work and play, encouraging 24/7 work hours unless a conscious effort is made to use technology as tools to control working conditions, rather than expand the workday (Honoré 2004). Telecommuting, for example, can give rise to freedom and flexibility from traditional, physical geographical boundaries, yet may induce psychological constraints, such as anxiety about 'proving' one's productivity outside traditional work places or isolation if face-to-face relationships are replaced by cyber communities. While popular and academic debates over the benefits and limitations of technologies abound, one group questioning the consequences and implications of our shift to a globalised 'fast' culture are the contrarians who embrace 'simple' or 'slow' lifestyles.

This chapter commences by introducing the slow and simple living movements, describing their origins and lifestyle choices which counter much dominant ideology exhibited in mainstream Western culture. It proceeds to highlight recent Australian news media articles discussing trends known as 'downshifting' and 'treechanging'. Downshifting has been described as a backlash to hyper-urbanisation, driving some inner-city residents in major metropolitan areas, such as Melbourne and Sydney, to make a 'treechange' which like 'lifestyle migration' involves seeking refuge in 'the country', otherwise known as 'the bush', in pursuit of the so-called 'simple life' beyond 'the big smoke' (Lingane 2007; Osbaldiston, this volume). Next, it offers primary-collected qualitative data from interviews conducted with more than 50 'treechangers' thematically analysed to examine if and how members of this newly labelled social group that news media assert as desiring to escape the 'rat race' of city lifestyles (Morley 2008, p. 32; Patterson and Carne 2007, p. 28; Pilcher 2008, p. 5) exhibit sentiments consistent with the pursuit of downshifting or a slow lifestyle. Overall, the chapter seeks to identify if discernable patterns exist among the treechangers interviewed regarding 'place' and 'lifestyle' to answer the question: Do treechangers' experiences reflect simple or slow ideology?

Western lifestyles and the 'Slow' and downshifting alternatives

Psychologists and leisure researchers have used the concept of 'lifestyle' not only to identify the social patterning of how individuals or groups live life (Cheng, Yang, Ting, Chen and Huang 2011; Hawkins, Best and Coney 2004) but also to identify one's agency, or ability, to affect and determine what to do with one's time and where to do it (Cook, Yale and Marqua 2002). Lifestyle research has historically been accompanied by quantitative investigations of time and its use. Since the early twentieth century, international social scientists have conducted time-use investigations (Harvey and Pentland 1999) which have led to landmark sociological time-use research (Robinson, Converse and Szalai 1972) based on the diary methodology (Alaszewski 2006; Robinson 1999), which captured the first snapshots of how contemporary Westerners spent their everyday lives. Early psychological investigations (Perreault, Darden and Darden 1977) of time use also focused on its quantification, as did early leisure analyses (Plummer 1974; Wells and Tigert 1971) used in advertising and marketing, which emerged post-1960s from the newly founded 'leisure studies' academic discipline.

Much contemporary lifestyle research continues the positivist trajectory of charting how individuals spend their time. This has perpetuated the production of statistical data about how specific lifestyle activities affect various aspects of individual well-being, such as sports and college students' fitness levels (Cheng et al. 2011) or leisure activities and Croatian citizens' well-being (Brajsa-Zganec, Merkas and Sverko 2011). Some time-use analysts have claimed that the new self-chosen identities that individuals can pursue, typically hobby-based, as a result of increased leisure time has made searches for happiness and freedom redundant (Blackshaw 2010). Critics (Roberts 2011) point out the lack of evidence to support such widespread claims as well as the class-based inequality in opportunities to pursue work conditions or leisure preferences. In addition to Roberts' (2011) sociological critique, I would add that time-use research conducted with a leisure studies' lens consistently fails to theorise 'lifestyle' as a holistic element rather than a work/non-work dichotomy.

Alternative lifestyles represent a popular cultural rejection of mainstream stereotypes of the work/leisure dichotomy. Two alternative lifestyles (which can academically be labelled social movements) gaining momentum are the Slow Movement (henceforth 'Slow'), with its backlash against globalisation and renewed advocacy of localism, and the Simple Living Movement (Dominguez and Robin 1992) (henceforth 'Simple'), with its rejection of materialism and consumption. Although each espouses different ideology, both encourage introspection, believe in individuals' capacity to change their lives, have philosophical roots grounded in individualism and advocate the emancipating capacity of seeking alternative existences.

For Simple followers, this might mean freeing oneself from the more-is-better mentality (Wachtel 1989) or identifying what work we do for wages and/or fulfilment so as not to 'consume our way to happiness' (Dominguez and Robin 1992, p. 231). This backlash to US consumerism reached such a widespread level in the 1990s that voluntary simplicity was identified among the top-ten national trends (Simcon, De Graaf, Wann, Naylor and Horsey 1997) and psychologists coined a new disease, 'affluenza' (Goldbart and Di Furia 1997), to describe the guilt that accompanied excessive wealth held by most first-world citizens. As the decade ended, downsizing (Schor 1999) came to be recommended as an antidote to excessive modern lifestyles epitomised by the 1980s' so-called excess.

As the simple movement was emerging in North America, in Europe the slow movement was also developing during the 1980s. Begun as the slow food movement in Italy, Slow originated as a countermovement to fast food (Petrini 2001). Blamed for its nostalgic romanticism, disengagement with food policy, 'othering' of ethnic food, classism, socio-economic privilege and elitism, slow food has received its share of criticism (see Donati 2005). Despite this, Slow ideology has transcended its exclusive focus on food in 1986 when founded and since has been applied to every aspect of life, complete with how-to-live manifestoes alerting readers to the dangers of multi-tasking (Richards 2011), step-by-step maps for having slow careers (Gelardin, Muscat and Whitty 2010) and even slow cities where one can do everything slower. Slow cities, which also emerged in Italy, are said to value people and experiences as well as exhibit certain attitudes toward life in general.

So what attitudes characterise Slow, in contrast with fast? The descriptions offered by Honoré (2004, pp. 14–15) are illustrative:

Fast is busy, controlling, aggressive, hurried, analytical, stressed, superficial, impatient, active, quantity-over-quality. Slow is the opposite: calm, careful, perceptive, still, intuitive, unhurried, patient, reflective, quality-over-quantity. It is about making real and meaningful connections – with people, culture, work, food, everything. The paradox is that Slow does not always mean slow.

Foucaldian interpretations of Slow similarly characterise the concept as 'an attitude that stems from a way of caring for the other and that it can be translated into practice or a mode of living' (Tam 2008, p. 217).

As a philosophy, a way of being and a purpose for living, both Simple and Slow transcend specific activities; they are lifestyle choices. Slow and simple are grounded in individual identity rather than in the collective action characteristic of traditional social movements such as unionism. Therefore, they may be classified as new social movements. Living slowly or simply arguably become an identity, much like being vegetarian, or any other chosen 'lifestyles', although the degree to which the identity is transient or enduring is debatable. In describing the history of the slow movement, Honoré states: 'many people decide to slow down without ever feeling part of a cultural trend, let alone a global crusade' (2004, p. 14). This concept is recent but not new. As French social theorist Jean Baudrillard (1981) asserted, consumption bestows social legitimacy upon those who consume certain brands and images, which in turn fosters social identities.

Consumption, or lack of consumption, may be understood as a practice which confers a sense of group membership (Fox 2001) and social identity when lifestyles achieve the status of consumable goods (Ragusa 2005). This may, but does not have to, lead to support for widespread social change which, in contrast, is the fundamental purpose of old social movements (Snow and Oliver 1995). Lifestyles can have long-term consequences for individuals and societies; Slow and Simple are actions that transcend categorisation as mere leisure pursuits. To assume emerging slow trends, as described by the not-buying-it gurus of popular books including *Enough Is Enough: Exploding the Myth of Having It All* and *Simplify Your Life: 100 Ways to Slow Down and Enjoy the Things That Really Matter*, illustrate that an anti-capitalist backlash may be misleading for several reasons. First, the philosophy underpinning these new social movements, indeed counter-movements, lies far deeper than a mere rejection of Madonna's 'material world' by a collectively organised social group, such as unionists of bygone decades. The Slow movement is not anti-capitalist. According to Carlo Petrini, who founded the slow food movement in Italy, 'Being Slow means that you control the rhythms of your own life ... and today I want to go fast, I go fast; if tomorrow I want to go slow, I go slow' (cited in Honoré 2004, p. 16). Rather than abolish capitalism, Slow seeks to humanise it.

The notion that one can self-determine or select aspects of capitalist exchange is not limited to slow movement ideology. Critical empirical research has questioned the *a priori* assumption that contemporary time use is engulfed by commodification. For example, Williams and Windebanke's (2003) empirical study of domestic service provision in the UK was grounded in their critique of specific time-use studies' overestimation of the amount of time individuals spent in paid employment as well as an extensive literature in gender and voluntarism research which refuted assertions (Harvey, 1982) that monetary exchange has invaded nearly all realms of social and personal life. By evoking literature on alternative economic spaces which operate under profit and non-profit motives, divergent rationales for monetary spending and identifying non-economically motivated exchanges in the formal economic sphere, Williams and Windebanke (2003, p. 250) counter the stereotype, 'the commoditised economy is stretching its tentacles ever outward to colonise more spheres of life' and pave a path to explore how individuals today may self-determine how, and when, commodification suits their desires and lifestyle.

Second, in contemporary society, living slowly, simply or downshifting does not necessarily mean sacrificing comfort or enduring hardship. For instance, economist Clive Hamilton's study in the UK entirely defined downshifting in relation to employment (reduced hours, work cessation or changed career) and subsequently found 'a large class of citizens who consciously reject consumerism and material aspirations' (Hamilton 2003, p. x). Replicating the UK study in Australia, he found 'A smallish proportion of people gave as their reason for downshifting a desire to live a less materialistic lifestyle or a desire to live a more environmentally friendly lifestyle', as he told the *Australian Broadcasting Corporation*. It may thus be problematic to further describe this group as 'People who go beyond materialism, quite explicitly as a matter of principle. And they are the people who are most likely to undertake a radical change, to do the seachange, to go to an intentional community such as Maleny. To live quite radically different lives' (Australian Broadcasting Corporation n.d.). As international research revealed (see Schor 1999) and Hamilton (2003) notes, people choose to downshift for a variety of personal and structural reasons. For example, North American research found periods where employees were overworked (Schor 1999), yet recent studies (Roberts 2011) alert us that widespread downshifting has failed to materialise in either the USA or the UK despite increased opportunities for part-time employment. It remains unknown if Australian treechangers exhibit behaviours or existential desires that are characteristic of downshifting. Hence, equating sea/treechange with downshifting may, or may not, be problematic. Finally, there seems to be an erroneous stereotype perpetuated throughout history, as well as by Australia's mass media, equating geography and development with lifestyle pace. The stereotype is that simple lifestyles are rural, country and slow, while exciting and fast lifestyles are lived only in cities. Tired of the fast life? Move to the country. 'Suburban dwellers are pulling up stumps and heading bush for laid-back living. The lure of lifestyle and affordability are putting city folk on the road to country Victoria' (Cogdon 2008, p. 12). As the following section on 'treechange' describes, however, much energy and marketing is currently being put into selling the country's rural vistas. Furthermore, more often than not, great effort is made to assert how cosmopolitan country life can be: 'a rural life does not have to mean a simple life, with new housing estates and homes to rival, if not surpass, metropolitan's best' (Cogdon 2008, p. 12). Such movement, in this instance, shows the degree to which Australia parallels the UK, whereby 25% of Britons, equally spread across socio-demographic categories, who claimed to have downshifted in the past decade, were noted by an economist as 'immediately dispel[ling] the most widespread myth about the phenomenon, *viz.* that it means selling up in the city and shifting to the countryside or a small town to live a life closer to nature' (Hamilton 2003, p. 12).

Treechange in popular culture

In 2004 the term 'treechange' was popularly coined to label those who relocated within Australia from the city to the country, in contrast with 'sea change', adapted from a TV series and subsequent lifestyle choice common among retirees wishing to relocate to the coast. In 2008, 'downshifters' were reported as 'a new demographic category' (Cenigh-Albulario 2008, p. 3) in the Australian news media, despite the concept of downshifting being described in detail in a book entitled *Downshifting* (Saltzman 1991). Hence, not only does the relationship between Australian treechangers and downshifters seem to remain unclear among journalists, but the global history of counter-movements seems largely unknown. The term treechange perseveres in popular cultural outlets today, specifically business/marketing campaigns, news media and real-estate advertisers. Yet, more than being a descriptor to sell landscapes and lifestyles, 'treechanger' came to be adopted by individual Australians as a social identity and/or lifestyle aspiration (Ragusa 2010).

The familiarity of 'treechanging' in Australian popular culture can be evidenced by its adaptation by local and national government. Spin-offs of the term, namely 'C-change' (where 'C' stands for 'city'), have recently been used to promote government agendas. In 2009 the Australian federal government committed $1.2 million to promote seven regional cities in a marketing initiative with the explicit purpose of 'tempt[ing] Sydney-siders to relocate'. Described as 'four years in the making', in 2009 the councils associated with evocities capitalised on the perceived popularity of the sea/treechange phenomena by encouraging Sydney-siders to move 'to a regional city', as opposed to 'the country', not with the aim of attracting individuals interested in a slower or simpler lifestyle but rather as a competitive push by regional cities to convince urbanites that 'there was more than "the bush" over the Great Dividing Ranges', the Dubbo council noted (Dubbo City Council 2009, para. 2). In light of local and national government agendas, the fundamental objectives of Evocities is to divert a proportion of Sydney's population to each of the seven regional 'cities' which have, according to councils' population statistics, achieved an average annual growth rate of between 1% and 2%. Urban relocation would thereby simultaneously achieve the dual purpose of regional rejuvenation and metropolitan decentralisation. To help to achieve this, the website is replete with stereotypes, such as living with less traffic, having a 'great lifestyle', experiencing a 'welcoming and safe community', and having all the 'diverse' and 'beautiful' landscapes at your doorstep (Evocities n.d., para. 2).

Contextualising the present study

Since 'we are living in an age of communication revolution – using machines that far outpace human capacity, talking, writing, and typing to one another at greater speed than ever before' (Freeman, 2009, p. 196), the association of treechange with slowing down seems dubious. As reflected in the media, 'Sure, there's the sea change movement and the treechange movement, but will this be the start of an evolutionary slide back into the simple life? Hardly, we carry too much in our genes, such as mobile phones, credit cards and iPods' (McFadyen 2008). Freeman's (2009, p. 198) demand for the creation of a 'slow communication movement' evoked the insights gained from the slow food movement of the 1980s, particularly how productivity changes our environment, landscapes and way of existing. Yet, asking technophiles to de-mechanise during an historical era when technology is used to promote 'flexible' workplaces, indeed to *sell* treechange destinations, seems unlikely. 'Telecommuting is also making it possible for people to treechange, and anecdotal research suggest mobile phone coverage is a key determinant in choice of destination' (Stirling 2008, p. 9). As an academic quoted in *The Australian* added, 'People are increasingly using telecommunications, which allow them to plug into a whole range of opportunities from home or from a base in a regional centre – it doesn't matter whether you're in the hurly burly of the metro area, now you can telecommute to different things' (Budge cited in Stirling 2008, p. 9). Given the widespread reporting in the Australian media of treechange as a form of slowing down and downsizing, and growing academic research on lifestyles and time use, as well as Australian definitions of downsizers as those seeking less employment, no employment or a radical career/lifestyle change (Hamilton 2003), the current research next contributes primary data for the broad research question: Do treechangers experiences reflect simple or slow ideology?

Methodology

Between 2007 and 2011, 53 telephone interviews were conducted with self-identified treechangers in New South Wales (NSW) and Victoria (VIC), Australia, after university human ethics committee approval was sought and obtained (protocol 2007/179). The research design, sampling frame and participant selection criteria were created to permit access to individuals living in geographically distant, rural and remote locations without research grant funding and minimal intrusion upon participants' time since no compensation for participation was provided. Purposive and snowball sampling techniques were used, as suitable for exploratory, non-representative qualitative research (Walter 2010; Flick 2009), and provided access to an otherwise hidden, hard-to-access population (Bouma 1996) due to a lack of national statistics on in-migration trends illuminating local migration trends. Local radio, specifically the Australian Broadcasting Corporation, printed flyers and electronic media, namely listserves, electronic forums and newspapers, were the recruitment strategies used. Three participation criteria were established based upon popular and academic conceptualisations of treechangers. First, individuals were required to have lived in a major Australian city as an adult for typically a decade or longer. Second, they had to have moved to a rural or regional and inland location in NSW or VIC for self-defined 'lifestyle' reasons. Third, each had to meet the ethics committee's requirements.

The research instrument was informed by existing literature and prior research. Specifically, 30 open and closed questions were created in 2007 in light of insights garnered from the limited amenity migration research in Australia. Knowledge gaps informed by local and national policy and my concurrent research investigating media representation of treechangers (Ragusa 2007, 2008) informed the refinement of interview questions in 2008, although care was taken to retain all original questions to enable analysis across interviews. Every participant was asked the same original question schedule to permit continuity of topic coverage (Rubin and Babbie 2008), and a limited number of questions were added over time to accommodate emerging trends and insights. Instrument construction permitted the use of probes, and a structured interview schedule ensured that leading questions were avoided (Fowler and Mangione 1990). The interview length ranged from 20 to 60 minutes. Participant anonymity was assured, no participants experienced distress as a result of participation and all gave informed consent.

All interviews were recorded using an iPod, transcribed by research assistants and coded. Descriptive statics were generated by SPSS (analytics software) from demographic data collected to describe the treechangers. Qualitative data were thematically coded after the collection of all interviews to permit refinement of the initially developed coding system so that emergent themes unrelated to specific questions could be identified (Sarantakos 2005). This chapter presents local, specific experiences from the treechangers interviewed that answer the research questions previously posed. Subsequently, as qualitative sociological research, it does not seek to produce universal theories or hypotheses (Crabtree and Miller 1992) related to all treechangers.

Findings

Descriptive statistics are presented first to offer a demographic profile of participants. Key insights from two key themes are then discussed:

- what lifestyle factors treechangers articulated as sufficiently important to motivate them to leave city life in search of greener, or perhaps browner, Australian pasture;
- what treechangers hoped to achieve personally through their relocation.

Demographic profile

Some 57% of participants were women, 84% partnered and 61% had at least one child at the time of the interview. The average age of participants was 51, with the youngest aged 24 and the oldest 70. Overall, participants were well educated: 88% had completed certificates and degrees beyond Year 10 themselves and 66% of their partners achieved this same level of education. Some 67% were born in a city and more were born in Sydney (35%) and Melbourne (15%) than in any other city. A smaller percentage (17%) were born overseas, in either Europe (the UK or Germany) or North America. The majority of all participants (73%) moved from Sydney (42%) or Melbourne (31%) to their treechange destination into a house in a country town or its suburbs (59%) rather than to a hobby farm or farm. Although most (78%) purchased, rather than rented, their home, 48% expected to move again in the future and another 10% were undecided if they would stay or leave their treechange destination. Only 50% expected to stay a maximum of five years in their current location despite 100% employment rates (94% full-time employment among non-retired interviewees and 6% part-time) for those interviewed and the same for their partners. Partners, however, were less likely to work full time (72%), and had higher part-time employment rates (15%) or no desire for employment outside the home (13%), than participants.

Qualitative thematic analysis

Research findings revealed that time is an intrinsic motivation to leave city life. Although not one interview question mentioned the concept of time, nor enquired about the pace of living, nearly all treechangers independently identified time and pace of living as paramount to their lifestyle expectations and aspirations. Collectively, treechangers' pursuit of country life evidences a deep desire to slow down, consistent with, yet divergent from, slow movement ideology as explored below.

Seeking … a 'slower' pace of living?

When simply asked to 'describe your previous lifestyle', treechangers consistently responded with a discussion of time. 'City life is really chaotic, it's really fast, it's very expensive. In country life, you know we have no traffic lights in Yak. It's an alternative life to living in the city' (TCer-E [treechanger id code] 2007). Indeed, a 'slower', more 'relaxed' lifestyle was a common expectation that city-dwellers had of country life. 'I did imagine it to be slower pace, maybe a little bit boring' (TCer-M 2008) was the expectation that a 20-something Sydney-sider in international marketing had of her treechange location. Other Sydney-siders, such as a 30-something male construction worker and a female marking professional, had the same expectations: 'I thought it would be slower, I thought that there would be more leisure time and what appealed to me would be the less travel time' (TCer-N 2008). A retired police officer with a heart condition who relocated for a 'slower pace of lifestyle' elaborated: 'My expectation was that it should slow down. I did have a period of ill health in Sydney and I was quite happy to slow down because of that. My expectation was to take it easier; my expectation always was to continue work at a slower pace' (TCer-A 2007).

City life left most individuals feeling that they had insufficient discretionary time to pursue meaningful activities, which were always defined in contrast with work. 'Meaningful' time use varied from involvement in groups, social activities or sports (TCer-M 2008) to sufficient time spent with friends and family, such as the sentiment expressed by a father to have 'time with family, my nuclear family, being able to spend more time' (TCer-J 2008). The city was stereotypically characterised by many as fast-paced and hectic, leaving its dwellers time-poor: 'In the city, because it's so hectic, you don't get to spend that much time with your partner' (TCer-E 2007). In contrast, romantic notions of country life equated it with a slower, more contemplated existence. Reflecting on her move from Canberra to Beechworth, one treechanger commented: 'I guess one of the delights is going downtown and always meeting someone you know and having the time to stop and talk' (TCer-I 2008). In this particular instance, not only is it necessary to believe one has sufficient time to stop and have a conversation, but the geography means that one has the ability to run into individuals previously known. In this instance, it is likely such an interaction could be experienced in either country or city locations. For example, one might readily frequent a café in a suburban neighbourhood in Canberra and encounter other 'regular' patrons, neighbours and so on, which is a common Australian experience irrespective of location. Hence, it is the perceived quantity and/or use of time, and willingness to engage in conversation, which seems to dictate that urban and rural social interactions are equated with geography.

The search for a slow, 'quieter lifestyle' where it is 'easy to get around' and 'friendlier' lured one academic from Sydney to Bathurst in search of something small and low maintenance. 'I am 59 and I just need a place to retire into. I am not looking for something that requires a lot of work' (TCer-V 2009). Unfortunately, his treechange resulted in 'a neighbour problem where I have been renting, but where I am buying I expect to find everything I am looking for' (TCer-V 2009). Similarly, another Sydney-sider who mentioned 'slower paced' as the best thing about her treechange and also chose to rent in a country town complained: 'we have loud neighbours that put the music up loud on either side. They are not the type to ask to turn it down. In Sydney we didn't have that problem' (TCer-O 2008). She also thought that 'the main reason [to buy rural lifestyle property was] to get away from neighbours' noise' (TCer-O 2008).

While the stereotype of slow country towns and fast cities persist, individual stories reveal that ideas about when it is suitable to 'slow down' are inconsistent. In other words, although historical and contemporary demographic data show that Australians prefer to live in cities during their young adulthood (see Ragusa 2010), the broad age range of treechangers sampled reflects a pocket of individuals with potentially counter-mainstream ideals. One young, single mother from Sydney commented: 'I miss the night life and the action but [although] it is great to visit, I couldn't live there permanently and do that again' (TCer-R 2009). For her and her young son living on 10 acres, the slower pace of country life was more suitable:

> I am not so stressed anymore so that is having a greater impact on my kid too. I am not this screeching mother anymore. I am relaxed and spending more time with him and taking him to places like cricket and I would never had been able to do this in the past.
>
> (TCer-R 2009)

In contrast, a family of six considered making a treechange earlier, but opted not to because they thought their children would find country life too slow. 'We could've done this earlier, but we would have had four children probably getting a little impatient with a small town life and the opportunities and they probably would of gone into Albury or Melbourne or been desperate to get away' (TCer-I 2008). Indeed, sometimes country 'slow' was equated with boring. According to one young mother from Sydney,

> I thought it was going to be boring. I didn't think there would be much to do, but I was willing to do it for my son's sake and it would be better for me and healthier and we would make better use of our time with more simple pleasures.
>
> (TCer-S 2009)

A mother-to-be echoed similar sentiments about boredom yet moved for very different reasons:

> I thought that life would be a bit slower. I thought that it would be more relaxed. I was concerned that I would get bored particularly on weekends. On a Sunday or Saturday afternoon the main street shuts down, all the shops close and the streets are quite empty, and I thought that would be hard to deal with.
>
> (TCer-B 2007)

Another ex-Sydney-sider's aspirations exhibited anything but downsizing. The wife of a member of parliament, she noted the move to the country meant that 'we can actually afford a bigger house than what we could in Sydney' (TCer-B 2007). For her, the best aspects of country life all related to time:

> Time. Availability of time; having an extra few hours in the day because I am not commuting and then the absence of traffic hassles and also I mean that during the week getting to and from work and weekends as well, so, being able to visit your friends more freely. It is easier to get around town to see people. Being able to do things that I normally would not have the opportunity in Sydney because of the availability of time; cooking for example. I do more cooking now than I did in Sydney so I think I eat better, I have more time to cook whereas in Sydney I used to eat out a lot more.

Several treechangers mentioned a general sense of casualness in country lifestyles.

> Just being relaxed and the friendly feel and the common courtesy, that is something both me and my sister have noticed. Here, people, you just look like you are going to cross the street and people stop. In Brisbane or the Gold Coast they would much rather run over you.
>
> (TCer-V 2009)

Some, such as a local council worker in rural VIC, became 'slow' converts, 'The pace is just way more relaxed and easy going, and I actually got to the point where I hate going to the city' (TCer-T 2009). These insights beg the question: What accounts for the perception that one has enough or too little time?

Lifestyles and the perception of time ... the complexity of having 'enough' time

The search for a better lifestyle, one slow enough to engender meaning-ful interactions and self-directed time use, yet not so slow as to feel bored to death, hinged on individual perceptions of time and its importance. In most situations, what constituted a desirable pace was contingent on the issue at hand. For example, when trying to make a dental appoint-ment in the country, slow was undesirable, whether in Albury, 'it is hard to get into the dentist, it is quite annoying that doctors are all booked out' (TCer-X 2009), or Orange, 'I did get a dentist here just for a basic check up for my little bloke. That was just by coincidence. They hap-pened to ring up someone that no longer works here and I managed to get an appointment. Apparently it is hard to get dental here' (TCer-R 2009). After obtaining a highly sought appointment, however, slow service was perceived by some as advantageous, as in Griffith where the 'Dentist it is better. It is more personal. People have more time to talk to patients' (TCer-I 2008).

Whether people in the country actually have more time was not the research focus; how individuals perceive country versus city life's pace was the greater interest. An unexpected, yet emerging, trend was the lack of agency, or control, that many individuals perceived they had to lead a slow life in a city. Rather than perceiving that they are in charge of how they spend their time, the majority cited seemingly unavoid-able structural reasons for being time impoverished: commuting, traffic, work hours, childcare arrangements, children's extracurricular activities and so on. Although most treechangers wanted more time to pursue 'meaningful' activities prior to moving, they felt too time-poor due to unavoidable demands that city environments placed on their daily lives. Very few participants acknowledged the role their own time-use values or decisions played in creating their situations. One British woman who 'really appreciate[s] the differences between country and city' noted that it is up to individuals to balance their lives, 'even when I was full time, I loved my work, but I loved my home life and recreational or leisure time and I balanced them well ... I make the effort' (TCer-Q 2009). When asked if she thought it was a city/country difference or individual issue, she responded: 'individual'.

Another participant who noticed it was changes she made that caused substantial change in her lifestyle reflected: 'I was frantic in Adelaide, just go, go, and going around and getting nowhere, just surviving, whereas in Griffith, because my circumstances changed but also because

I made lifestyle changes about quality rather than quantity, I am more relaxed' (TCer-R 2009). Another exception noted: 'I have slowed my lifestyle a little so I have time to join a service club like Rotary' (TC-2007).

Not everyone saw the contribution that their decisions made to their perceived lack of time. For example, one mother described her lifestyle in Canberra as 'Absolutely flat out with four children doing everything. We were up at 5:15 every morning taking them to rowing. In the last eight years they all did senior college and so we were both working full time' (TCer-I 2008). Yet, rather than associating her lack of time with parenting choices, which would leave most people time-weary, she faulted city life for the lack of volunteerism in contrast with the country:

> There are a number of people that we have met in the last six months that are willing and able to give time voluntarily on community projects. In the city...nobody had time or very few people had time and the cry was for people to turn up...very few people had time to put into voluntary work...it is such a change... there seems to be a lot more effort put into doing things for other people.
>
> (TCer-I 2008)

Aside from differences in specific time-use activities, whether shuffling children to sports or volunteering, some saw contemporary Australian lifestyles as more similar than different:

> I have realised that no matter where you live life is very similar. You do similar things you get up, you go to work, you see your friends, you see your family, you clean your house, you do your washing, you go to dinner, you go to the cinema. Life is pretty much the same no matter where you live.
>
> (TCer-B 2007)

Nevertheless, one activity commonly accused of taking up more time than was acceptable, regardless of location, was employment.

The overworked Australian

Regardless of age, gender and profession, Sydney-siders generally agreed that 'You spent too much time at work and not enough at home' (TCer-N 2008). This was due to the very long hours that full-time work and commuting demanded. 'In Sydney, because working hours were so long and commuting adds to the time on top of that, it's really hard to have any quality time together' (TCer-B 2007). Comments such as 'I was at work at 8.00 until 7.00 pm at night' (TCer-B 2007) typified the workday of most Sydney-siders employed full time. A feeling of being over-worked described many urbanites, irrespective of the city left behind. An ex-Londoner, now an organic pig farmer in rural Australia, moved to achieve a better 'quality of life' since her husband and she 'were working quite long hours. Our children had a nanny. We didn't see a lot of them and I think we thought that moving to a farm would be a good way to change that' (TCer-Z 2011). For many, moving to the country resulted in more time spent with family, such as the ex-Sydney-sider who established a business and suddenly found instead of spending 'maybe a few hours at night' with his partner, the treechange enabled them to be 'together all day everyday and it's a really nice experience' (TCer-E 2007).

Consistent with slow movement ideology, relocating to the country did not necessarily result in less work. For many, the key difference was an individual belief of being in control of deciding how many hours, as well as the conditions, one would endure for a pay-check. The move from Sydney to Junee resulted in one treechanger 'working so many hours at the moment I am just going to work, coming home and doing work; that includes the weekends', yet still describing one of the best outcomes of the move as 'just feeling relaxed, even though I am working longer hours I feel relaxed' (TCer-O 2008). In contrast with a 7.00 am start at a construction job in Melbourne, one TCer spoke of being 'fortunate enough the job I have is a five-day job and I don't have to start here until 8.00 in the morning. I usually get here earlier. I leave here at 7.00, which is enough time to spend with the kids before you go, and I am home by 5.30', which was in addition to 'managing a property that is bigger than a quarter-acre block' (TCer-C 2007).

To equate a 'slow' lifestyle with a slow pace of life defined by less time spent working would be erroneous. As the Junee resident elaborated further, it is the freedom to decide one's own pace, rather than the duration of hours, that is responsible for perceptions of decreased work pressure,

> I think it is a slower pace because if I had to work back (I worked back till after six o'clock tonight and I put in a ten-hour day and I have to work tonight), but I am not thinking that I have to leave by 3.45 otherwise I will be sitting in traffic for two hours. I can stay as long as I need to at work and not have to worry about traffic, so that pressure is off a little bit.
>
> (TCer-O 2008)

A theatre director from Adelaide also noted how the anticipated slower pace of life failed to materialise: 'I am finding the demands of work to be more than I expected which is meant that I am doing more. I am actually enjoying it more than I expected, but that is also throwing off the family work balance' (TCer-F 2007).

Country life did not translate into the anticipated slower pace of work irrespective of occupation. Speaking about work–life balance, a young professional in Bathurst commented: 'It has gotten worse in the sense that work has dominated everything...it has been pretty full on...Because you don't know as many people ... perhaps work is more likely to take over...Maybe if I was still in Perth I would still be busy but you would still make time to do other stuff' (TCer-L 2008). A 60-something farmer also expressed sentiments of feeling tied to the job: 'I can't get away for more than a half a day because I have to look after the animals. We [he and his wife] can't go away together at all. And if I'm here on my own and I have to go to town, I have to come back the same day' (TCer-Y 2009).

Despite long hours, self-directed employment, in the number of hours and work conditions, was perceived to be very important to satisfaction:

> I work for myself and I work from home. There is no routine and I work hours that suit myself and I have a lot more time to do things that I want to do, whether that is lunch with friends in the middle of the day and working in the afternoon or in the evening.
>
> (TCer-B 2007)

For this individual, however, geographic location was not responsible for her job flexibility: 'I had a very flexible employer who did not want me to leave and so I would work one week from home in Griffith and then every second week from the office in Sydney. The back and forwards got a bit tiresome but the flexibility was great' (TCer-B 2007). The ability to create a personally rewarding career contributed to individuals' satisfaction with a treechange. As one Sydney-sider soon realised, 'if I wanted to stay in the area the only thing I could do was run my own business' (TCer-E 2007). Although running a business actually resulted in longer hours, the ability to spend more time with his partner was worth the long work hours: 'We're together 48 hours a day. We're here seven days a week' (TCer-E 2007). Because they could spend more time together, the extra work was described as 'an amazing change and we've adapted to it very, very well' (TCer-E 2008). Still, affordability was crucial to the realisation of their dream: 'We bought this place in Yak, three-bedroom and the shop and it was 160,000, and that was about six years ago, and you know that was really cheap' (TCer-E 2007).

Downshifting or conspicuous consumption?

All interviewees could articulate lifestyle factors prompting their move, yet beyond listing undesirable attributes of city life and stereotypical hopes for the country alternative, few mentioned a desire to fundamentally change either their standard or way of living. A Sydney-sider said: 'I was thinking more of the things I was getting away from rather then things that would be here, so not the commuting time, the air would be cleaner' (TCer-U 2009). Subsequently, hardly any treechangers rejected capitalist pursuits or sought less employment simply because they made a treechange. Most ex-urbanites took their strong work ethic to rural locations, hoping mainly to avoid specific undesirable realities of dense urban environments, such as traffic, dense living conditions and long commutes. In other words, the treechangers' dreams failed to manifest in downshifting *per se*. Few interviewees rejected contemporary consumerism or cultivated a deep desire to live remotely or 'off the grid', or sought a romanticised notion of yesteryears. What analysis did reveal was the conflicting desire to 'live slow', as in choose-your-own-destiny, while living 'large'.

A contemplated pursuit of reduced consumption did not prompt any treechangers' move from the city to the country, nor did attributes of specific locations attract them. In all but the rarest of instances it was a vague sense of improved life satisfaction associated with the countryside that prompted relocation. With most treechangers being middle aged, it was a sense of being fed up with the negative aspects of city life that made them accept the limited creature comforts as a reality that accompanies country living, such as 'adapting to being more relaxed about what I can't have when I am shopping' (TCer-T 2009). Some were more willing than others to forego urban comforts in exchange for a slower pace of living:

> It was more about the comfort that we were used to at our home in Adelaide and we wanted to make sure, I particularly wanted to make sure that my family was comfortable, that they were not doing without because the move was significant and I definitely did not want our standard of living to drop ... we certainly looked for a house that was contemporary in its style and design architecture, offered a reasonable garden and outside amenities.
>
> (TCer-F 2007)

It is also a misconception that suburban life is intrinsically different in Australian country towns and metropolises. As an individual who relocated from Sydney to Griffith entirely for work reasons noted,

> my basic lifestyle it is still very similar, except here I only have to drive two kilometres here instead of twenty, that's important, I spend a good less time in traffic which is important that is one thing that I don't miss about Sydney is spending time in damn traffic.
>
> (TCer-A 2007)

Several treechangers moved to increase their purchasing power. Housing topped the list for Sydney-siders: 'Selling up in Sydney... we could buy a little cheaper here. It has improved our lifestyle because of the economics of living in the country, which I think is cheaper' (TCer-A 2007); 'I would say one of the top factors was the affordability... now that 100 Sydney suburbs have a median house value of over a $1 million dollars, that is more than any Sydney-sider will ever know' (TCer-K 2008). A few Melbournians expressed similar sentiments: 'You could get a larger house with a smaller mortgage in Bendigo' (TCer-P 2009); 'We could not buy a house in Melbourne and that was when interest rates were 17%, and that was definitely a factor of why we moved to the country. It was the only way we could buy a house' (TCer-T 2009).

Although the pursuit of housing which hugely surpasses its capacity to offer modest shelter is an obvious act of conspicuous consumption, the pursuit of career advancement is an unforeseen aspect of treechanging that also counters downshifting ideology. Despite treechangers' clear desire for a 'slower' lifestyle, closer examination of work, beyond the quantification of hours worked, demonstrates the hope for 'more time for leisure, job security and lower price of living' (TCer-M 2008) alongside the active pursuit of economically rewarding careers and professional advancement.

> I reckon if I was in Sydney working for the ABC I would be on a six-month contract. I have a lot of job security in this position and I know that I am going to get a lot of opportunities to learn how things work from the inside out as well. In Sydney there are so many people hustling about to get the one gig, so, it is too hard. You don't get the chance to really prove what you can do.
>
> (TCer-W 2009)

The misconception that moving to the country is akin to retirement is dispelled by further young treechangers who experienced career advantage by living in the country:

Living here in the country has enabled me to join a couple of boards. I don't think I would have had that opportunity in Sydney whereas here in Griffith the local boards are happy to have my marketing expertise. They haven't had anyone with as much marketing experience.

(TCer-B 2007)

For some, not only does the country offer career advantages, but their treechange was a strategic decision: 'Well I moved here [Bathurst from Perth] for work, entirely for work, so...the experience will make me more attractive on the job market' (TCer-L 2008). Another explained:

I think I have made different choices and I think because I have a number of qualifications, I think my chances of securing a better paid position are better in the country. This sounds very snobby, but there is less people with my breadth of experiences and qualifications. I think that I was a little fish in a big pond in Adelaide, whereas in Griffith I am a big fish in a [little] pond.

(TCer-D 2007)

'Potential professional field' (TCer-I 2008) was noted by yet another as one of the best five things about where you live now.

Relocating one's career to the country does not come without change, however. Just like the individuals who accepted the rural realities of fewer shopping opportunities and restaurants, so, too, did a treechange require work adjustments: 'I changed my focus back to rural research...I have continued since then. Being in a rural area is a great advantage' (TCer-P 2009). For a mother of three university-age children, the lack of opportunities to spend money coupled with a quiet atmosphere were conducive to writing: 'You don't spend much, either, staying home and writing...not being in a hurry is probably an advantage' (TCer-I 2008). And: 'Here the kind of high level marketing roles aren't really available...which is why I chose to set up my own marketing consultancy business' (TCer-B 2007). This professional's clients were from 'mostly Sydney, but I am trying to change that and that is just because where my circle of contacts have been, but it is changing' (TCer-B 2007). Others traded in career advancement for job security: 'I don't feel like I am stuck in a career race anymore...I am not freelancing casual contract working. It's a real sense of security and that is important to me' (TCer-W 2009). As some found,

Although the career choices aren't as great...the work is there instantly because there is a shortage for people to fill the positions. It is harder to get people in the country so although your choices might be limited, if you have your qualifications, there is no trouble getting work even in a field that is not quite your own.

(TCer-U 2009)

This sentiment was echoed by a retired police officer:

I thought it was going to [slow down] but the reality is it has not, and I think that is only because we have moved to a country town that has plenty of work. There was a whole bunch of things I could of done. In fact, if I didn't take the job I have. I had three other options, so I guess what I am saying, the work options were pretty good.

(TCer-A 2007)

Conclusions

This chapter sought to determine whether treechangers in Australia exhibited characteristics typical of downshifting and/or slow ideology. Qualitative sociological analysis of interview data suggests that the treechange movement largely fails to be an expression of downshifting given the tendency of urbanites to pursue high levels of material comfort and wealth, evidenced by property consumption and the continuation of long work hours, albeit with less time spent commuting. Interview data do suggest, however, that this in-migration phenomenon is, at least in part, pursued for ideals associated with slow movement ideology, particularly the desire to individually determine one's lifestyle pace – whether that is a fast-tracked career, making time to join social clubs or choosing how many hours to devote to a meaningful, and often more secure, job.

The opportunities and experiences that a treechange affords are as varied as the destinations chosen and the individuals seeking a lifestyle change. Yet, despite individual differences, two key patterns are discernible. First, the action of 'taking charge' of one's destiny, regardless of how it ultimately turns out, appears to be an experience that few regret. Even those who hated their treechange or loved aspects of the city so much they intended to return one day engaged in aspects of self-reflection which caused them to notice previously taken-for-granted aspects of their lives or alternative ways of living. Nevertheless, the research failed to show that making a treechange resulted in decreased consumerism. Citing Hamilton's research, the *Sydney Morning Herald* reported:

> The significance of a tree or sea change is having the courage to make the transformation in the first place ... Once you have done that then you are changed forever. You have broken out of the work-spend cycle and adopted a different attitude. Whether your tree change is forever does not really matter; the point is to buck convention and make the change.
>
> (Ducker 2008, p. 21)

The current study does not reveal whether making a treechange either permits one to break out of the work–spend cycle or even encourages one to do so. Rather, the qualitative data complement much statistical data and have revealed that most waking hours are spent working for money (see Honoré 2004). Although all treechangers sought to escape traffic, pollution and the undesirable aspects of dense urban living, all continued to drive cars, often commuting even longer distances; all remained active participants in a capitalist economy; and none reported making significant changes counter to dominant Western lifestyle trends.

In seeking to examine if treechangers' experiences reflected simple or slow ideology, two unexpected findings resulted:

- several treechangers moved to the country because of the work opportunities it provided in contrast to cities;
- many treechanger accounts reported working even longer hours in contrast with their city jobs.

Both findings counter stereotypical beliefs that country life can be equated with a simpler lifestyle and slower pace. Surprisingly, those individuals who worked the longest hours reported being the most satisfied with their treechange. According to slow movement expert Honoré (2004, p. 189), 'everyone needs to earn a living, but the endless hunger for consumer goods means that we need more and more cash', which causes many to seek higher incomes and/or longer hours rather than to work less. This is a plausible theory yet it remains un-evidenced. Did the treechangers who were interviewed work longer hours because of their endless hunger for consumer goods? Maybe, but those who willingly worked the longest hours did so to (i) permit them to live in a specific location or (ii) permit employment autonomy, whereby they controlled their working conditions. This difference highlights the complexity of treechange as a social phenomenon routinely oversimplified in popular culture. Treechange enables some to 'live large', climb the corporate ladder, buy a bigger house or afford travel. For others, a treechange is more characteristic of a rejection of Marx's commodity fetishism in pursuit of a more authentic self, guided by self-actualising work, whether this involves a longer or shorter length of time devoted to paid labour. Ultimately, perceptions of 'enough' time, how and where to spend it, and which activities are most/least meaningful are driven by historically and culturally contingent values, beliefs and social norms. Lifestyle dissatisfaction is arguably the key driver behind treechangers' actions, yet reducing treechange to a counter-movement synonymous with a rejection of consumerism, materialism, careerism or even workaholicism would be as inaccurate as describing all urbanites as hippies.

References

Alaszewski, A., 2006, *Using Diaries for Social Research*, Sage, London.
Australian Broadcasting Corporation, n.d., *Downshifting*, Canberra, ACT, viewed 22 September 2010, http://www.abc.net.au/religion/stories/s1115995.htm.
Baudrillard, J., 1981, *For a Critique of the Political Economy of the Sign*, C. Levin (trans.), Telos Press, London.
Blackshaw, T., 2010, *Leisure*, Routledge, Abingdon.
Bouma, G. D., 1996, *The Research Process*, 3rd edn, Oxford University Press, Oxford.
Brajsa-Zganec, A., Merkas, M. and Sverko, I., 2011, 'Quality of life and leisure activities: how do leisure activities contribute to subjective well-being?', *Social Indicator Research*, 102, 81–91.
Cenigh-Albulario, L., 2008, 'New breed packing up to flee the 'burbs': the baby boomers – a special advertising report', *The Australian*, 19 September, p. 3.
Cheng, J. S., Yang, M. C., Ting, P. H., Chen, W. L. and Huang, Y. Y., 2011, 'Leisure, lifestyle and health-related physical fitness for college students', *Social Behaviour and Personality*, 39(3), 321–332.
Cogdon, K., 2008, 'Place to be', *Sunday Times (Perth)*, 1 February 2008, p. 12.
Cook, R. A., Yale, L. J. and Marqua, J. J., 2002, *Tourism: The Business of Travel*, Prentice Hall, Upper Saddle River, N.J.
Crabtree, B. F. and Miller, W. L., 1992, *Doing Qualitative Research*, Sage, Newbury Park.
Dominguez, J. and Robin, V. 1992, *Your Money or Your Life*, Penguin, New York.
Donati, K., 2005, 'The pleasure of diversity and slow food's ethics of taste', *Food, Culture & Society*, 8(2), 91–106.
Dubbo City Council, 2009, *$1.2M Federal Funding Announced for EvoCities Project*, Dubbo, New South Wales, viewed 22 September 2010, http://www.dubbo.nsw .gov.au/BlogRetrieve.aspx?BlogID=2424&PostID=42559.
Ducker, A. 2008, 'When tree is not enough', *The Sydney Morning Herald*, 23 February 2008, p. 21.

Evocities, n.d., *Lifestyle*, New South Wales, viewed 22 September 2010, http://evocities.com.au/quality-life/

Flick, U., 2009, *An Introduction to Qualitative Research*, Sage, UK.

Fowler, F. and Mangione, T., 1990, *Standardized Survey Interviewing*, Sage, Newbury Park.

Fox, R. F., 2001, *Mediaspeak*, Praeger, Westport.

Freeman, J., 2009, *Shrinking the World: The 4000-Year Story of How E-mail Came to Rule Our Lives*, The Text Publishing Company, Melbourne.

Gelardin, S. D., Muscat, E. J. and Whitty, M. D., 2010, 'Slow career: mapping out a slow and sustainable lifework process', *The Business Renaissance Quarterly*, 5(1), 31–54.

Hamilton, C., 2003, *Downshifting in Britain: A Sea-Change in the Pursuit of Happiness*, The Australian Institute, Canberra.

Harvey, A. and Pentland, W., 1999, 'Time use research', in W. Pentland, A. Harvey, M. Lawton and M. McColl (eds.), *Time Use Research in the Social Sciences*, Kluwer Academic/Plenum Publishers, New York, pp. 3–18.

Harvey, D., 1982, *The Limits to Capital*, Oxford, Blackwell.

Hawkins, D. I., Best, R. J., and Coney, K. A., 2004, *Consumer Behavior: Building Marketing Strategy*, McGraw-Hill, New York.

Honoré, C., 2004, *In Praise of Slow: How a Worldwide Movement Is Challenging the Cult of Speed*, Orion Books, London.

Lingane, D., 2007, 'Country buyers on the march', *Sunday Times Perth*, February 2007, p. 12.

McFadyen, W., 2008, 'The story still has the power to transfix', *The Age*, March 22, http://www.theage.com.au/news/opinion/the-story-still-has-the-power-to-transfix/2008/03/21/1205602653979.html

Morley, P., 2008, 'Country life is perfect – city slickers find best of both worlds in regional areas', *The Courier-Mail*, May 2008.

Patterson, K. and Carne, L. 2007, 'The great escape to Boonah – lifestyle changes bring boom times', *The Sunday Mail*, 2 February 2007, p. 28.

Perreault, W. D., Darden, D. K. and Darden, W. R., 1977, 'A psychographic classification of vacation lifestyles', *Journal of Leisure Research*, 8 (3), 208–224.

Petrini, C., 2001, *Slow Food: Collected Thoughts on Taste, Tradition, and the Honest Pleasures of Food*, Chelsea Green Publishing Company, White River, VT.

Pilcher, G. 2008, 'Lifestyle dreams go south', *Herald-Sun*, 5 March 2008, p. 5.

Plummer, J. T., 1974, 'The concept and application of life style segmentation', *Journal of Marketing*, 38, 33–37.

Ragusa, A. T., 2005, 'Social change and the corporate construction of gay markets, in *The New York Times* Advertising Business News', *Media, Culture & Society*, 27(5), 653–676.

———, 2007, 'Not all boomers can ski: Australian news media's depiction of baby boomers and "tree change" ', *The Australian Sociological Association Conference Proceedings 2007 Auckland*, The Australian Sociological Association, Swinburne University, Melbourne.

———, 2008, 'Media symbolism, knowledge production and image creation of tree changers in Australia: Tracing the historical development of a new social group and its impact on Australian landscapes', *Proceedings of the Urban History and Planning Conference Sippy Downs*, University of the Sunshine Coast, Queensland.

————(ed.), 2010, *Interaction in Communication Technologies & Virtual Learning Environments: Human Factors*, Information Science Reference, Pennsylvania.

Richards, C. 2011, *International Institute of Not Doing Much*, www.slowdownnow.org, viewed 8 June 2011.

Roberts, K., 2011, 'Leisure: the importance of being inconsequential', *Leisure Studies*, 30(1), 5–20.

Robinson, J. P, 1999, 'The time diary method: Structure and uses', in W. E. Pentland, A. S. Harvey, M. P. Lawton and M. A. McColl (eds.), *Time Use Research in the Social Sciences*, Kluwer Academic Publishers Group, New York, pp. 47–89.

Robinson, J. P., Converse, P. E. and Szalai, A., 1972, 'Everyday life in twelve countries', in A. Szalai (ed.), *The Use of Time: Daily Activities of Urban and Suburban Populations in Twelve Countries*, Mouton, The Hague, pp, 113–144.

Rubin, A. and Babbie, E. R., 2008, *Research Methods for Social Work*, 6th edn, Thomson, Belmont.

Saltzman, A., 1991, *Downshifting: Reinventing Success on a Slower Track*, HarperCollins, New York.

Sarantakos, S., 2005, *Social Research*, 3rd edn, Palgrave Macmillan, Basingstoke.

Schor, J. B., 1999, *The Overworked American*, Basic Books, New York.

Snow, D. A. and Oliver, P. E., 1995, 'Social movements and collective behaviour: social psychological dimensions and considerations', in K. S. Cook, G. A. Fine and J. S. House (eds.), *Sociological Perspectives on Social Psychology*, Allyn and Bacon, Boston, pp. 571–599.

Stirling, J., 2008, 'Tree change takes roots', *The Australian*, January 2008, p. 9.

Tam, D., 2008, 'Slow Journeys: what does it mean to go slow?', *Food, Culture & Society*, 11(2), 208–218.

Wachtel, P., 1989, *The Poverty of Affluence*, New Society Publishers, Philadelphia.

Walter, M. (ed.) 2010, *Social Research Methods*, 2nd edn, Oxford University Press, Melbourne.

Wells, W. D. and Tigert, D. J., 1971, 'Activities, interests and opinions', *Journal of Advertising Research*, 11(4), 79–85.

Williams, C. C. and Windebank, J., 2003, 'The slow advance and uneven penetration of commodification', *International Journal of Urban and Regional Research*, 27, 250–264.

7
Sensuality, Sexuality and the Eroticism of Slowness

Barnaby B. Barratt

The notion of slowness, as applied to the erotic potentials of the body, raises some slightly different, but nonetheless seriously interesting, questions compared with its appearance in the 'slow food' or other movements. There is not – to my knowledge – a consciously political movement representing the advocacy of slow sex, although I will suggest that the contemporary Euro-American engagement with tantric practices and other rites of body-based spirituality come close to meeting this criterion.[1] Although *slow sensuality* is arguably a mode of 'alternative hedonism', rarely is its pursuit, as the cultivation and the critique of transcendent processes, comprehended as a catalyst for socio-cultural transformation, even if it might become such a catalyst. Understood as an essentially private engagement, the pursuit of slow sensuality is akin to mystical practice, which has traditionally constituted a bewildering domain for the social sciences, accustomed as they are to examining the structures of belief. Particularly challenging is the claim of mystical practice to conjure dimensions of experience that are beyond belief, beyond scientific conceptualisation or rationalisation, and indeed promissory of a profound experience of life that is transcendent and, so to speak, 'pre-conceptual' (indeed, an experience that has critical momentum against the conceptual pretensions of transcendent belief systems). Here I will discuss some of the possible significance of slow sensuality, asking what we might make of the notion of *slowness* in the light of the postmodern retrieval of the elementariness of our experiential embodiment, the fundamentality of bodily experience and the genuinely unsurpassable momentum of human erotics.

In this context, one hesitates to write of 'slowness' as a concept, especially since what is proclaimed, by the polyglot practitioners of slow sensuality, is the potential of the embodied force of desire to comprise an experience that subverts categories such as fast/slow – categories which, in this globalised era of technological and social acceleration, are routinely conflated with progress/stagnation, and so forth. If *the sensuality of embodied experience is the truthfulness of our being* in some foundational sense, then the slowness with which our personal and communal selves engage the world erotically may well have this sort of subversive potential (Barratt 2010a; cf. Foucault 1988–1990). The radical nature of sensual slowness is that it claims to undermine its own conceptualisation, requiring a mode of awareness that is otherwise than ordinary self-consciousness (which is composed of concepts and narratives). It thus indicates the limits of self-consciousness. The claim of slow sensuality is that it can only be understood as a defiance or counteraction to the prevailing socio-cultural acceleration of a globalised and technologically alienated world – even if this intention is not rhetorically explicit. Indeed, slowness might be defined as the corporeal reality that liberates precisely by exposing the limit of our cognitive aspirations to transcendence, of our utopian fantasies about another time and place, and of our objectification by the technological commodities that have escalated throughout a transnationally advancing capitalist economy. Slow sex claims to achieve all this by returning awareness to its grounding in embodied experience. In sympathy with this possibility, I will argue here that how we *fuck* comes to have profound significance for the potential of any radically powerful socio-political, cultural and psycho-critique.[2] I will try – in as scholarly a fashion as the topic permits – to establish the spiritual and socio-political significance of fucking, to argue the transformative potential of its frequent and slow engagement, and then to assess certain aspects of the potential of *slow sensuality* not only as a counter-cultural praxis but also as a possible source of far-ranging and deep-rooted change.

To write approvingly of the implications of slow fucking is not necessarily to make moralising judgments condemnatory of the 'quick-fuck'. I do not wish to excoriate those episodes in which the temporal distance from excitement to climax (for a man, an ejaculatory release with minimal full-bodied orgasmic repercussions; for a woman, perhaps no more than a complementary spasm) is minimised so that physical relaxation may be quickly achieved and attendant fantasies gratified. But it is necessary to contrast these modalities in order to expose the possible socio-political, cultural and psychological significance of each.

Prolegomena to a phenomenology of fucking

As a beginning, let us establish the tenet – consistently verified by clinical and sexological observation – that how we fuck portrays and even epitomises the deepest structures and processes by which we engage our inner selves and our outer worlds. Although every individual is fractured with conflicts and contradictions, there is putatively a holistic connectedness to the many aspects of our functioning. How we fuck is reflected and refracted in how we think, how we eat, how we walk, how we dance, how we engage in life's commerce and – perhaps most tellingly – how we come to terms with our death (Barratt 2004a, 2009, 2010b). All these acts express our capacity for compassion, appreciation and grace, as well as expressing the anguish and torment with which we live from cradle to grave (Barratt 2004b). In fucking, the repertoires of self-pleasuring (from the sensuality of nakedness, the erotics of the bath, the enjoyment of springtime fragrances, the relief of foot massage, to the caress of the genitals) exhibit our sense of being-in-the-world, the quality of the processes of self-care from which we may extend our selves to others, whether in a spirit of care for them and for their pleasures or with other intentions (Barratt 2005). How we then involve ourselves with the bodies of others, in the ebb and flow of receiving and giving pleasure – from the way in which we interacted with the bodies of primary caretakers to the manner in which we engage our lovers – exhibits the most basic processes and modalities with which we express and project ourselves in the world.[3]

In short, there is fundamentality to embodied experience. However much we become estranged or alienated from our experiential embodiment by the infusions of aggressivity, by the structures of language, by the mechanisms of 'higher' cognition or by the devices of our socialisation, becoming 'strangers to ourselves' (Kristeva 1991), our bodily sensuality remains the ground, the *fons et origo*, of our being-in-the-world. How we fuck – in the sense that I am deploying this notion – epitomises the most basic way in which we treat our bodily sensuality and in which we caringly attend to, or suppress and repress by means of narrative structures, our awareness of this embodied experience. As Freud famously wrote, the I is 'foundationally the bodily I' (1923, p. 255, my translation).

On the functions of fantasising

Characteristic, indeed defining, of the quick-fuck is the accompaniment of fantasies, as narratives that kidnap our attention and distract us from bodily sensations. The act of the quick-fuck indulges the figments of imagination as much as, or perhaps even more than, the brio of the flesh. Whatever their manifest content, these fantasies are redolent with themes of irresistible desirability, insuperable prowess, conquest or subjugation, superiority or submission, rebellious defiance toward the anti-sexual forces of socialisation, the lascivious transgression of taboo and so forth. All of these might aptly be categorised under the modern motif of mastery, with all its variants of capitalist and statist ideology. They are the themes that characterise human relations in late capitalism – ideological bytes that sustain and perpetuate the mechanisms of commodification, domination and exploitation.[4] Fantasies are, in conventional psychoanalytic terminology, a construct of the organised and organising aspect of mental functioning ('ego structure') that alleviates the anxiety of conflict by forming compromises between competing forces within our mental world. Psychoanalytic investigation offers three insights about the deeper functions of such fantasising.

First, these fantasies juggle the organisation of desire around the forbidden allure of incestuous wishes. One way or another, the fantasy must involve an 'object' that is close enough to the body of a primary caretaker to be arousing, yet far enough from that body to permit arousal. The earliest experiences of the primary caretakers' embodiment, which is commonly taken to mean the maternal body, constitute the prototype for all subsequent desires of both men and women – a prototype which is invariably held ambivalently due to the later encounter with the incest taboo. This is perhaps the insight of psychoanalytic inquiry most resisted by the public and by non-psychoanalytic scholars (as well as not a few allegedly psychoanalytic ones). The ambivalence is often palpable. As Freud's patient said, 'you ask who this person in my dream could be – it's *not* my mother!' (1925, p. 11, my translation), or as one of my patients disclosed, 'I've only ever been attracted to red-haired women, which is strange because there is no one in my life who has red hair, except my mother.' As clinical experience amply demonstrates, the varieties of passage through Oedipal complexities are multifarious, resulting in all the diversities of adult orientation, but *invariably* – whether for hetero-erotic or homo-erotic proclivities, in men and in women – sexual arousal can be traced back to forces of *both* attachment to *and* avoidance of the repetition of sensual experiences with primary caretakers.[5]

Second and correspondingly, the fantasised scenarios have roots in primary or primal scenes. For example, the fantasy of irresistible desirability is typically discovered, on deconstruction, to counter some earlier anxiety and despair around feelings of exclusion, rejection, being undesired and undesirable, or 'castrated'. This is regularly the warp and woof of psychoanalytic exploration. It has caused some psychoanalytic theorists to become overly entranced with the notion of 'the ego's capacity for mastery', to the point where they become almost oblivious to the tragic reality that the nature of the repetition compulsion – which is surely one of Freud's greatest and most central contributions – is such that the ego's sense of mastery is more or less delusional and thus evidences its ongoing captivation by forces beyond itself.

Third, these erotic figments conjure our bisexuality (more precisely our *polysexuality*) for they serve not only overtly to gratify our conscious wishes but also covertly to satisfy those whom we have suppressed and repressed (Barratt 1984, 2005). For example, it is a commonplace of psychoanalytic insight that the appeal of hetero-porn to ostensibly hetero-men is not just that they can identify with the 'stud' who is seen to be fucking the 'babe', but also that they can unconsciously imagine themselves as she who is being fucked. To give another example, manifestly fantasising about entering a partner anally also indulges the latent thrill of being thus penetrated. Often a fantasy serves to gratify the psychic wish for an act that one has no intention of engaging in, or even fears engaging in, behaviourally; there is a crucial distinction between indulging a wish in thought (marked as fantasy) and indulging it in action, although the former can, in the context of psychic reality, be as gratifying as the latter.

What does it mean to assert that all human beings are inherently polysexual? For obvious reasons of strategic diplomacy as well as his personal commitment to bourgeois values, Freud wrote of 'polymorphous perversity' that characterises every childhood. On the basis of this (with the influence of contemporary thinkers as diverse as Francois Peraldi and William Stayton), I developed the notion of *polysexuality*, which is Freud's concept freed from his value judgments, from his pathologisation of erotic repertoires other than the penile-vaginal, and from the tendentious perspectives of adaptation and maturation (Barratt 2005). Freud articulated his insight in a manner infused with bourgeois prejudices, producing what Gayle Rubin once humorously called the 'teleology of the missionary position'. However, the critical impetus of Freud's notion should not be lost; namely, that *every* human starts life with the potential for *every* sort of sensual enjoyment, and that the vicissitudes of ontogenesis gradually – and perhaps we may add tragically – narrow each individual's actual and possible repertoire of erotic pleasures.

To give one obvious example, what is commonly called 'heterosexuality' is founded on the suppression and repression of 'homosexual' desires (and vice versa). This theory of pluripotentiality does *not* imply that our sexual ambitions are a matter of preference or choice, for our sexual patterning comes to be established as 'hard-wired' by our earliest experiences. The theory is profoundly important in showing how we all, in one way or another, live deprived of our full erotic potential – in various degrees of estrangement/alienation from the sensuality of our embodied experience (Barratt 2005, 2010a). Inevitably, we all sustain ourselves only in a condition that I have called 'castratedness' (Barratt 2004a, 2010b). This theory is also essential in understanding the reassuring role of fantasy in appearing to establish firmly the dominance of some erotic repertoires over other potentials for pleasure that have been lost, or at least suppressed and repressed. Fantasy secures the ego organisation's delusional sense that things are assuredly one way and not otherwise.

With respect to the sensuality of our embodiment, fantasies thus have a double effect. They may serve to rouse the body, but they also distract the subject's awareness away from the sensations of the body's arousal. They may stimulate the flesh, but they are also an avoidance of the sensuality of the flesh. Once a fantasy is engaged, it typically sets the pace for the sexual act, seemingly appropriating the rhythm of bodily sensations and co-opting them to its own design. There are limits to this appropriation, for the body has its own 'say' in the course of events. It is nonetheless conspicuous how fantasy – one might again specify that the fantasy is invariably a compromise formation constructed within and by the 'ego organization' – attempts to assert control, or indulge the delusion of control, over the sensual functioning of the body. I do not intend to reintroduce an outdated Cartesian dualism here, but merely to underscore the way in which fantasy is an effort to govern the sensuality of embodied experience, and that this effort occurs – obviously – on the temporal dimension. In this respect, every fantasy re-enacts the Cartesian delusion of mastery, and in some sense reflects the current socio-politics of its *episteme* or era.

The superficially masterful motif of the quick-fuck is such that the act must both relieve the physical itch and fulfil the functions of the fantasy as efficiently and expeditiously as possible. Thus, an effective sexual fantasy does several things at once: it reassures the self-conscious subject about his/her relationship to the forbidden; it gratifies some compensatory scenario by an egotistic mode of mastery; it reasserts the subject's overt sexual identity and thus strangulates or channels the energies of an inherent polysexuality by marshalling the subject's erotic momentum into a particular sexual identity against the exuberant polypotentiality of its embodiment; *and* it takes the subject out of awareness of his/her embodied experience.

The implications of slow sensuality

Fantasy is the stuff of the quick-fuck. But what of the cultivated practice of slow fucking? We may define this as sensuality characterised by what some sexologists have called the three 'P's. Slow fucking is *processive* (facilitating a focus on the sensuality of embodied experience, as contrasted with the goal-directedness that characterises fantasy); oriented to *pleasure* (facilitating the intensification of, and the focused awareness of, sensual pleasure, as contrasted with the aim of relief from tension); and *playful* (meaning that it is whimsically at the leisurely caprice of our body's erotic energies, rather than under the organised governance of clock-time or the terminus of a narrative structure).

It might be thought that slow fucking opens us to a wider psychic 'timespace' in which fantasies would fester and flourish with even greater power and profusion. To assume this would be to make a crucial error. It makes logical sense, but not 'bodymind sense' (so to speak), to think that the slower the pace of sensual activities, the greater the room for the narratological construction of fantasies. The contrary is more accurate. Of course, it is hypothetically possible to prolong intercourse by a sustained sequence of fantasies (although sexological and psychoanalytic observation suggests that this is quite arduous and rarely accomplished). However, in the sense I am discussing it here, the very slowness of slow fucking requires a loosening or releasing of the grip of fantasies over the subject, thus eliciting a renewed awareness of the erotic energies of embodied experience. We can conjecture (because there is a paucity of research on this topic) that in contrast with the quick-fuck, sensual slowness is accompanied by a significantly different pattern of the neurophysiological release of endorphins and hormones, such as oxytocin, and that this release blocks the 'higher' cognitive functions involved in conceptualisation and the narratological production of fantasies. Moreover, orgasming causes a transient loss of what is commonly called consciousness (hence the well known French reference to *le petit mort*). Consciousness, as I am using the term here, involves a narratological structure profoundly discrepant from the awareness of embodied experience.[6]

To sustain the sensuality of slow fucking requires presence and awareness incompatible with the narratological imperative that builds edifices out of pasts and futures. It removes the 'subject' from the realm of thetic or *apophantic* consciousness. Thus, whereas the quick-fuck depends on the production of fantasies, slow fucking requires the subject to surrender to the rhythms of the body's erotic energies and to attend to them with awareness. As fucking becomes slower, bodily awareness increases and the role of fantasies diminishes or is even extinguished. Concomitantly, by requiring the subject's awareness of the sensuality of embodied experience, slow fucking cannot be accomplished without a 'clean and clear' emotional connectedness that some would call 'Love' (see Barratt 2009). Lacking the infusion of aggressivity that characterises the quick-fuck, its prerequisite is the working-through, the *aufhebung*, of hostile or sadistic incursions into the act. This process characterises the progression from 'phallic sexuality' (for both men and women, this is the quick-fuck) to the potentials of 'genitality' (which I am characterising as slow fucking). To take this further, consider the cultivation of multiple or extended orgasmicity in both men and women, which could be said to be the apotheosis of slow fucking, and which exemplifies an authentic genitality of which few individuals are capable. Extended orgasmicity takes subjects figuratively, and perhaps literally (if one concedes the literality of subtle energy systems), 'out of their heads'. It dissolves the ego organisation's differentiation between 'me' and 'not-me', creating a transcendent experience of fusion or dedifferentiation with the energies of the universe.

Admittedly, there is only a small psychoanalytic literature on these processes of slow fucking, and its conclusions are somewhat mixed. Michael Balint's 1948 paper remains the most useful discussion, and is to be credited with preserving, against the conservative tide of mainstream psychoanalytic writing, the distinction between phallic sex and fully orgasmic 'genitality'. Otto Kernberg more recently entered this discussion, but he is so convinced of the insuperability of aggressive and sadistic forces within our psychic constitution that he cautions that the experience of transcendent fusion during orgasm will likely lead to violence. Kernberg seems to take Nagisa Oshima's 1976 Franco-Japanese film *L'Empire des Sens* (based on an event in the 1930s in which a man embarks with his female servant on an obsessively torrid relationship that ends in castration and death) as evidence for his contention (see Efron 1985). It seems to be this eminent psychoanalyst's view that one should never take fucking too far, or that one does so at one's peril. However, the 'evidence' on this point, and the extraordinary drama that seems to have captured Kernberg's attention, are a far cry from the cultivated praxis of slow fucking.

Slow fucking is the much publicised, and greatly misunderstood, key to tantric sex – which is principally not a 'sex act' at all, in the conventional sense, but rather an erotic spiritual praxis.[7] It is in its power to deliver what might, in a pedestrian terminology, be called an 'altered process of consciousness' that slow fucking acquires its significance as a somatic-spiritual process with implicit socio-political implications. Its sheer leisureliness exhibits the way in which the erotic energies of embodied experience defy governance by the forces of socialisation and acculturation. It would be exceedingly challenging – perhaps impossible – to generate an authoritative historical and sociological account of the various initiatives that have intentionally and methodically cultivated the practices of slow fucking.[8] Records rarely exist and some documentation, such as that produced by religious organisations, tends to be imbued with anti-sexual ideologies (as with the materials on witchcraft archived by the Inquisition). However, the praxis seems almost always to have been counter-cultural. As with the erotic-mystical practices of the Taoist, Sufi, Kabbalist, Gnostic and certain indigenous traditions, not only are these beliefs and ritual practices often cast as a secretive protest against a predominant ideology – frequently practised as a private defiance of publicly prevailing values – but the specifically sexual dimension of these practices is invariably shrouded and their methods transmitted almost entirely from adept to novitiate in an oral tradition that was, and is, guarded diligently. However, what we do know of the history and sociology of the tantric movement illustrates instructively the counter-cultural impetus of slow fucking.

What is most misunderstood about tantra in contemporary Europe and North America is that it is foremost a set of methods for meditation, most of which are not what anyone in the West would conventionally call 'sexual' (Barratt 2006). Their purpose is to cultivate an acute awareness of what are comprehended as the subtle erotic-spiritual energies that circulate within us, through us and throughout the universe. The intent of those tantric practices that do involve touching and the deliberate facilitation of energy awareness through what we would commonly recognise as sexual acts, solo or partnered, is still primarily the cultivation of what might be called a transcendent but embodied condition of awareness. Thus, if tantric practices are defined as any method of meditation that releases the subject from imprisonment in our egotism's 'chattering mind', then tantric sex definitely exemplifies what I am describing as slow fucking and the cultivation of transcendent processes of orgasmic awareness.

These practices have almost invariably been opposed, often quite viciously, by religious orthodoxies, and their history is one of recurrent persecution. Tantra survived in Tibet because of the country's relative isolation, and perhaps also because the explicitly sexual methods were only practised by the elite members of certain specific groups (most tantric practice being pursued under conditions that would commonly be regarded as abstinent). Tantra is believed to have flourished in South Asia from about the fourth to the eleventh centuries of the Common Era, and survived mostly in secretive cults, which were successively attacked by the Brahmanic authorities, by the theistic hegemony of Muslim invaders and by the anti-sexual zeal of Christian missionaries.[9] Although rarely articulated or organised as such, tantric practice was, and arguably still is, a spiritual-erotic protest against prevailing ideology. It stands against the ideological construction of persons as property, against patriarchy, against the social distinctions of class and caste, and against the oppressiveness of institutionalised marriage. It would be a mistake to suggest that these politics have only an arbitrary connection with the tantric advocacy of slow fucking.

Politics and the 'energies' of eroticism

This brings us to the question of whether and in what way slow sensuality might have a transformative impact beyond the personal growth and spiritual enlightenment of the individual practitioner. Since Marx wrote of mysticism and empiricism as the twin characteristics of bourgeois thought, leftist theorists have tended to discount the contribution of such private practices to progressive social change. However, in addition to whatever one assesses as the significance of the modalities of 'alternative hedonism', there is another way to approach this issue: by examining the extent to which transformative movements limit their impact when they do not permeate beyond the level of the individuals' cognitively held belief system, beyond the level of ideology, to the deeper level of their sensual relationship with their own embodied experience and with that of others.

Wilhelm Reich, at least in his early adulthood, perhaps remains a paramount twentieth-century spokesperson for such a viewpoint (although the clinical work of Otto Gross, Sándor Ferenczi, Otto Rank, Wilhelm Stekel, Georg Groddeck and even Theodor Reik perhaps contextualise his contributions). Prior to his emigration to the USA, after which his work drifted in a more arcane direction, Reich, as the foremost socialist psychoanalyst, was quite lucid in his theorisation of the connection between orgasmicity and social change. The 'character armored' individual, closed down with respect to his or her capacity for orgasm (and correspondingly, in the terminology of these notes, imprisoned by fantasies and limited to the quick-fuck), is the product of the suppressive and repressive acculturation that is required for the ideological perpetuation of an oppressive social formation. A genuine socialist revolution – the overcoming of dehumanising aspects of capitalism, the ideology of property, the objectification and exploitative treatment of people in the interests of capital accumulation – will not occur unless the sensuality of our embodiment is concurrently liberated.[10]

For Reich, in his Vienna and Berlin years from the early 1920s to 1933, this meant the establishment of clinics for the provision of contraception and the eradication of venereal diseases, as well as support for the equality of women. These commitments were vigorously undertaken not only on medical grounds but out of a belief that fucking needed to be anxiety-free and egalitarian. Reich supported energetically the sexual rights of young people, and advocated the establishment of locations where adolescents who lacked privacy at home could go to fuck freely and enjoy such activities in a leisurely manner, rather than be limited to quick-fucks in back alleys or other surreptitious venues. These community-based efforts were understood as preliminary but necessary steps toward widespread and revolutionary social changes. Reich is rarely ranked as a major figure in social and political theory, yet we should entertain his candidacy if only because few other theorists consider the significance of sexuality in the processes of social change (even in post-1960s social and political theory, exceptions to this egregious oversight are rare). There is no evidence that Reich knew much about spiritual traditions such as tantra, but he was acquainted with the pioneering work in somatic awareness undertaken by Elsa Gindler and Heinrich Jacoby, and probably would also have been influenced by the emphasis on the body represented by the controversial and marginalised ideology of *freikörperkultur* (see Barratt 2010a). My point is that his insights into what I am now calling slow fucking are remarkable, even if somewhat inchoate.

Drawing on Freud's work on libidinality, Reich articulates how the foundations of pathology in erotic restriction and constriction are endemic to the social and economic conditions of the patient. Orgasmicity is not just nature's inducement for procreation (if that were the case, humanity might never get beyond the strangulated climax of the quick-fuck). Rather, it is the essence of health, a resource of subtle emotional energies that is commonly drained by the construction of symptomatic formations and character armouring. Humans lose their 'orgastic potency' precisely because of the suppressive and repressive consequences of adaptation to, or maturation within, oppressive social and cultural circumstances. This loss is the cause, catalyst and consequence of inner anxieties and outer rigidities, fuelling the ideologies of hatefulness, sadism, exploitation, greed, fascism, racism and – we might add – the individual's readiness to accede to his or her objectification, the rendering of individual as commodity. The socio-political remedy is a full-scale attack on bourgeois morality and the economic structures that support it; the individual corrective is a treatment that frees the subject for an ethical and vibrant sexual life, released from conflicts and inhibitions. When such treatment is successful, 'body armor' dissolves, breathing deepens throughout the body, movements are softer, somatic awareness increases and – in the terminology of these notes – slow fucking becomes possible.[11]

Reich's notorious discovery of 'orgone' developed out of Freud's early writings on *libidinality*. While Freud cast his formulations psychically in terms of the erotic energies of the individual body, Reich cosmically expanded the notion to denote a universal power of life, comparable to Carl von Reichenbach's Odic force, to Henri Bergson's *élan vital* and to other precursors. It is interesting that contrary to Carl Jung, neither Freud nor Reich seem to have had much acquaintance with Dharmic-Taoic cosmologies or with indigenous philosophies. Yet the notion of libidinality can be considered a Western rediscovery of the subtle energy systems that are known to non-Western experience (as *prāṇā* in South Asia, as *lom* in parts of Southeast Asia, as *chi* or *ki* in East Asia and so forth). Significantly, these subtle energies are both/neither material and/nor non-material, and thus it is suggested that experience of them challenges or indeed subverts the casting of this distinction. If nothing else, this proclaims a metaphysics of experience – in Freud's terms, a metapsychology, which riffs on the translation of *psyche* as soul – that is vehemently anti-narratological.

Subtle energy is not to be debated, only to be experienced by means of a cultivated awareness of the sensations within our embodiment. Tellingly, Freud seems to have retreated from the powerful notion of libidinality after about 1914, when his theorising became more systematic and inherently conservative. Almost all the psychoanalytic movement followed him in this retreat, which is why the significance of sexuality within psychoanalytic discussions became progressively discounted through the course of the twentieth century. This is, in my view, a retrogressive shifting away from postmodern discovery to a nostalgic retrieval of Cartesian dualism and modernist scientificity (Barratt 1984, 1993).

Sexual practices and ideology critique

Awareness of one's own libidinality, of the subtle energies that course within, and perhaps through, our embodiment, requires the sensuality of slow fucking, and a relaxing of the grip of narratological consciousness. This is the claim of the spiritual and socio-political 'movement', such as it is, that advocates and appreciates slowness in our erotic life. The concomitant claim is that any social movement that pushes for cultural transformation limits itself if its proposals remain on the level of narrative and narratologically motivated actions. Rather, deep-rooted change requires a reconfiguration of our relationship to embodied experience – a radical shift from the imposition of new narrative structures to the anti-narratological processes of attending to our potential for awareness of embodied experience.

From an anthropological and sociological point of view, it is difficult to assess whether slow sensuality and the methods prescribed by Reichians and post-Reichians, by Tantrikas and neo-Tantrikas, as well as by a diverse collocation of other individuals and groups, might eventually amount to a historically founded and perhaps contemporarily burgeoning movement. From an academic standpoint, it is perhaps impossible to evaluate whether there is truthfulness to the claim of certain erotic practices to subvert the dichotomous structures of modern narratives, or that these practices thus challenge the paramount relevancy of belief systems, ideologies and narratives by offering alternative processes of living an ethical and authentic life that might generate profound and pervasive socio-cultural transformation. In a certain sense, the very nature of a 'belief' in slow sensuality – and the trenchant insistence on the primacy of cultivating an awareness of embodied experience – shields itself from evaluation.

While the cultivation of slow sensuality may not be fully or legitimately comparable to other initiatives that constitute the culture of slowness – the movements toward slow food, amenity migration, seachange/treechange, downshifting and anti-consumerism – it does make a powerful statement against the commodification of the body that characterises the globalised ideologies of corporate capitalism. Consider here three idealisations of the body that certainly characterise the dominant – Western, capitalist – culture. There is the media ideal, which emphasises spectatorial value, in the tyrannical aesthetics of cosmetology and fashion, or in the brute mechanics of professional sport. There is the medical ideal, which values the body as a sort of living cadaver, acknowledged only in terms of its anatomical and physiological functions. And there is the economic ideal, which treats the body for its value either as a unit of labour within the workforce or for its consumptive capacity. It is unarguable that the cultivation of each of these requires that fantasy be superimposed upon the now strangulated rhythm of subtle energies, and that awareness of the sensual experience of embodiment be overridden by narrative structures. It is in this context that the cultivation of slow fucking may be understood as a praxis that defies the ubiquitous forces of objectification and commodification. Whatever their intention or articulation, those who advocate, appreciate and practise slow fucking are making a socio-political statement enactively.

Contrary to Leonore Tiefer (1994), sex is not merely a socially constructed act, although it is important to analyse it as such; not just because of irreducibly biological components but because there are esoteric dimensions to our sexual expression (although this is scarcely believable to those who have not personally experienced the power of subtle energy systems that flow within and through our embodiment). The cultivation of slow fucking, as a way of accessing such energies, may not constitute a 'movement' that would satisfy the definitions of contemporary social sciences, but one cannot evade the conclusion that its practitioners are engaged in processes that have socio-political significance in that they are profoundly contrary to the cultural norm.

On a final note that might be an amusing example of commodification were it not so appalling, consider one of the chants that is – I am told – currently used by the military during marching manoeuvres: 'This is my dick and this is my gun; one is for fighting, the other's for fun'. Here is an example of the instrumentalist ideology indicted so powerfully by Max Horkheimer, by Herbert Marcuse and by their successors. When the penis becomes a tool by which to achieve an end, and the vulva-vagina merely becomes an excitable receptacle that is to be conquered – the common situation which is the soulless centre of the quick-fuck in its hetero-manifestation – fantasy reigns supreme and the awareness of the sensuality of our embodied experience is obliterated. This is the requirement that sustains the military-industrial complex. Oppression can persist to the extent that we block our awareness of embodied experience. Against such ideologies that suppress and repress this experience is where the cultivation of slow fucking shows its counter-cultural potential.

Notes

1. Carl Honoré (2004) mentions how Albert Vitale, a noted Italian entrepreneur, started a 'slow sex movement' in the last years of the twentieth century, but this appears to have fizzled into a campaign against pornography with an unidentified number of supporters. However, the influential text by Parkins and Craig (2006) omits any discussion of sexuality. Recently, Nicole Daedone (2011) declared her 'One Taste' program to be a movement advocating slow sex, and in the USA she has become a popular proponent of orgasmic meditation, although her focus is on facilitating female orgasmic capacity. There are other popular works along these lines (e.g. Powell 2008; Richardson 2011). These somewhat scattered initiatives seem both indicative of the fact that there is, within our contemporary Western culture, a growing interest in slow sensual practices of various sorts, and evidence that, at this time, these initiatives have not yet consolidated into what one would confidently designate a socio-political movement.

2. Despite the risk of offending the academy, I will use the word 'fuck' to convey the full earthiness of this dimension of experience in a manner that other terminologies perhaps evade ('make love', ' copulate', 'have sex', 'engage in intercourse', 'be intimate'). For the present purposes, I will define the term as incorporating or encompassing any physical interaction that intentionally aims toward the cultivation of pleasure and that is *safe, sane,* and *consensual* (Barratt 2005). Thus, in this context, rape is excluded, as would be any suicidal act of 'bareback' intercourse. But included would be all manner of penile-vaginal, penile-anal, oral-oral, oral-genital and other interactions, including epidermal erotics (such as massage) and every sort of possible touching (including autoerotically).

3. The testimony of sexological investigation is that becoming a virtuoso at self-pleasuring is the essential preparation for virtuosity in pleasuring others. Psychoanalytic and spiritual wisdom suggests that masochism is not love, but that the capacity to love an 'other' is crucially contingent on the capacity to love oneself. This is not advocacy for narcissistic preoccupation, in which the world of others is subordinated to the overweening demands of the self – a condition born of fundamental fear and anxiety. Rather, it is to acknowledge the simple truth that self-pleasuring is indispensably fundamental to all authentic love-making.

4. My understanding is not only indebted to the early Marx but specifically to the writings of the Frankfurt School, as well as to the contemporary work of Mark Taylor and Timothy Reiss on the historical and cultural significance of the motif of mastery or domination. There have been many studies of sexual fantasy, most too popular to be serviceable as scholarship; those that are more scholarly are grievously cautious about examining wider and deeper cultural and political implications. Jack Morin (1995) remains useful, although his work lacks the power of a psychodynamic perspective. Many of the psychoanalytic works on this topic are theoretically parochial, but some of the better ones would include the various works of Robert Stoller (e.g. 2009).

5. An important empirical study undertaken in the 1960s – which I believe remains unpublished, but which was frequently mentioned during my 1970s

studies at Harvard University with professors John W. M. Whiting and David Maybury-Lewis – categorised a range of ethnographically documented cultures according to the normative style of heterosexual intercourse. Having analysed a large amount of anthropological data from the Yale Human Relations Area Files, it was found that the only predictor of this variable is the culture's specific style of breast-feeding and weaning during infancy. It might also be noted that even an eminent sexologist such as John Money (1986), who was notorious for his anti-psychoanalytic polemic, consistently acknowledged, on the basis of his empirical investigations, that our adult sexual patterning is established in the crucible of our earliest experiences.

6. The distinction between *consciousness* as established by the narratological imperative and *awareness* as the process pertaining to our attention to embodied experience is discussed elsewhere (Barratt 1993, 2010a). Narratives are precisely the modality by which our ego organisation avoids listening to the wisdom of embodied experience.

7. Contrary to the 'bubble bath and scented candles' image of tantric practices that now pervades the popular market, which is – however, delightful – thoroughly misleading, it is provocatively helpful to remember that the Dalai Lama practises an abstinent form of tantric sex. The higher reaches of spiritual practice, in the Gelugpa tradition of Vajrayāna Buddhism, involve a disciplined mode of meditation that, without the involvement of touch, move the erotic energies of the universe through and around the practitioner's embodiment in a manner that may properly be described as transcendentally orgasmic. Other traditions – Taoist, Sufi, Kabbalist, Gnostic and indigenous – offer similar erotic methods of spiritual praxis (see Barratt 2006).

8. There have been some commendable efforts to document some of these movements and to discuss their significance in a scholarly manner (e.g. Evola 1983). However, most of the extant works in professional sexology are focused on the mainstream rather than the counter-cultural (e.g. Francoeur 1997), and most scholarly texts on the history of tantric spiritual practices tend to skirt around the sensual and sexual nature of these modes of meditation (e.g. Ray 2008).

9. There is a tendency toward nostalgic idealisation of this period of South Asian history, depicting it as the golden age that produced such wonderful erotic texts as the *Kāma-Sūtra*, the *Ananga Ranga*, the *Koka Shastra* and the entire literature of South Asian *Ars Amatoria*. Against this idealisation stands the evidence that the leisurely pursuits advocated in these texts were probably most available to an elite class supported by the labours of servants and slaves. What is also known about the less elitist tantric practitioners is that, from their earliest history, they defied the caste system, engaging in love-making across castes and, within the adult community, without ageist prejudice. Additionally, one practice in particular, the famous maithuna rite (in which partners switch and circulate in an elaborate celebration of slow fucking), was specifically intended to facilitate the practitioners' capacity to overcome jealousy and possessiveness; and in this sense it may be understood as an enactive critique of the establishment of marriage with its institutionalisation of women as property. It is also likely that such rites were homo-erotic as well as heterosexual, although this is not, to my knowledge,

anywhere documented. Finally, it must be noted that tantric practice almost always operated as a protest against patriarchy, at least in so far as the female is held to be equal to, or even superior to, the male. When tantra is designated the 'left-handed' path, the designation not only contrasts its practices with the 'right' and the orthodox but also suggests the egalitarian directionality of its socio-political impact.

10. Wilhelm Reich's socio-political writings are somewhat haphazard and polemical, often most blatant in pamphlets written during the Berlin years, one of the best of which is *The Sexual Struggle of Youth* (which precipitated an intensification of the Nazi campaign against his work). Most of these are not available in translation, although the collection edited by Lee Baxandall under the title *Sex-Pol 1929–193*, is helpful. The 1927 book entitled *The Function of the Orgasm* (later translated as *Genitality in the Theory and Therapy of Neuroses*), his 1932 *The Invasion of Compulsory Sex-Morality*, his 1933 *The Mass Psychology of Fascism* and his 1936 *The Sexual Revolution* all clearly demonstrate Reich's understanding of the crucial mediations between the personal and the socio-cultural levels. Even the later, near rantings of 1948, published as *Listen, Little Man*, are of interest, especially since they surfaced just a couple of years before Theodor Adorno's et al. (1951) more measured, but nonetheless powerful, appraisal of obedience to fascism in *The Authoritarian Personality* (Adorno et al. 1951). Still actively read today, by clinical trainees and others, is *Character Analysis*, which, despite now being a classic of continuing importance, sadly lacks the political punch of the other works (cf. Reich 1961, 1971a, 1971b, 1980, 1986). Myron Sharaf's (1994) authoritative biography of Reich is commendable, although perhaps not as extensive as one might wish in his exegesis of Reich's significance as a social and political *ur*-theorist.

11. This presentation of Reich's ideas is somewhat extravagant and extrapolative on my part. It must be noted that Reich never – to my knowledge – addressed directly the distinction between the quick-fuck and slow fucking, and he wrote little or nothing about the role of fantasy in the blocking of erotic potentials. Also, without excessive licence, it cannot be claimed that he clearly envisioned the polysexual nature of human erotics; rather, he was, like Freud, quite focused on the penile-vaginal variant. However, one point is clear: Reich understood that how one fucks has pervasive and profound socio-political and cultural, as well as psychological, implications and ramifications.

References

Adorno, T. W., Frenkel-Brunswick, E., Levinson, D. J. and Sanford, R. N., 1951, *The Authoritarian Personality: Studies in Prejudice*, W.W Norton, New York.

Balint, M., 1948, 'On genital love', *International Journal of Psychoanalysis*, 29, 34–40.

Barratt, B. B., 1984, *Psychic Reality and Psychoanalytic Knowing*, Analytic Press, Hillsdale.

——, 1993, *Psychoanalysis and the Postmodern Impulse: Knowing and Being since Freud's Psychology*, John Hopkins University Press, Baltimore.

————, 2004a, 'Desire and death in the constitution of I-ness', in J. Reppen, J. Tucker and M. A. Schulman (eds.), *Way Beyond Freud: Postmodern Psychoanalysis Observed*, Open Gate Press, London, pp. 264–279.

————, 2004b, *The Way of the BodyPrayerPath*, Xlibris/Random House, Philadelphia.

————, 2005, *Sexual Health and Erotic Freedom*, Xlibris/Random House, Philadelphia.

————, 2006, *What Is Tantric Practice?*, Xlibris/Random House, Philadelphia

————, 2009, *Liberating Eros*, Xlibris/Random House, Philadelphia.

————, 2010a, *The Emergence of Somatic Psychology and Bodymind Therapy*, Palgrave MacMillan, Basingstoke.

————, 2010b, 'Ganesha's lessons for psychoanalysis: Notes of fathers and sons, sexuality and death', *Psychoanalysis, Culture and Society*, 14, 317–336.

Daedone, N., 2011, *Slow Sex: The Art and Craft of the Female Orgasm*, Grand Central Life, New York.

Efron, A., 1985, 'The sexual body: an interdisciplinary perspective special issue', *Journal of Mind and Behavior*, 6(1), 1–88.

Evola, J., 1983, *The Metaphysics of Sex*, Inner Traditions, New York.

Foucault, M., 1988–1990, *The History of Sexuality* (3 vols), Vintage, New York.

Francoeur, R., 1997, *The International Encyclopedia of Sexuality* (3 vols), Continuum, New York.

Freud, S., 1923, 'Das Ich und das Es', *Gesammelte Werke*, 13, 237–289.

————, 1925, 'Die Verneinung', *Gesammelte Werke*, 14, 11–15.

Honoré, C., 2004, *In Praise of Slowness: Challenging the Cult of Speed*, HarperOne, New York.

Kristeva, J., 1991, *Strangers to Ourselves*, Columbia University Press, New York.

Money, J., 1986, *Lovemaps*, Irvington Publishers, New York.

Morin, J., 1995, *The Erotic Mind*, HarperCollins, New York.

Parkins, W. and Craig, G., 2006, *Slow Living*, Berg, Oxford.

Powell, J. N., 2008, *Slow Love: A Polynesian Pillow Book*, Ponui Press, Santa Barbara.

Ray, R. A., 2008, *Touching Enlightenment: Finding Realization in the Body*, Sounds True, Boulder.

Reich, W., 1961, *Wilhelm Reich: Selected Writings*, Farrar, Straus & Giroux, New York.

————, 1971a, *The Invasion of Compulsory Sex-Morality*, Farrar, Straus & Giroux, New York.

————, 1971b, *The Sexual Revolution*, Farrar, Straus & Giroux, New York.

————, 1980, *The Mass Psychology of Fascism*, Farrar, Straus & Giroux, New York.

————,1986, *The Function of the Orgasm: The Discovery of the Orgone*, Farrar, Straus & Giroux, New York.

Richardson, D., 2011, *Slow Sex: The Path to Fulfilling and Sustainable Sexuality*, Destiny Books, Rochester.

Sharaf, M., 1994, *Fury on Earth: A Biography of Wilhelm Reich*, De Capo Press, Cambridge.

Stoller, R., 2009, *Sweet Dreams: Erotic Plots*, Karnac, London.

Tiefer, L., 1994, *Sex Is Not a Natural Act and Other Essays*, Westview Press, New York.

8

Creativity Takes Time, Critique Needs Space: Re-Working the Political Investment of the Consumer through Pleasure

Roberta Sassatelli

Introduction

The debate about consumption, and its organisation, including its spatiality and temporality, is quite rich today in and beyond academic circles. Such debate is fuelled not only by polemical or celebratory writing but also by much, often good, empirical research which addresses some relevant theoretical issues (Lewis and Potter 2011). Still, on the whole, the debate about consumption remains rather fuzzy. This is partly due to the lack of a common understanding of what we mean by consumption and to the different emphasis given to its many semantic relatives. To summarise, for the majority of the social scientists working on consumption empirically, it is understood as the use and appropriation of commodities for the creation of meaningful worlds. With the notion of *consumer society*, instead, critical theorists have singled out particular aspects of contemporary culture which fall under the rubric of *consumerism*: possessive or acquisitive individualism, a market dominated by massification, the production of waste and commodity obsolescence, the increased dominance of promotional culture even in the public sphere, the dominance of commodity sign values, the commoditisation of the consumer and so on.

Authors as different as Theodore Adorno, Jean Baudrillard and, more recently, Zygmunt Baumann consider consumption largely within the rubric of consumerism. In one way or another, what critical thinking proposes is very much what philosopher Hannah Arendt adumbrated in her celebrated *The Human Condition* (1958), in particular in the chapter entitled 'Consumers' society': consumption features as a process of worldly alienation. Arendt signals a pressure to move away from the use of goods to commodity acquisition, with no time to actually come to terms with one's own purchases, to have them work effectively and to make home for oneself in the world. In a consumer society, she writes, 'the rate of use is so tremendously accelerated that the objective difference between use and consumption, between the relative durability of use objects and the swift coming and going of consumer goods, dwindles to insignificance' (Arendt 1958, p. 125). Clearly she was working on the assumption that 'to say *user* rather than consumer is still to express a relevant distinction', as Raymond Williams (1976, p. 70) says in his highly influential dictionary of culture in the 1970s. The notion of use/r here appears to single out the utilisation of goods independently of their market value, whereas consumption is inherently related to commoditisation. This dualism brings with itself a particular set of oppositions which work in terms of temporality: use is conceived as reasoned or motivated appropriation which requires time as opposed to hasty, mindless consumption; use is portrayed as realisation of values, replenishing or fulfilling, rather than the consuming generation of waste diminishing value and creating emptiness.

Both of these different semantic universes have been taken on board by contemporary studies of consumer practices and cultures, in the recognition that the heavy metaphoric aura (Wilk 2004) around consumption may actually get in the way of understanding what people do when they purchase, employ and possibly throw away commodities. This is partly because, to the social scientists of today, the notion of consumption is very broad: it is both use and acquisition, it concerns both necessities and luxuries, adumbrates both successful appropriation and frustrating waste, is both egoistic and altruistic as well as both private and public – ultimately, while it dialogues with commoditisation, it may bypass, reform or alter it. Indeed, much sociological and anthropological writing suggests that despite the dangers of consumerism as a dominant cultural strand in Western societies, people as consumers still try their best to use commodities, both durable (e.g. furniture) and consumables (e.g. food), to feel at home. The commodity form has indeed been rescued from its doomed quarters in critical approaches, and phenomena such as critical or political consumption – from consumer boycotts to ethical purchase networks – have been indicated as promising seeds for alternative ways to organise commodity circuits and the market.

Social scientists have also tried to take consumer practices at face value – that is, to understand their meanings for people, suspending moral judgment, even though a moral dimension typically emerges, and in different guises, from the very encounter with people and practices. Thus, considering the variety of the cultures of consumption which humans build together in their ordinary lives rather than consumer society as an abstract foremost cultural mechanism, many of us point to consumption practices as a terrain of *ambivalence*. In other works (Sassatelli 2001a, 2001b, 2007), I have looked at how this ambivalence has been inbuilt into prevalent notions of the consumer and consumption, and how this has happened as a function of the way they were constituted together with production and the cash nexus in the consolidation of modernity. However, simply referring to the ambivalence of consumption may appear far from final. Here, thus, I want to take a step ahead. And to do so, I will have to come back on a more normative terrain. In particular, in this chapter I shall focus on a critical appraisal of the ambivalence of consumption, reflecting on how to consider consumer practices from an angle on their temporality.

Indeed, facing structural unbalances in the commodity circuit as they are evident today, it is necessary to engage more closely with consumer power, its workings and its dimensions. Different, contrasting arenas converge in the commodity circuit: the cultural and the economic, at least. While the cultural arena of the commodity may allow for consumers to articulate meanings deploying creativity and critique, the economic arena pushes for surplus to be generated and monopolised in the hands of producers. The set up of the economic arena partly thrives on the relative disarticulation of the cultural arena, whereby (some) symbolic creativity and even critique among consumers fuels economic surplus generation. It also accounts for the unbalances of power between consumers as individual and often individualised actors and producers as industries and corporate actors. What is more, it promotes a novelty-gripped, obsolescence-driven, territory-disarticulating temporality of consumption which structurally limits consumers' creativity, enjoyment, critique and ultimately power. Addressing the power of consumers, I start by considering the scope of what normally goes under the notion of 'political consumerism', placing it in the context of a wider politics of consumption. I propose that embracing all too naïvely the investment of consumers with political power and responsibility may, quite paradoxically, divert our attention from the politics of consumer practices as embedded in time and space. Temporality in particular points to the importance of a reflection on two elements which feature as taken-for-granted cornerstones in the standard economic theory jigsaw: taste and pleasure. While the former is made to correspond with revealed preference, the latter is rendered through a hydraulic, individualistic model of satiation. Neither assumption allows for the processual and situated nature of consumption. It is such a view that we to build on in order to provide a critical view on the politics of consumption. Holding a processual view of consumption, heterodox economist Tibor Scitovsky was among the first to criticise neo-classic consumer sovereignty from the standpoint of pleasure rather than duty. Drawing on his work, I will explore the dualities of comfort vs pleasure, standardisation vs individualisation and generalised vs specialised knowledge in relation to the current debates about alternative ways of consuming. An argument for creativity, as realised through processes which slow down the pace of consumption and embed it reflexively in social relations, is developed. As against consumerist views which end up equating the serial fulfilment of transient desires as the realisation of individual happiness, slowness and embedment are considered to be key elements for the appropriation of taste and the realisation of wider-than-self Self capable of facing our ever-smaller world.

Engaging with consumer power

Standard economic theory has dealt with consumer power under the fundamental rubric of consumers' sovereignty. Here consumers as individualised beings have the power to get what they want from producers and ultimately rule the market. If this is a crude vignette of what mainstream neo-classical economic theory has put forward, such theory holds nonetheless quite a simplistic view of power. Such a view leaves little space for control and conflict, persuasion and protest. To be sure, persuasion and protest are key elements of power as a relationship mediated though, and an effect of, the sum of strategic positions and inequalities in a given society (Foucault 1975). Both characteristically concern consumption. The persuasion of consumers though sophisticated promotional techniques, and the subsequent manipulation of their wants and tastes, have been the object of broad structural critiques of consumer society launched by critical theories of a cultural-Marxist variety, at least from the Frankfurt School onwards. Consumers' protest as mobilisation against, or in favour of, specific companies or producers' initiatives has been addressed by a number of empirical studies of consumer practices. In the stronger sense, they show that consumption concerns power because social actors may deploy their consumer choices to make their voices heard for a number of political issues related to the distribution of resources, the value of labour, the exploitation of natural resources and common goods and so on. The fact that practices of consumption can be constituted as a space for forms of political action has been used, with some reasons, against traditional critical views considering that advertising is able to commend consumption as an alternative to political rebellion (cf. Lasch 1991).

Sociologists, anthropologists and political scientists have recently been very interested in the political investment of the consumer, considering how various forms of 'political consumerism' may broaden the repertoire of political mobilisation and what is the significance of the use of the market for political and environmental reasons. As we know, 'political consumerism' is not new – for example, as early as the late eighteenth century, English women used their consumer power to support abolitionism (Micheletti 2007; see also Friedman 1999; Glickman 1997; Cohen 2003). Still, contemporary 'political consumerism' has been recognised as different: in the 'magnitude of the efforts (the numerous issue areas), the size of their constituency (the global community but primarily the rapidly growing middle class), and the more public interest of their mission (its focus on human rights, farm animal treatment and global common pool resources)' (Micheletti 2011). Indeed, the scope of contemporary political consumerism is global, or at least supranational, extending along the long interdependency networks which have been developing with economic dis-embedment. The dialectic of globalisation (Robertson 1995) is at the heart of contemporary forms of political consumerism: as we know, global capitalism has tended to raise local hackles, provoking resistance in many different forms, including fundamentalist ones. As globalisation proceeds, it is especially large multi-nationals that have become the targets of growing critical attention within environmentalist organisations and the alter-global movement. In introducing innovations which alter the routines of consumption, in expanding the relevant human community, in promoting the dis-embedment of economic from socio-cultural processes, globalisation creates a space to address both commodities as vectors of social relations and the re-embedment of economic process.

Let's explore briefly the field of political, critical or ethical consumerism. Symbolic initiatives against multi-national companies and the boycotting of global brands, branded respectively 'discursive' and 'negative' political consumerism, have been increasingly joined by 'positive' initiatives (Micheletti et al. 2004), or 'buycotting' (Friedmann 1999) – that is, the purchase of alternative products such as ethical finance, organic food or Fair Trade goods. Critical consumption practices now seem to concern a wide sector of the population in developed countries, but the fact that they typically thrive on middle-class publics is often considered limiting and drawn back to the power of consumer practices and taste of generating social hierarchies among consumers.

The scope of political or critical consumerism has also been criticised on the grounds that what draws consumers to ethical products may not be a strong political consciousness; that well-meaning initiatives may not be consequential in terms of specific or global welfare or environmental targets; and that much of what can be done in terms of structural change needs to be accompanied by policies and regulation as well as grassroots mobilisation. Certainly, it would be mistaken systematically to attribute a deliberately political intention to all 'responsible' consumer choices (Sassatelli 2006). Many of the practices which come under the umbrella of political consumerism may be conducted by consumers who have in mind meanings and objectives other than strictly political ones, with variations having to be explained also in terms of local histories and circumstances. For example, in the UK, alternative distribution networks, including second-hand shops, not only respond to a politically conscious middle-class consumer but also attract disadvantaged urban groups that may not be able to afford to shop via formal channels (Williams and Paddock 2003). Likewise, the demand for organically grown vegetables typically mixes private health concerns with some degree of environmental consciousness, and comes from diverse sources, including a large vegetarian movement as well as health-conscious or gourmet carnivores (Lockie and Kristen 2002). In Italy, a large proportion of those who buy Fair Trade goods in supermarkets, for example, do so because they 'like' the products or consider them 'better quality', or just 'by chance' (Leonini and Sassatelli 2008).

Awareness of these dynamics helps to address the possible conflicts which may indeed emerge from different components of critical consumers' actions: such as between the support for Fair Trade and ecological consideration in terms of food miles, or the support of local, sustainable agriculture. This is particularly relevant as there is now a growing awareness that as Fair Trade has gone mainstream, it has had difficulties in always keeping its promises to help producers in developing countries (Lyon and Moberg 2010). Works on global anti-sweatshop campaigns (Micheletti and Stolle 2007) and on their appropriation by US company American Apparel (Littler 2009) seems to point to the fact that wide public resonance, and even commercial success, may not always correspond to a real improvement in the working life of garment workers. More broadly, it is important to be sensitive to the localisation of dissent and to the possible particularistic, or nationalistic, outcomes of the political investment of consumption. And it is important to be sensitive to the political legitimation function that endorsement of, for example, Fair Trade initiatives may have for local or national political leaders, quite independently of the effectiveness with which these initiatives impact on the needy populations they are intended to help (Clarke 2007). This points to the role of politics *strictu senso*, of global and local governance, and of local/global regulation policies.

In his brilliant book *Coca-Globalization*, anthropologist Robert Foster (2008) follows a highly standardised, often contested, commodity, Coca-Cola, throughout global commodity networks and their local ramification in Papua New Guinea, and considers the role that commodity and commodity networks criticism have on the glocalised construction of commodity value. This book can be taken as an appreciation of, and a cautionary tale relating to, the belief that the 'consumer' now translates to a global scale the duties and capacities of the citizen, as reckoned by authors such as Beck and Gernsheim (2001). Foster looks at shareholder activism and responsible investment as increasingly important options to facilitate consumers' action on issues outside the jurisdiction of local and national politicians. However, he notes that these options indeed respond to the notion of corporate citizenship that corporations themselves promote, and he concludes that 'no matter how much good corporations can do and have done, doing good will never be their "core activity" [...] The legal mandate and main purpose of corporations is to enhance market value for the owners of the corporation' (Foster 2008, p. 227). The model for such options is charity, and when economic recession threatens profits, charitable practices may swiftly vanish. Such a depressing ending occurs more easily for issues which are not of immediate relevance, like the well-being of faraway workers and common pool resources whose vulnerability does not yet impinge on consumers' daily life.

Foster's book warns of the importance of the regulation of long commodity networks, embracing both production and consumption. The field of research which has coagulated around issues of consumers' power and responsible consumption seems now mature enough to place emphasis precisely on governance and the regulatory frameworks which may institutionalise political consumerism (see Bevir and Trentman 2007) and normatively entrench considerations of justice in global commodity networks. The latter rests on the political negotiation of forms of knowledge, auditing and procedures that translate economic externalities into endogenous components of commodities and commodities networks. Clearly, an analytical shift in focus from political consumerism to the politics of commodity networks is wanting. A politics of commodity networks should acknowledge both the power and the limits of consumers' protest while recovering a space for the role of persuasion, thus mapping intricate and differentiated networks as they interlock in both the economic and the cultural arenas. This is required not only because grassroots protest and symbolic strategies, such as sub-advertising, become pray to 'cool hunting', but also because political consumerism does not simply realise a new 'global citizenship', working on pure universalistic, cosmopolitan and humanitarian grounds. A political moment, in terms of both representation and governance, is needed.

Such a move clearly entails a focus on the role of both civil society (movements, political and cultural intermediaries) and political bodies (at local, state and supra-national level). Indeed, in line with some of the more promising developments within economic sociology, it entails conceiving of the market itself as an embedded socio-economic formation charged with normative dynamics, rather than an abstract mechanism made of individualised individuals and corporate entities operating in purely instrumental fashion. Issues of governance (of commodity networks) and representation (of consumers) have started to come to the fore in order to problematise the political investment of the consumer as a consumer-citizen. This is partly because the scope and nature of political consumerism is still highly contested. In her influential book *Political Virtue and Shopping* (2003), political scientist Michele Micheletti framed the issue through the notion of 'individualized collective action'. This was meant as an analytical tool to capture 'the essence' of a form of 'citizen engagement that combines self-interest and general good'. In a more recent paper, she (2011) proposes a new, different label: 'individualized responsibility taking'. This linguistic move signals the necessity of the role of collective agents – social movements and the like – in the translation of individual responsibility into political action. It thus stresses more clearly that to be effective, a politics of consumption must include civic engagement in addition to market-based efforts (see also Micheletti 2003, pp. 161 ff). In doing so, it moves some way in the direction of the perplexities that were generated by her previous work as to the real impact or effects of individual consumers' ethical choices. And it shifts attention from the individual weighting of what is useful with what is right, to the social dynamics that render subjective pondering truly political – that is, negotiated in public as explicit means of interrogating our ways of going about social and economic organisation. The mediating role of cultural or political intermediaries and the translation of new visions of individual responsibility into regulatory frameworks are crucial to determining the scope of political consumerism.

Still, even with her recent contribution, Micheletti well epitomises the one unchanging feature of much reflection on political, ethical or critical consumption: the emphasis on duty. Taking responsibility for the world is a commitment, a modality of action oriented to outcomes and results. It is neither a dutiful pleasure (which somehow combines involvement in a pleasurable present and positive long-term outcomes) nor a pleasurable duty (a good thing for others and the world which nevertheless makes us happy to the point that we can't easily give it up and substitute it with something equally satisfying but less good). Indeed, the notion of 'individualized responsibility taking' is wanting in that it is predicated on a dualistic emphasis on duty and responsibility as opposed to pleasure and happiness: ultimately, self-interest is portrayed as opposed to common good, and doing right is seen in the light of either a sensible sacrifice or a charitable obligation. And yet, renouncing to pleasure may have its costs: charity, again, is a frail model in moments of crisis, and regulation obviously becomes the only way to sustain it, with increasing pressures in terms of efficient auditing.

The emphasis on regulation and governance in the field of critical consumption studies is timely and well justified. Surely one way to stabilise consumer practices, and in particular to internalise concerns for fairness and the environment, is to regulate commodity circuits so that these concerns are literally taken into account (in legal requirements, setting of targets and budgets, running of procedures, etc.) and, indeed, promoted. Consumers' grassroots ethical initiatives may otherwise be easily subsumed within externalising, instrumental, profit-driven market logic. Still, such emphasis is also clearly based on reducing the scope of individual choice, something which may appear unpalatable to liberal sensibilities. More broadly it does not exploit to the full the creative power of consumers' practices, their importance as involving meaningful worlds for participants and their capacity to work through pleasure as much as duty. Together with regulation, it is thus important to consider in which way ethical/critical consumption may offer strong intrinsic incentives to participants, stabilising taste and knowledge, which in turn contributes to fixing alternative social and commodity networks. In other terms, we should consider how consumption can be organised in ways that allow for immediate, self-rewarding creativity as well as well-being larger than immediate, fast-consumed satiation, which generate a rat-race, and an obsolescence-driven thirst for easy-to-digest commodities.

This entails taking seriously the pleasures of consumption, considering ethical consumption not just like a means to do something else, however important this might be (participation to the polis, changing the world, etc.). A new focus on pleasure, and on the different possible qualities and definitions of pleasure, becomes fundamental. Only thus is it possible to allow for the mixture of motivational logics (altruistic or otherwise) which impinge on individual consumer practice at large (see e.g. Zelizer 2009), and which is arguably even more implicated in practices of a 'responsible' variety. The strength of consumption as an ordinary practice lies by and large in the fact that it is framed as finality in itself. While we cannot equate 'genuine' critical choices with political vote, we should not disqualify the intrinsic pleasures of ethical shopping as simply the ultimate distinctive fashion of the well-off. Shopping ethically and critically may enable us to make choices which matter to us in everyday life in ways which political voting may not (Schudson 2007). Many consumer choices matter in themselves for what they allow us to do and to be, for whom they make us relate to and how, rather than for their possible larger effects on macro realities (world justice, global environmental issues, etc.). And yet, what is at stake in many critical consumption initiatives is precisely that people's lives can be re-organised entirely, starting from a number of apparently banal, practical choices: this will require and induce a different management of time, space and social relations, which will be more fulfilling for the individual and promote collective, sustainable 'happiness'.

Slowness, creativity and critique

Let's go back to mainstream economic reasoning and consider how taste and pleasure are dealt with. Even in mainstream economics there has been an increasing attempt to overcome the individualistic, instrumental view of consumer sovereignty portraying the actor as an isolated maximiser of utility who knows very well how to get satisfaction from the market. Particularly influential was the work of Amartya Sen (1977, 1985) who has tried to include altruistic motivations, power structures and cooperative/conflictual forms of interaction (see also Hirschman 1985). These moves have certainly been very important. However, I'd like to suggest that today the most relevant issue when considering the scope of critical consumption, and consumer practices more in general, is not the tempering of instrumentalism with altruistic motivations. Dominant economic theory, epitomised by Gary Becker's (1996) *Accounting for Tastes,* indeed includes some altruistic effects through an extended individual utility function. Yet, it is still characterised by an equation between revealed preferences and taste – that is, what people buy is an accurate reflection of their original, true wants. This has the effect of removing persuasion from the picture: consumers are autonomous beings who will stop wanting only if they are truly and happily satisfied. Satisfaction itself is seen as the elimination of discomfort: a perspective which reifies pleasure as the discrete 'filling in' of a gap in a linear sequence of clear-cut options. There is, thus, little space for a relational and processual perspective on pleasure, one which defines pleasure as an interactive learning process of mutual shaping between social beings, social practices and (socially mediated) objects. As I shall show, only such a perspective can help us toward a critical appraisal of consumption today.

Particularly promising to correct a reified view of pleasure and take on board a relation and processual perspective are, I suggest, some aspects of the work of heterodox economist Tibor Scitovsky. In his major work *The Joyless Economy* (1992, orig. 1976), he underlined that the growth of material culture does not automatically translate into more happiness.[1] In particular, he asked what the price of economic progress was, suggesting that economic growth in the West has provided genuine gains in living standards, but that these have not translated into fertile leisure, thereby enhancing human happiness. On the contrary, it is especially the pursuit of fertile leisure and creative activities – at once time intensive and less dependent on standardised commodities – which appears to be squeezed by the logic of market expansion (see also Bianchi 2003; Di Giovinazzo 2008). To an extent, Scitovsky appears to side with Arendt, as mentioned at the beginning of this chapter, in considering fast, waste-producing, obsolescence-driven commodity culture a major shortcoming of contemporary societies. And yet there are significant differences. As is well known, Arendt (1958) equated on the one hand consumption with labour (itself connected with the biological processes, whereby *animal laborans* produces consumer goods, non-durables necessary to keep the human organism alive), and, on the other, use with higher-order forms of production typical of the *homo faber* (through work, humans produce the artificial environment as home for themselves, with use objects, durables mostly, which are needed for the *zoon politicon* to fix speech and memory). For Arendt the commodity form and commodity circuits seemed inevitably to bring forth consumption as a waste-creating, de-humanising activity antagonistic to the superior functions of the *zoon politicon*. The *zoon politicon* still had to do with objects, but make use practices needed to be removed from the fast, disembedding circuits of the market. While assigning an important role to the public promotion of art, creative leisure and sport, Scitovsky took a critical but less adversarial position to the market and the commodity form.[2] The problem is not so much commoditisation or consumption per se, but how these are organised. Individual consumption skills are indeed important in Scitovsky's argument, on the assumption that consumption can be organised differently. This can be done, he reckons, if we revise the idea of individual pleasure as mechanic satiation which is at the basis of mainstream economic reasoning.

In many ways, Scitovsky's stance is puzzling when placed on the backdrop of the current debates on consumption and its politics: neither does he side with the collectivist criticism of contemporary consumer society which considers consumer culture as alternative to politics, sees the latter as the sole area where humanity may flourish, and human flourishing as linked to the public provision of public goods rather than consumer sovereignty; nor does he side with the libertarian apology of contemporary consumer society which, sceptical of politics and the political identification and provision of public goods, totally relies on individual sovereignty and freedom to consume. On the contrary, while he strongly criticises the idea of consumer sovereignty, he still considers that human flourishing can be pursued through it, or better through the critical shaping of individual tastes. Juliet Schor (1996) is right in commenting that Scitovsky's book focuses on individual pleasure and does not give enough consideration to public goods acknowledging more systematically the existence of biases toward private consumption as against free time and the environment. And he does not give sufficient attention to the pleasures of political participation, as Hirschman (1996) suggests. Scitovsky himself (1996) is quite ready to agree on these points, and stresses the importance of Schor's 'structural critique' of American consumerism. 'She correctly notes' – writes Scitovsky (1996, p. 598) – 'that competitive spending on positional goods is a zero-sum game that can never add to one's comfort or contentment as long as everybody else also spends on it. All this does is to use up hard-earned income and absorb resources that could better be used' (see also Schor 1998 and Gross 2000).

That has long been an important argument for the political regulation of consumption, based on the recognition that, in contrast to neo-liberal slogans, the common good does not automatically follow from the pursuit of individual interests. Against such a celebratory stance, in his well-known work *The Social Limits of Growth*, Fred Hirsch (1977) showed that the democratisation of luxuries and superfluous private goods which mark status may become a pointless and dangerous game. Only recently has the great majority of the population had access to this 'positional' kind of consumption which was previously reserved for privileged groups. The opening up of the possibility of competition within the field of consumption for the majority of the population has not, however, cancelled out social differences: for while the least favoured groups now consume to display, their relative positions have yet to change. This also has the complex effect of heating up demand, leading to social and economic instability as well as environmental hazards. Indeed, the emphasis on consumer sovereignty, private consumption and individual satisfaction has tended to blind many to the role of what Manuel Castells (1977) has called 'collective consumption' – that is, consumption of public goods provided by political institutions to the whole population – to which we can add the consumption of natural goods and environmental commons. The crisis of the welfare system led many to believe that that everything could be privatised with excellent results in terms of economic efficiency, only to realise that certain goods – those which amount to the diffuse minimum necessities in a given society (water and roads, but also education and health) – cannot be efficiently produced, distributed and consumed through the mechanisms of the market alone, which in the long term generates strong economic inefficiencies, as Sen (1977, 1985) convincingly argued.

To be sure, such structural collectivist critiques of consumerism – coupled with Schor's (1996) emphasis on the lack of a real market for leisure time sustained by employers denying opportunities to trade income for leisure – are very important, and increasingly so facing the urgency of global environmental issues. However, Scitovsky's structural individualistic critique of consumerism addresses issues of individual pleasure and sovereignty in ways which are quite powerful. His work is best read as an attack against naïve visions of consumer sovereignty, questioning the all too direct relationship between consumption and happiness postulated by neo-liberals in particular by stressing that revealed preferences and tastes are not simply coterminous. His

> concern was to explain why many well-to-do people, able to afford everything they would need for a full and satisfactory life, nevertheless end up with a feeling of emptiness and boredom.

> This contradicted economists' traditional, simple-minded assumptions that each of us (1) knows what is best for him- or herself, and (2) aims rationally to achieve or at least approximate it within his or her available means

explains Scitovsky (1996, p. 599), 20-something years after the first edition of his book. Consumers are not, at least not always, the best judges of themselves and their pleasure (Scitovsky 1992, p. 7), and the economy may be organised in ways that what they come to prefer is not what really satisfies them (Ibid., XII). The postulate of the correspondence between taste and revealed preferences was shown to be at best an elegant device (mainstream) that economists deploy to avoid answering uncomfortable questions of a political nature, questions dealing with power as influence on taste and structural limitations interfering with the formation of preferences in line with the attainment of pleasure. Holding a processual view of action, Scitovsky would concur with what is today the practice turn in consumer theory: as preferences are shaped by the process of consumption in the encounter between consumers and goods, it is how this encounter is organised through various institutional arrangements which matters (Sassatelli 2007 and 2010). On these premises, it is dubious to say that preferences are revelatory of a defined taste as well as that production merely responds to demand. As demand is, at least partly, shaped by production, there is the political need to promote the demand for certain goods: 'the big question is how to motivate people to prefer benign to malignant activities and make such choices on their own initiative' (Scitovsky 1992, p. 296). What emerges from market competition as it is currently organised is a particular structural configuration of material culture and subjectivity which triggers the divorce between taste and revealed preferences, shaping what people may want even though this may not produce more happiness. Indeed, in today's consumerists markets, 'many people are unaware of their need for enjoyable activity, and in any case lack the skills that most such activities require to be enjoyable' (Scitovsky 1996, p. 599).

Indeed, in late capitalist societies the economy has been organised so as to boost a trade-off between comfort and pleasure. In standard economic theory, all consumer satisfactions are treated as if they were alike and modelled on a simple, mechanistic notion of satiation, whereby maximum pleasure is reached with the maximum reduction in excitement. On the basis of a mechanistic anthropology whereby the human being features as a hydraulic machine reacting to the need of eliminating (physical) discomfort, pleasure coincides with an (instantaneous) moment of satiation. On the contrary, we should start by acknowledging, with Sen (1977), that utility is plural in nature. There are different utilities, which generate different effects both on individual welfare and on public goods. This is why a politics of utility – or, in other terms, pleasure – is central. And central to this is the factoring in of temporality. Indeed, in line with classical Greek philosophy, Scitovsky considers that critical reflection about what one wants is crucial to the pursuit of happiness: this opens a space for exiting the immediacy of substitutable utilities as defined by market options, and consider not just satisfaction of a given need but present pleasures that may result as comparatively more encompassing, long-lasting and sustainable in the future. Once we overcome the idea of pleasure as passive satiation, the components of the good life are not simply 'outcome oriented' activities aiming at relieving pain and stress, but also self-rewarding activities requiring skills and that are, to some degree, renewable and self-sustainable in their projectual force. 'The distinction between actual desires (for commodities and life styles) and scrutinised desires (taking full note of the need for constructive stimulation) has bearing on some of the most basic concepts of social analysis', notices Sen (1996, p. 486) about Scitovsky's contribution. But such distinction here is not to be conceived in terms of a practical or normative alternative: the challenge is to combine immediate pleasure and long-lasting, sustainable well-being. In other terms, this is not a reactionary call for abstaining from, or deferring, pleasure. It is the recognition that only some immediate pleasure is organised as to be sustained and renewed in the long run, and that only sustainable pleasure is real – that is, truly beneficial across time. Such a position involves a particular view of individual pleasure as developing in the process of looking for, finding and learning about things. It is as a process, through activity and critical appropriation, that pleasure is produced. This requires some form of self-discipline as linked to the active learning of (consumption) skills. Thus while comfort is linked to goods that save time, effort and skill (and thereby produce instantaneous satiation of a want), pleasure is linked to goods and modalities of consumption that require time, effort and skills (and thereby enrich one's own faculties and produce long-term well-being).

Recognising that consumption needs time, and that the spending of time in consumption can produce skills which may be deployed creatively, is fundamental and goes to the heart of a further distinction: that between standardised goods which provide novelty by obsolescence and pleasure goods which work in a more individualised fashion, providing novelty by learning, creativity and relationality. Now, we should be clear that pleasure goods are such not just, nor mainly, for their objective, intrinsic qualities, but for the way consumption is organised. These goods are indeed pleasure circuits, entailing ways of consuming which enhance the critical acquisition of skills through lively interpersonal relations. Let me illustrate this by contrasting pleasure circuits with 'sterile ownership', a classical disease of consumer capitalism for Simmel (1990), fuelled by the growth in commoditised material culture, the standardised diversity of objects and their continual marginal innovation.[3] Consumers may indeed find themselves with objects which are useless and meaningless or even alienating, and they may be upset by having discarded an object which still represented them. In such a situation, the consumer legally owns the object but does not possess it emotionally; such an object can certainly provide the extrinsic pleasures of status competition but offers nothing in terms of intrinsic pleasure and personal fulfilment. Such a paradoxical configuration is evident when we consider that consumption as appropriation requires time. Thus forms of sterile ownership may be a feature of economies where leisure time is the shortest for the moneyed elite. A study of consumption patterns in contemporary 'liberal market' societies by Sullivan and Gershuny (2004) indeed shows that expensive leisure goods (sophisticated cameras, camping equipment, sport accessories, etc.) are purchased by time-pressured high-income earners and are often left unused, remaining in storage at home as symbols of a potential future and a wished-for self-identity These luxuries do contribute to consumption expenditure at the macro-economic level, and of course produce a number of unwanted externalities (external diseconomies or costs on the environment, for example, or on perceived deprivation as induced by status competition) even though they remain unused. As such they do not straightforwardly produce pleasure: being only virtually consumed, they offer some symbolic support in daily life only to be bearers of frustration; they phantom consumption skills to make an impression rather than favouring the critical learning of skills which may allow for future, renewable pleasure.

This study is particularly salient because the goods mentioned are precisely of the sort that may let consumers to be critical, active and reflexive about their pleasures. A camera needs (consumption) skills to be used, and while we may soon be back on the market to buy extra accessories, what matters in terms of sustainable pleasure is learning to use and make the most of it. Likewise, golfing equipment is meaningful in that its real pleasure relates, like much consumption, to the socialisation which develops through play, to the rituals of play and to the added effect of interaction among participants. Interaction in consumer practices may amount to what, in economic terms, may be defined as 'external economies'. External economies of this sort are 'especially important in the area of stimulation and excitement, because many of their sources depend on human interaction, which his often of a type that is enjoyed by all those who interacts' (Scitovsky 1992). Goods such as the arts, sport and social games require (consumption) skills and are typically organised via sustained social interaction, and they are thus 'relational goods'. They point to the fact that the value of consumption lies in its being not only an individual process of discovery but also a way of sharing and communicating knowledge, memories, narratives and emotions. As is apparent, for example, in the commercialisation of leisure activities, fitness and sport (see Sassatelli 2010), commercialism typically instrumentalises social relations in order to promote the fastest appropriation of goods possible via a 'must-have', 'must be' or 'status symbol' logic which can easily be rendered in monetised terms, rather than allowing the time and informality which promotes relationality *per se*. There is thus the need to prioritise the flourishing of the 'relational' component in consumption, even at the expense of commercialism, and indeed promote the de-coupling of the consumption of pleasure goods from monetary logic by recognising the social value of alternative systems of provision. Much of this is happening around the idea of 'critical consumption', indeed is predicated on a relational logic. Thus a number of different critical consumption organisations place emphasis on consumer choice not only as a political action but also as one which may provide pleasure by being decoupled from the commercial logic of fast consumption and by the conscious re-embedment of pleasure into social relations (Sassatelli 2006; Leonini and Sassatelli 2008). Even Slow Food emphasis on 'conviviality' responds to this logic, and around this lingers much of its attempt to promote the refinement of taste as an ethical, humanist pursuit of consumers' skills as opposed to a distinctive class practice (Sassatelli and Davolio 2010; cf. Lindholm and Lie, this volume).

Recognising that taste is shaped in the encounter between goods and people, we have to place emphasis not only on the institutional structure of such an encounter (from consumerist commercialism to gift relations) but also on the skills which it requires and promotes. Consumption skills or knowledge are a fundamental issue to address for a critical appraisal of contemporary consumer culture. They also, clearly, entail a temporal dimension in that the acquisition of skills implies a number of resources, including time. All in all, the storing up of consumption knowledge is a serious affair which may be demanding both on time-pressured elites and on the money-short working classes. Scitovsky posits an insidious gap between generalised knowledge, which is needed for everyday consumption, and specialised skills, which are required in the work environment. The skills required in the work environment are intensive, often technical in nature, and geared to solving specific, practical tasks, while generalised knowledge is more extensive, less technical and more about the meaning, the value and the connections between elements, and respond generally to aesthetic and ethical sensibility. Resources, both collective and individual, are spent to make us become good workers, while little is devoted to make us become good consumers. Even back in the early 1970s, Scitovsky (1972, p. 64) lamented that the education system

is increasingly aimed at providing professional training in production skills, rather than the general liberal arts education, which provides training in the consumption skills necessary for getting the most out of life. The changing aims of education are responsible for our increasing productivity. They also explain the paradox that, as progress frees more and more of our time and energies from work, we are less and less well prepared to employ this free time and energy in the pursuit of an interesting and enjoyable life.

Recent debates on education and commercialisation, and on the effect of neo-liberal policies on teachers' capacity to teach how to learn and how to extract pleasure from learning point in a similar direction (Connell 2009). Such debates could be enriched by considering anew our relation to the world of commodities on both the production side and the consumption side. In his well-known book *The Social Life of Things*, Arjun Appadurai (1986) is right in stating that consumption and production knowledge do not coincide, but we should avoid inferring from this that consumption knowledge and skills are essentially good. With the consolidation of modernity, people's knowledge as consumers generally becomes 'infinitely more varied than their knowledge as producers', yet it might just be as much piecemeal and reactive. 'Modern consumers are the victims of the *velocity* of fashion as surely as primitive consumers are the victims of the stability of sumptuary laws' which prescribe what to consume (Ibid., 32, my emphasis). This entails that, although more varied, consumption skills may never become sufficiently reflexive to allow for the successful, fertile appropriation of goods and sustainable pleasure.

Concluding remarks

These observations point to the importance of factoring temporality into the definition of pleasure: awareness, novelty by learning (which entails relationality) and creativity are central elements for the configuration of pleasure which can marry immediate involvement and longer, sustainable projects of well-being. This argument provides a structural individualist critique of the contemporary institutional organisation of the encounter between subject and objects. It recognises the power of such an encounter and calls for a politics of pleasure which deconstructs the idea of pleasure as repeated, instantaneous satiation, not against sacrifice or altruism but against the subject's sustainable and, thus inevitably, relational well-being.

In *The Culture of Speed*, John Tomlinson (2007, p. 158) suggests that

> what we have to confront [...] is not just zones of acceleration, but a broad condition of immediacy which, whilst providing no coherent narrative, none the less offers many prompts, cues and incitements. The attractions of immediacy are strong because they *do* deliver the comforts [...] that have been long promised in the cultural imagination of modernity. But in moral terms, it is the cultural assumptions and expectations of effortlessness, ubiquity and endless delivery in a fast-paced, technologically replete and telemediated world that now need to be challenged. The intrinsic complacency of immediacy needs to be disturbed because it provides no existential resources with which to respond to the contingency of modern existence and to meet the surprises that await us.

He turns to a rather broadly defined 'slow culture' to suggest possible alternatives, stating that a focus on 'balance' and 'the need to draw breath in order to take stock and examine our lives' are what characterise the discourse of slow' (Ibid., p. 152). In broader terms, a focus on the creative, slow appropriation of commodities resonates with the growing body of literature in philosophy and the social sciences which suggests that people's well-being could be reformulated on grounds other than increasing expenditure, starting from notions of 'quality of life' which will often thicken up a short-term, individualistic, competitive and private vision of individual choice with environmental or communitarian contents (Nussbaum and Sen 1993). This may imply some form of 'voluntary simplicity' or 'downshifting' in consumption, rejecting upscale spending and long working hours, to live a simpler, more relaxed life and to enhance personal fulfilment, socio-economic equality and environmental awareness (Etzioni 2004).

The emphasis on simplicity is in many ways all but regressive: it is an emphasis on slowness and embeddedness which amounts to the deepening of consumers' knowledge, where the redundancy that allows for the elaboration of taste as a reflexive, critical practice does not come from sophistication or distinction but from the embracement of the relational nature of commodities. An emphasis on slowness may take place in order to discover new pleasures and enhance personal satisfaction, as well as to further socio-economic equality and environmental awareness (see Soper et al. 2009). Clearly, seen in this light, critical consumption practices do have potential for social change.[4] While such potential needs to be considered case by case, it is evident that critical cultures of consumption of different varieties represent a crucial reservoir for political mobilisation, but should not be equated with it, partly because they are broader and much more mundane than political consumerism strictly speaking (Sassatelli 2004, 2006, 2009). Critical or ethical commodities and commodity circuits embody a critical dialogue with many aspects of consumer capitalism, including the notion of consumer sovereignty. But they do not throw this notion away. Rather, they consider consumer sovereignty to be a political project larger than the market as narrowly defined. They thus attempt to modify consumer capitalism from the inside, the starting point of these initiatives being that consumer choice is not universally good and it certainly is not a private issue.

Notes

1. Since the mid-1970s a stream of studies in economics on the 'paradox of happiness' have developed. These have provided both empirical grounding and theoretical sophistication to the idea that a growing level of material prosperity does not provide for growing levels of perceived well-being (see Bruni 2008; Easterlin 2001). Recent developments in economics, from game theory to behavioural economics, have also tried to recognise the temporal dimension, factoring in a processual view of action (see Nisticò 2005 for a perspective sympathetic to Scitovsky; see also Steedman 2001). For a recent review of those trends and aspects in the economic theory of consumption which may go beyond utility maximisation, see Swann (2002).
2. This becomes even clearer in the second edition of *The Joyless Economy*. The subtitle of the first edition published in 1976 was *An Enquiry into Human Satisfaction and Consumer Dissatisfaction*, whereas that of the second edition published in 1992 shifted to *The Psychology of Human Satisfaction*, with the opposition between consumer (dissatisfaction) and human (satisfaction)

disappearing. A broad critical discussion of Scitovsky's book can be found in the symposium published by *Critical Review* (1996:10(4)) to celebrate 20 years since the first edition and featuring, besides Scitovsky himself, Albert Hirschman, Juliet Schor, Amartya Sen and other important contributors.

3. The idea of sterile ownership thus adumbrates the gap between consumer practices as the use of goods, and demand as the purchase of commodities. It also hints at the lack of reciprocity between consumption as subjective culture and consumer culture as objective or material culture. This lack of reciprocity means that even successful appropriation in ordinary life may have perverse effects. Indeed, the increased pressure on individual consumer choice may have unintended cultural effects. Miller (2004) illustrates this by setting a puzzle: why do Western women dream of colourful dresses and increasingly buy black, grey and plainly unadorned clothing? His reply points to the fact that choice has become so overwhelming that it might be given up altogether, or indeed strictly regimented, by resorting to hegemonic codifications: the 'little black dress' is seen as an anxiety-reducing response to the variety of clothing available and the de-classificatory trends in the fashion system.

4. This is probably even more evident when people refuse to embrace the role of 'consumers' while acting as recipients or users of public services or collective goods. For example, it is evident in consumers' protests of an explicitly political variety which have been directed at basic services or commodities provided by the state, such as water, and involving civil disobedience actions, such as the refusal to pay (Morgan 2007). Such protests often entail the attempt to refuse the identity of the consumer and reclaim that of the citizen, such as when health services get privatised, as in the case of the UK (Clarke 2006). The latter suggests that the current political investment of the consumer as a consumer-citizen is, at least partly, a response to state neo-liberal rhetoric addressing the citizen-consumer only to reduce the former to the latter. Here we have the refusal not only of embracing standard, consumerist, free-market views of consumption and the consumer, but also of whatever consumer choice might be imagined: water, health, air and so forth simply do not look very much as choices.

References

Appadurai, A., 1986, 'Introduction: commodities and the politics of value', in A. Appadurai (ed.), *The Social Life of Things. Commodities in Cultural Perspectives*, Cambridge University Press, Cambridge, pp. 3–63.

Arendt, H., 1958, *The Human Condition*, New York, Dubleday Anchor Books.

Beck, U. and Gernsheim, E., 2001, *Individualisation*, London: Sage.

Becker, Gary S., 1996, *Accounting for Tastes*, Cambridge Mass.: Harvard University Press.

Bevir, M. and Trentmann, F., 2007, *Governance, Consumers and Citizens*, Palgrave, Basingstoke.

Bianchi, M., 2003, 'A questioning economist: Tibor Scitovsky's attempt to bring joy into economics', *Journal of Economic Psychology*, 24(3), 391–407.

Bruni, L., 2008, 'Le sfide della felicità, economia, beni e relazioni umane', in P. Rebughini and R. Sassatelli (eds.), *Le nuove frontiere dei consumi*, Ombrecorte, 2008.

Castells, M., 1977 [1972], *The Urban Question*, Edward Arnold, London.

Clarke, J., 2006, 'Consumers, clients or citizens? Politics, policy and practice in the reform of social care', *European Societies*, 8, no.3, 423–444.

Cohen E. 2003. *A Consumers' Republic. The Politics of Mass Consumption in Postwar America*, Knopf, New York.

Connell, R., 2009, 'Good teachers on dangerous ground: towards a new view of teacher quality and professionalism', *Critical Studies in Education*, 50(3), 213–229.

Di Giovinazzo, V., 2008, 'From individual well-being to economic welfare. The Scitovsky contribution to the explanation of a joyless economy', *European Journal of Economic and Social Systems*, 21(1), 57–81.

Easterlin, R., 2001, 'Income and *happiness*: towards a unified theory', *The Economic Journal*, 111, 465–484.

Etzioni, A., 2004, 'The post-affluent society', *Review of Social Economy*, LXII(3), 407–420.

Foster, J.R., 2008, *Coca-Globalization. Following Soft Drinks from New York to New Guinea*, Palgrave Macmillan, New York.

Friedman, M., 1999, *Consumer Boycotts: Effecting Change through the Marketplace and the Media*, Routledge, New York.

Glickman, L.B., 1997, 'Born to shop? Consumer history and American history', in Glickman, L.B. (a cura di) *Consumer Society in American History. A Reader*, Cornell UP, Ithaca.

Hirschman, A.O. 1985, 'Against parsimony: three easy ways of complicating some categories of economic discourse', *Economics and Philosophy*, 1, 7–21.

Hirschman, A., 1996, 'Melding the public and private spheres: taking commensality seriously', *Critical Review*, 10(4), 533–550.

Lasch, C., 1991, *The Culture of Narcissism*, Norton, New York.

Leonini, L. and Sassatelli, R., 2008, *Il Consumo Critico*, Laterza, Bari.

Lewis, T. and Potter, E., 2011, *Ethical Consumption: A Critical Introduction*, Routledge, London.

Littler, J., 2009, *Radical Consumption: Shopping for Change in Contemporary Culture*, Open University Press.

Lockie, S. and L. Kristen 2002, 'Eating green', *Sociologia Ruralis*, 42(1), 23–40.

Lyon, S. and Moberg, M., eds, 2010, *Fair Trade and Social Justice*, New York, UP, New York.

Micheletti, M., 2003, *Political Virtue and Shopping: Individuals, Consumerism and Collective Action*, Palgrave, London.

———, 2007, 'The moral force of capitalism: anti-slavery and anti-sweatshop', in K. Soper and F. Trentmann (eds.), *Citizenship and Consumption*, Palgrave, Basingstoke, pp. 121–136.

———, 2011, 'Responsibility taking in politics,' in M. Micheletti and A. S. McFarland (eds.), *Creative Participation. Responsibility-Taking in the Political World*, Paradigm, Boulder.

Micheletti, M. and Stolle, D., 2007, 'Mobilizing consumers to take responsibility for global social justice', *Annals of the American Academy of Political and Social Science*, 611, 749–769.

Micheletti M., Follesdal, A. and Stolle, D. (eds.), 2004, *Politics, Products and Markets: Exploring Political Consumerism Past and Present*, Transaction Publishers, New Brunswick.

Miller, D. 2004, 'The little black dress is the solution, but what is the problem?', in K.M. Ekström and H. Brembeck (eds.) *Elusive Consumption*, Oxford: Berg.

Morgan, B., 2007, 'Consuming without paying: stealing or campaigning? The civic implications of civil disobedience around access to water', in K. Soper and F. Trentmann (eds.), *Citizenship and Consumption*, Palgrave, Basingstoke, pp, 71–86.

Nisticò, S., 2005, 'Consumption and time in economics: prices and quantities in a temporary equilibrium perspective', *Cambridge Journal of Economics*, 29, 943–957.

Nussbaum, M. and Sen, A. (eds.), 1993, *The Quality of Life*, Clarendon Press, Oxford.

Offer, A., 2006, *The Challenge of Affluence*, Oxford University Press, Oxford.

Robertson, R., 1995, 'Glocalization', in M. Featherstone, S. Lash and R. Robertson (eds.), *Global Modernities*, Sage, London, pp, 25–44.

Sassatelli, R., 2001a, 'Tamed hedonism: choice, desires and deviant pleasures', in A. Warde and J. Gronow (eds.), *Ordinary Consumption*, Routledge, London, pp, 93–106.

———, 2001b, 'Trust, choice and routine: putting the consumer on trial', *Critical Review of International Social and Political Philosophy*, 4(4), 84–105.

———, 2004, 'The political morality of food: discourses, contestation and alternative consumption', in M. Harvey, A. McMeekan and A. Warde (eds.), *Qualities of Food*, Manchester University Press, Manchester, pp.176–191.

———, 2006, 'Virtue, responsibility and consumer choice: framing critical consumerism', in J. Brewer and F. Trentmann (eds.), *Consuming Cultures: Global Perspectives*, Berg, Oxford, 219–250.

———, 2007, *Consumer Culture: History, Theory and Politics*, Sage, London.

———, 2009, 'Representing consumers: contesting claims and agendas', in K. Soper, M. Ryle and L. Thomas (eds.), *The Politics and Pleasures of Consuming Differently*, Palgrave, London, pp. 25–42.

———, 2010, *Fitness Culture: Gyms and the Commercialisation of Discipline and Fun*, Palgrave

Sassatelli, R. and Davolio, F., 2010, 'Consumption, pleasure and politics: Slow-Food and the politico-aesthetic problematization of food', *Journal of Consumer Culture*, 10(2), 1–31.

Schor, J., 1996, 'What's wrong with consumer capitalism?', *Critical Review*, 10(4), 495–508.

———, 1998, *The Overspent American: Why We Want What We Don't Need*, Harper Perennial

Schudson, M., 2007, 'Citizens, consumers and the good society' *Annals AAPSS*, 611, 236–49.

Scitovsky, T., 1972, 'What's wrong with the arts is what's wrong with society', *The American Economic Review*, 62(1–2), 62–69.

———, 1973, 'The place of economic welfare in human welfare', *Quarterly Review of Economics and Business*, 117(2), 7–19.

———, 1992, *The Joyless Economy*, Oxford University Press

———, 1995, *Economic Theory and Reality: Selected Essays*, Elgar

———, 1996, 'My own criticism of *The Joyless Economy*', *Critical Review*, 10(4), 595–605.

Sen, A., 1977, 'Rational fools', *Philosophy and Public Affairs*, 6, 317–344.

———, 1996, 'Rationality, joy and freedom', *Critical Review*, 10(4), 481–494.

Sen, A.K., 1985, *Commodities and Capabilities*, Amsterdam, Elsevier.

Simmel, G. 1990, *Philosophy of Money*, 2nd Edition, London: Routledge [orig. second ed. 1907].

Soper, K., Ryle, M. and Thomas, L., 2009, *The Politics and Pleasures of Consuming Differently*, Palgrave Macmillan, Basingstoke.

Steedman, I., 2001, *Consumption Takes Time: Implications for Economic Theory*, Routledge, London.

Sullivan, O. and Gershuny, J., 2004, 'Inconspicuous consumption. Work-rich, time-poor in the liberal market economy', *Journal of Consumer Culture*, 4, 1, 79–100.

Swann, P., 2002, 'There's more to the economics of consumption than (almost) unconstrained utility maximization', in A. McMeekin, K. Green, M. Tomlinson and V. Walsh (eds.), *Innovation by Demand: An Interdisciplinary Approach*, Manchester University Press, Manchester, pp. 23–40.

Tomlinson, J., 2007, *The Culture of Speed*, Sage, London.

Wilk, R., 2004, 'Morals and Metaphors. The meaning of consumption', in K.M. Ekstròm and H. Brembeck (eds.) *Elusive Consumption*, Oxford: Berg.

Williams, R., 1976, Keywords.

Zelizer, V., 2009, *Vite economiche*, il Mulino, Bologna.

Conclusion: Departing Notes on the Slow Narrative

Nick Osbaldiston

At the heart of this volume of work has been a culturally focused understanding of 'slow'. Beyond the political and economic veneer of this phenomenon lies a rich construction of finely tuned cultural codes and narratives which transform everyday life. Parkins and Craig (2006) knew this when they wrote *Slow Living*. The empirical aspect to their journey into the slow perhaps does not do it enough justice. The reality that this volume seeks to expose is that slowness has penetrated, embedded itself into and altered several of our social and individual practices. This goes beyond slow food, slow cities, slow travel or voluntary simplicity. It manifests itself in transport, consumerism, spatial engagement and even intimacy. The underpinning message is clear: slowing down is temporal, physiological, social and psychological. Engaging in slow sex, as Barratt explores (this volume), requires attention, care and an alternative approach to intimacy differentiated from mainstream sexual acts. Similarly, travelling under the guise of slow travel accentuates the whole experience over quick and rushed tourism akin to the postmodernist Western consumer (Urry 2002, 2011). Personal valuations of expectations in the tourist 'adventure' are redefined away from commercial ventures and group travel schemes. And yet, as Ryle and Soper illustrate above, rejuvenating sensations in travelling, even in the mundane environments of the city, produces a narrative that may well in the long term be a sustainable solution to traffic pollution. Of all the chapters here, cycling is the one empirically related example of slowness that is highly evident not only in numbers on the streets but also in town planning through the contestation and development of bike tracks.

Critics of this volume may suggest that approaching slowness in this way dilutes it somehow of its power. Without a rigid and clear theoretical model, we risk turning the slow into an abstract, fleeting and blunt concept which can be used to describe all activity that does not fall under the auspices of fast capitalism (Agger 2004). In other words, the slow adjective is broadened to the point where it becomes an empty signifier, filled with endless and ultimately meaningless interpretations. Once this occurs, the risk to deadening slows potential, as a pointed political/ethical critique of the modern predicaments of consumer-based capitalism grows significantly. From this point of view, slowness must be maintained as a type of revolt, a social movement instead of a mere cultural reaction. Organised movements like slow food are embedded in the political, a collective rejection of homogenised corporate food production and the wholesale takeover of local food traditions and cultures. From a Weberian perspective, they are built on charismatic foundations and survive through bureaucratic and rational organisation. Certainly today, 'Slow Food' has become a significant institution which has all the trimmings of a modern-day corporation, minus the sense of capitalistic greed.

There is certainly something seductive about this approach – a growing set of discontent groups forming to work actively against 'fast capitalism' in a new paradigm that has emerged in late or postmodern society. Perhaps it's the sceptical attitude toward our economic system that flourishes in the social sciences and humanities which produces this admiration. Or perhaps it's the mammoth and, at times, overwhelming narrative of climate change that causes us to celebrate campaigns aimed at redefining values and goals for whole economies and societies. Certainly this is one of the more pressing matters which remain relatively unattended by some of our largest nation-states. However, what this book does show is that the intentional act of altering personal relations and engagements with the social are changing outside of the organisations and social movements. There is a theme which has been broken into conceptual pieces and fed into cultural practice. That wider theme Lindholm (2008) has called authenticity (cf. Taylor 1991; Osbaldiston 2012; Vannini and Williams 2009), and the contestation over it causes him to question some of the ethics of slowness period (see Lindholm and Lie, Osbaldiston and Ragusa, this volume). Yet this broad paradigm helps us to bind together the preceding chapters. It does not necessitate, however, losing the critical edge that is associated with slowness as defined by others. In these final departing remarks, I seek to explain this a bit further, referring to the thematic of the chapters as well as their empirical content.

Alternative speeds?

Without question, the narrative of authenticity through 'slowing down' has its roots in history. While we could return to the Greeks or even Christianity's earliest beginnings, contemporary history demonstrates these things more eloquently for a modern audience. Of all those engaged in this practice, it was perhaps Henry David Thoreau's adventures in *Walden* that provide rich expressions of slowness that are found in our slow movements today. His very rejection of city life was focused on a narrative, fed by a spiritual sense and transcendental connection to nature, which promoted simplicity as a way of life. It required a change of practice that is reflected in some ways to our slow narratives above. This is exemplified in the oft-quoted portion of text from *Walden* below:

> I went to the woods because I wished to live deliberately, to front only the essential facts of life, and see if I could not learn what it had to teach, and not, when I came to die, discover that I had not lived. I did not wish to live what was not life, living is so dear; nor did I wish to practise resignation, unless it was quite necessary. I wanted to live deep and suck out all the marrow of life, to live so sturdily and Spartan-like as to put to rout all that was not life, to cut a broad swatch and shave close, to drive life into a corner, and reduce it to its lowest terms...
>
> (Thoreau 1965, p. 82)

The quest of *Walden,* as we all know, ended in failure for Thoreau. Yet the American wanted to exemplify through his own actions, perhaps more than anything else, a critique of the 'machine' that was society and the simplicity that was nature (Paul 1962, p. 101). Society is here not simply an organising animal requiring of its people social obligation to broad collective norms, as is apparent in Durkheim, but rather it involves the direct transformations of social practices that provoke rushed attitudes, the rationalisation of life through money economies and the noise and pervasiveness of industry. This is demonstrated quite significantly in his latter critiques, such as *Life Without Principle*:

> This world is a place of business. What an infinite bustle! I am awaked almost every night by the panting of the locomotive. It interrupts my dreams. There is no sabbath. It would be glorious to see mankind at leisure for once. It is nothing but work, work, work. I cannot easily buy a blank-book to write thoughts in; they are commonly ruled for

dollars and cents...I think there is nothing, not even crime, more opposed to poetry, to philosophy, ay, to life itself, than this incessant business.

(Thoreau 1965, p. 712)

Within this quote alone, we foreground some of the more recent critiques of contemporary lifestyles exacerbated by an even faster and more intense form of industry and capitalism than in Thoreau's time. Tomlinson (2007) and Agger (2004), among others, have criticised the insatiable and encompassing goliath that is 'fast capitalism' which serves to agitate consumer desires and produce consistent activity in the market place. Instantaneous communication technology further compresses time and space allowing, ironically, for less time as we confront the continuous demands of email, messaging and other work-related matters. In order to keep up, individuals are required to be flexible, technologically adaptable and available in a 24/7 economy (cf. Schor 1998; Hochschild 1990, 1997). The rhetoric of work–life balance is contested, perhaps, by a realisation for many that 'work is life'.

It is not the intention of this volume to provoke a pointed critique of 'fast capitalism'. However, it is hard to escape it when engaging with some of the slow narratives. Humphery (this volume) demonstrates this criticism when he briefly discusses 'consumer rage' at slow customer service – something we are all accustomed to. Further, as Schor (this volume) attests, there are wider implications of unsustainable growth in relation to an unfettered consumer-based market at the micro level. Waste, in this case waste in textiles, drives ecological problems as we struggle with our mostly Western obsession with cheap goods that have a high turnover and short lifespan. This, she argues, is being challenged through 'connected consumption' patterns that re-use goods through trade among consumers. This has expanded in the recent global economic downturn. Yet our problem of waste, which is, for instance, a problem in marine ecology with regard to plastics, not only has societal implications but also influences our global ecology (see e.g. Blight and Berger 1997; Robards, Piatt and Wohl 1995 for discussions on marine bird populations and plastic ingestion).

We shall return momentarily to the potential for slow narratives to challenge current ecological problems. Returning back to the narrative that underpins Thoreau's writings, there is a sense that he feels a growing inauthenticity among society through technological and economic advance. The way forward, to rejuvenate the self and return it back to a deep and meaningful existence, is through simplicity. I would hesitate to suggest that this is precisely what the slow narrative proposes today. What we have witnessed in this volume reflects little of the rejectionist sentiments of Thoreau's thoughts, except for maybe some of the more counter-cultural amenity-led migrants found across the world (see Moss 2006). What we do find in common among them, however, is a desire for slower forms of lifestyle. Whether that is in micro-areas, such as cycling or within consumer products, or larger areas, such as environmental or place-based migration practices, what underpins this cultural revolution is the same quest for authenticity that drove Thoreau.

From this perspective, the culturally located critique of capitalism has continued but has been broken into the various postmodernist aspects of our very complex lifestyles today. Before outlining this further, it is worth considering this by discussing what the slow does not involve. The premise is that the slow involves some type of cultural concern with an aspect of 'fast capitalism' that disables enjoyment of certain everyday activities, or at least makes them unpleasant. This would counter any notions of stillness or idleness which would reflect immobility in a mobile world (Bissell and Fuller 2011). However, this dialectic between moving and not moving is debatable:

> To prioritize an understanding of stillness where it is always captured as a *particular* relation to mobility – to commit to a relational politics of mobilities where stillness is just an effect, a function of, or an enabler of movement – overlooks and neglects other registers and modalities which still and stillness in habits ... We want to consider how stillness might emerge through other configurations of matter which are not necessarily reducible to the dialectic of mobility and immobility.
>
> (Bissell and Fuller 2011, p. 6)

Using this as a guide, *Stillness in a Mobile World* opens up the paradigm of 'being still' through a range of compartments in society. This includes in manufactured spaces, such as airport 'junkspaces', where the stilled body is analysed in counter-position to speed orientated spatial configurations (Harley 2011, p. 38). Within this framework, the 'stillness' is opened up as a potentiality alongside other mobilities, such as running, rushing and impatient waiting (Harley 2011, pp. 38–39). This is a theoretical and conceptual transformation, however, not simply an act of performing the still on behalf of the individual who is often in these spaces forced into stillness (waiting for a plane, watching TV or reading a book, sleeping). Indeed, there is scope to consider that enforced stillness within the airport is entirely undesirable, such as when flights are delayed, when there are long lines at security gates or when having to endure uneasy waiting during landing cycles. This particular work also explores other aspects of the 'still', however, including politics, education and photography, each of which would appear to stand aside from the slow.

That the boundaries between the still and the slow are blurred is demonstrated, however, by Conradson's (2011) discussion in the same edited collection of the UK's retreat culture, which he argues is an 'orchestration of feeling'. Stillness here is a potentiality that is facilitated by spatial organisation and expertise in techniques of 'stilling':

> The orchestration of feeling was no simple matter, however, and space was made for stillness in multiple ways. The hospitality offered to guests, including the good food and comfortable if not luxurious rooms, contributed to a relaxing and calming environment. The focusing and meditation techniques helped individuals become better attuned to their felt sense of being in the world, and to develop new ways of relating to this. The opportunity to inhabit a different temporality was also important. Most of the meditative techniques acted to slow the rhythms of one's thoughts, in part by recalibrating them to other bodily rhythms such as that of breathing. In addition, the regularly-spaced schedules for the sessions, meals and free time gave each day a sense of familiarity and navigability.
>
> (Conradson 2011, p. 83)

Participation in these ritualistic type events is counter-posed against the 'intensity of life and the challenges of coordinating employment, caregiving and recreational activities in space and time' (Conradson 2011, p. 72). Through escape, similar to my discussions of slow travel above, the individual embraces new temporalities that slow the mind, relax it and potentially refresh it for a return to the highly regimented world of city life. This narrative is certainly also reflected in those who seek permanent escape from the city by living in rural/regional environments (see Ragusa, this volume; Benson 2011; Osbaldiston 2012).

However, stilling the mind here is not linked to a wider cultural narrative, which I have delineated above as self-authenticity. There is a certain critique tightly woven into the motivation to 'do' retreats such as these. It is similar to Thoreau's argument, that life has become increasingly complex and sensually deadening. To re-awaken and enliven the senses again, we need escape into the countryside where, it must be admitted, stillness is produced. The main difference between 'slow' and 'still' here is that stillness is a side effect of slowness, a physiological and psychological alteration that is produced by participating in slow activities. If we examine the contents of this volume, we might see this further. For instance, again in Ryle and Soper's discussion of the cycling phenomenon, there is a production of pleasurable sensations which undoubtedly transform bodily and cognitive states – largely denied in automobility (Soper 2007). Further, in Barratt's chapter on slow sex, the transition in intimacy from fast to slow produces a 'different pattern of the neurophysiological release of endorphins and hormones such as oxytocin', which can alter the consciousness and the post-sexual experience. Other examples of the production of a stillness through the slow are evident in my chapter on slow travel and lifestyle migration, participant discussions in Ragusa's chapter on 'treechange' and theoretically in Sassatelli's consideration of consumer products that enable patience, learning and mastery.

Slowness, however, does not simply produce a stilled or altered consciousness or physiology. As Schor notes in her chapter on connected consumption and in her work on downshifting previously (Schor 1998), the slow here also enables a renewed appreciation of sociality. Not only does the transformation in economic practice potentially challenge mainstream consumerism but it also produces positive social relations through collaboration, sharing and cohesion. Similarly, slow food, the oft-cited leader of slowness, while reinvigorating difference in taste, also embraces local cuisine, tradition and a collective identity which is all consumed by the individual. As Lindholm and Lie have argued, the paradigm of slow food prioritises a rejection of fast-food techniques that allow no such connectivity of the individual to local traditions and tastes in food culture. Slow food also encourages social eating, which includes groups enjoying companionship at the table rather than the isolated individualised practices that occur in postmodern lifestyles (cf. Parkins and Craig 2006). I would argue that slow food epitomises the essence of the slow in suspending the intensification of individualised and isolated modern life through this act of collective enjoyment of food, albeit momentarily.

What this all boils down to is that slowness should be considered as shifting modalities of living to acquire more authentic moments that assist in developing the self. Simmel recognises such processes throughout his writings. The *Tragedy of Modern Culture* for him lay in the inability of modern processes and 'forms' to satisfy the need for acculturation (Simmel (1997[1912])). Objective culture has outgrown the individual's capacity to internalise and utilise the arts, objects, forms, laws and norms for their self-authentication. What I am proposing is evident in the push toward slow modalities today is an attempt to try to reverse this trend. By building into lifestyle choices activities that alter physiological, cognitive and social processes to produce meaning, stillness, attentiveness and enjoyment, the individual is attempting to recapture something lost to the everyday. That, I would argue alongside Lindholm (2008) and Vannini and Williams (2009), is self-authenticity – the very same thing which drove Thoreau to Walden Ponds all those years ago.

Alternative hedonisms? The future of our cultural revolt?

What is the future therefore of slow? One of the noticeable comments from Schor (this volume) is the manner in which the 'connected con-sumption' movement has opened up through the debilitating perfor-mance of the US market post-global financial crisis. As the fundamental tenets of economic growth in the neo-classical model begin to falter, adoption of more post-materialist-type sentiments become attractive and gather momentum. This certainly is not the case with all types of slowness that we have encountered here. One could hardly begin developing or purchasing high-quality homes in amenity-rich locations without the capital to do so. However, recessions are certainly times of critique as well, and this particular global financial incident has produced many, such as the Occupy movement. Critics of the slow, however, might suggest that the paradigm is built on fanciful idealism, or even a middle-class life project (see below). However, advocates such as Honoré disagree:

> Critics dismiss the slow movement as a passing fad, or as a fringe philosophy that will never go mainstream ... When the global econ-omy starts to roar again, or when the next dotcom-style boom comes along, will all the talk of slowing down go out the window as every-one rushes to make a quick buck? Don't bet on it. More than any generation before us, we understand the danger and futility of con-stant acceleration and are more determined than ever to roll back the cult of speed.
>
> (Honoré 2004, p. 276)

Despite Honoré's fervour, it is difficult to predict the impact of slow-ness on the everyday futures of a global society caught up in speed.

We merely have to witness the ever-expanding consumer market and the volatile nature of goods which upgrade daily to be wary of the future of slow. One of our more valuable corporations on the exchange is Apple, which stands shoulder to shoulder with natural resource giants in terms of market capitalisation. Its marque product, the iPad, which is to be remade into a 'mini' model soon, is forecast already to sell well over 20 million units in December quarter sales alone in 2012 (Padgadget 2012). Such a prediction speaks volumes about the intensity of our consumer desires. While these types of electronic 'gadget' may well enhance opportunities for collaboration, online community development and social media networking, they prove to us that the we are still in many ways dominated by technology and consumer products.

Despite this, as demonstrated earlier by Honoré (2004), there is optimism that through the slow 'revolution', if we may be inclined to call it that, there will be a sweeping change that will last through a rising generation, sceptical of unfettered economic growth and intense speed. From this emerges a belief that through slowness we might begin to challenge some of our most compelling problems across the globe today. This includes climate change and sustainability. Within this rubric, people are adopting techniques in areas such as transportation which while providing positive and refreshing sensations and enjoyment, also invite strategies for more sustainable, low-carbon solutions for the future. Kate Soper (2007) has described this type of revolt as 'alternative hedonism' – the use of hedonist pleasures once lost to advancement in modernity and time-saving technology to create new pathways for a sustainable future. Bike riding is one facet of this. Yet, such notions almost certainly embrace slow food, amenity-led migration, slow travel and other manifestations of the phenomenon. This on-the-ground solution operates in a way that reconfigures our enjoyment of the world to a more meaningful lifestyle while also providing ethical pathways for individual internalisation of ecological values and politics. In other words, it is via our own pleasure seeking that we can also embrace principles of conservation so important to global problems, such as climate change.

Still there are some, such as Tomlinson (2007, p. 149), who remain cautious about the impact of the slow phenomenon:

> It seems unlikely that the slow movement can in any direct way challenge the institutional grip of the condition of immediacy. However, the focus on the experienced problems of pace of life that it provides should not be discounted. For it is possible to discern within this discourse certain emergent values – the other aspect of Castell's

stipulation of the impact of a social movement – which might in the longer term be consequential. And if we, as we surely should, reject inevitabilism, then exploring such values, and the conditions of their cultivation, seems worthwhile.

From this we can assert that slowness is indeed an unlikely candidate for transforming our contemporary institutions, such as the state or a neo-liberal economy. In relation to the mammoth task of dealing with anthropogenic climate change, it most certainly will require more than the cultural will of 'pleasure seekers' and bike riders to halt dangerous levels of carbon dioxide pollution. Ironically, the slow paradigm moves too slowly to make any real impact on climate change. Slotted alongside macro-economic strategies such as carbon taxation or emission trading schemes and transitions to low-carbon-emitting power production, however, the slow narrative could assist in overwriting the postmodernist prose of consumerist tendencies and lead to an alternative future. A commitment to a slower form of consumerism, though, as Schor argues (this volume), provides pathways to an individually 'lower footprint' in the future that can grow collectively. It requires slowness to become a narrative that shifts the balance in consumer society away from the spectacle (Ritzer 2010) and instant gratification of fast capitalism (Tomlinson 2007). It will also require the confrontation of a highly innovative and creative consumer market place which, as Ritzer (2010, p. 210) notes, has found a new terrain for its proliferation on the internet. Here is where a vast amount of time and capital are expended every day.

Recent estimates, for instance, of time spent on the social networking site *Facebook* (which has become a haven for the advertising and marketing industries) have exploded to 53 billion minutes per month in the USA alone (Mack 2011). Further, the amount of money spent on video gaming (globally) totalled approximately $74 billion in 2010 and is tipped to exceed $112 billion by 2015 (Bilton 2011). These figures, along with the growth of other online activity, including shopping, gambling and media downloads, demonstrate that the world of capitalism has shifted. Ritzer's (2010) spectacles are no longer just found in the manmade wonders of Las Vegas and Dubai. Rather, they are discovered in living rooms, at work places and on mobile devices. As technologies which either sell a product (e.g. gaming) or allow for the advertising of products (e.g. *Facebook*) penetrate further into our private lives, the ability for slow narratives to challenge them becomes more complicated. Yet as Honoré (2004) suggests, it is through this ever-growing invasion of consumer-targeted technology that the slow narrative may gain further credibility and expand. Ironically, 'fast capitalism', as it grows faster, may also feed the attractiveness of the slow, and a desire for 'stillness'. I shall return to this point later.

Middle-class problems?

To conclude these brief departing remarks, I will consider the cynics. This group, embedded in a tradition of the social sciences to question power relationships and authority, arrive at a position of scepticism at the driving force behind the slow. Subsequently, any anticipations of its revolutionary potential are questionable. Throughout the collection of chapters here, this thought has been approached more than once. Lindholm and Lie (this volume), for example, in their discussions of the role of authenticity in slow food remonstrate over the authority of groups over others to delineate what authentic taste is. It is through this sensation that slow food gains its prominence, a rejuvenation of the palate though an education of the senses. Yet, the decision-making process regarding what is 'genuine' or 'authentic' in relation to local cuisines and traditions is value-laden and promotes opportunities for mainstreaming taste at the expense of others. Quite simply, through what appears to be an egalitarian movement, forces of authority which define what is authentic could potentially 'other' certain groups and practices in food production and consumption. Is this then a colonisation of 'food' in local settings?

Ragusa (this volume) is similarly wary of the attitudes of the consumers of slowness. Here she demonstrates empirically that 'treechangers' in Australia who have good intentions with respect to altering their normal behaviour post-migration (away from the city into the country) remain strangely unchanged in their daily practices. This group of people fail in mundane ways to acquire the 'still' mindset they initially set out to acquire in the country and continue with their middle-class habits and tastes. Further to this, I (this volume) call into question, through the works of Michaela Benson (2011) and Sharon Zukin (2008), the quest to authenticate, which may well be a quest to distinguish, in Bourdieusian terms. In particular, the practices of those seeking an 'authentic' getaway through either travel or migration are evidently practices of distinction derived predominantly from the middle classes.

There is little doubt that those exercises of the 'slow' described above can be seen as middle-class life projects. Scepticism then on the validity of slow culture is at times warranted. Sharon Zukin's (2008, 2010) work into the gentrification of places that once housed the poorer classes only to be retuned into chic and authentic looking suburbs through rejuvenation projects illustrates this further. This is a type of non-hostile takeover by the middle classes which squeezes out some of the most vulnerable people in our societies. Furthermore, the influence of the middle classes (and the rich) on sleepy and untouched country and coastal villages through lifestyle migration and second home buying has recently been the focal point of researchers tracking trends in inequality in housing, consumption and community (Osbaldiston and Picken, forthcoming; Benson 2011; Moss 2006; Costello 2006). In these instances, the quest to discover newer and slower forms of lifestyle while also developing wealthy and, at times, luxurious homes transforms small townships into meccas for the middle classes (Osbaldiston 2012).

Despite this scepticism, is there cause to dismiss slowness as just another 'fad' of the never-ending life projects of a middle-class culture? (cf. Rose 1996). The answer in my opinion is perhaps not. While we should not ignore that authenticity is contested between groups of difference, and perhaps also within groups (such as slow food – who decides within the group what is true local cuisine?), we must also acknowledge that the reaction toward hyper/fast consumer capitalism emerges from those who are likely impacted by it the most. Tomlinson (2007, p. 149) considers the criticism in the following;

> I think, in the first place, that it is important not to dismiss the movement as merely an expression of (otherwise comfortable) middle-class cultural anxieties and an apolitical, quasi-therapeutic response to these. The dominant stress on self-help – though it is, in both analytical and political terms, a weakness – can be understood as expressing the broader experience of immersion in a complex cultural condition which is most easily grasped, not in institutional abstractions, but in the data of individual experience . . . the problem resides within individual practices. In this sense, the slow movement is congruent with the condition of immediacy, matching both its mood of fluid complexity and over-determination, and the individualizing effects of both telemediatization and the shaping of consumption towards delivery.

We could use Tomlinson's (2007) scrutiny of the slow here as a baseline for the defence of it. For it is the very individualising practices that fast capitalism and hyper-consumerism enforce which create the potentiality for slowness to emerge. In other words, slowness is an 'individualised' practice (though it could be analysed as a social pattern of collectives) because the 'condition of immediacy' produces an individualised world (cf. Beck 1992; Lash and Urry 1994; Bauman 2001). We are, as Parkins and Craig (2006) also contest, freer today through the market to consume alternative lifestyles. Yet it is not simply freedom which provokes slowness but an unrivalled questioning of discourse, knowledge and, most importantly, mainstream understandings on how to live.

From this we might contend therefore that those who are more likely to be 'individualised' through the market and through practices associated with fast capitalism (i.e. over-stressed work conditions, longer work hours, higher mortgages and personal debts, positional consumption and metropolitan lifestyles) are also more likely to be the ones who become fed up with them and choose to seek alternative practices through the 'slow' paradigm. If we were to compare embracing slowness to embracing 'risk', we might find conceptual comparison in the theory of Deborah Lupton (1999, p. 157), who declared that heightened exposure to risk would necessarily lead to more 'risk-taking' ventures. Increased 'exposure' to the 'culture of speed' instils a highly individualised, fluid and reflexive self (cf. Parkins and Craig 2006). Subsequently, it is from within the system of speed itself that a reaction against it develops but does so through highly individualised forms.

While critics of the slow may find solace in declaring the movement/paradigm as a toothless tiger in the quest for middle-class authenticity, we depart this volume of work in a less cynical fashion. As Tomlinson (2007) contends above, those who are rejecting the 'fast capitalist' system and the culture of 'immediacy' are indeed the ones more fully engaged with it in the everyday. Thus, as Parkins and Craig (2006, p. 8) suggest, the 'everyday is the issue itself'. How slowness injects itself into individual actions is important. Practices as mundane as getting to and from work, eating, buying clothes, using material possessions and having intimate relations, through to the more extraordinary, such as travel and migration, have all in some way been reconfigured through the slow paradigm of meaningfulness, contemplation and authenticity (cf. Parkins and Craig 2006). As a 'culture of slow' gains more momentum, the future uptake of alternative practices could well alter our consumer landscape considerably.

References

Agger, B., 2004, *Speeding Up Fast Capitalism: Cultures, Jobs, Families, Schools, Bodies*, Paradigm Publishers, Boulder.

Bauman, Z., 2001, *The Individualized Society*, Polity Press, Cambridge.

Beck, U., 1992, *Risk Society: Towards a New Modernity*, M. Ritter (trans.), Sage, London.

Benson, M., 2011, *The British in Rural France: Lifestyle Migration and the Ongoing Quest for a Better Way of Life*, Manchester University Press, Manchester.

Bilton, N., 2011, 'Video game industry continues major growth, Gartner says', *The New York Times*, 5 July, viewed 12 April, 2012, http://bits.blogs.nytimes .com/2011/07/05/video-game-industry-continues-major-growth-gartner-says/.

Bissell, D. and Fuller, G., 2011, 'Stillness unbound', in D. Bissell and G. Fuller (eds.), *Stillness in a Mobile World*, Routledge, New York, pp. 1–18.

Blight, L. K. and Berger, A. E., 1997, 'Occurrence of plastic particles in seabirds from the eastern North Pacific', *Marine Pollution Bulletin*, 34(5), 323–325.

Conradson, D., 2011, 'The orchestration of feeling: stillness, spirituality and places of retreat', in D. Bissell and G. Fuller (eds.), *Stillness in a Mobile World*, Routledge, New York, pp. 71–86.

Costello, L., 2006, 'Going bush: the implications of urban-rural migration', *Geographical Research*, 45(1), 85–94.

Gowdy, J. M., 2008, 'Behavioural economics and climate change policy', *Journal of Economic Behavior & Organization*, 68(3–4), 632–644.

Harley, R., 2011, 'Airportals: the functional significance of stillness in the junkspace of airports', in D. Bissell and G. Fuller (eds.), *Stillness in a Mobile World*, Routledge, New York, pp. 38–50.

Hochschild, A., 1990, *The Second Shift*, Avon Books, New York.

———, 1997, *The Time Bind: When Work Becomes Home and Home Becomes Work*, Metropolitan Books, New York.

Honoré, C., 2004, *In Praise of Slowness: Challenging the Cult of Speed*, HarperOne, New York.

Lash, S. and Urry, J., 1994, *Economies of Signs and Space*, Sage, London.

Lindholm, C., 2008, *Culture and Authenticity*, Blackwell, Malden.

Lupton, D., 1999, *Risk*, Routledge, Hoboken.

Mack, E., 2011, 'Facebook sucks up American's time', *CNET News*, 12 September, viewed 14 March, 2012, http://news.cnet.com/8301-1023_3-20105184-93/facebook-sucks-up-americans-time/.

Moss, L. A. G. (ed.), 2006, *The Amenity Migrants: Seeking and Sustaining Mountains and Their Cultures*, CABI, Oxfordshire.

Osbaldiston, N., 2012, *Seeking Authenticity in Place, Culture, Self: The Great Urban Escape*, Palgrave Macmillan, New York.

Osbaldiston, N. and Picken, F., forthcoming, 'The urban push for environmental amenity: the impact of lifestyle migration on local housing markets and communities', in A. Ragusa (ed.) *Contemporary Rural and Regional Communities: Lessons from Australian Communities for a Global Audience*, Springer, London

Padgadget, 2012, 'iPad mini predicted to push overall iPad sales past 30 million this holiday season', *Padgadget*, 8 October, viewed 10 October, 2012, http://

www.padgadget.com/2012/10/08/ipad-mini-predicted-to-push-overall-ipad-sales-past-30-million-this-holiday-season/.

Parkins, W. and Craig, G., 2006, *Slow Living*, Berg, Oxford.

Paul, S., 1962, 'A fable of the renewal of life', in P. Sherman (ed.), *Thoreau: A Collection of Critical Essays*, Prentice Hall, Englewood Cliffs, NJ.

Ritzer, G., 2010, *Enchanting a Disenchanted World: Continuity and Change in the Cathedrals of Consumption* (3rd edn), Pine Forge Press, Thousand Oaks.

Robards, M. D., Piatt, J. F. and Wohl, K. D., 1995, 'Increasing frequency of plastic particles ingested by seabirds in the subarctic North Pacific', *Marine Pollution Bulletin*, 30(2), 151–157.

Rose, N., 1996, *Inventing Ourselves: Psychology, Power and Personhood*, Cambridge University Press, Cambridge.

Schor, J., 1998, *The Overspent American: Why We Want What We Don't Need*, Harper Perennial, New York.

Simmel, G. 1997[1912]. 'The concept and tragedy of culture', M. Ritter and D. Frisby (trans.), in D. Frisby and M. Featherstone (eds.), *Simmel on Culture: Selected Writings*, Sage, London, pp. 120–130.

Soper, K., 2007, 'Rethinking the "good life": the citizenship dimension of consumer disaffection with consumerism', *Journal of Consumer Culture*, 7(2), 205–229.

Taylor, C., 1991, *Ethics of Authenticity*, Harvard University Press, Cambridge.

Thoreau, H. D., 1965, *Walden and Other Writings of Henry David Thoreau*, Random House, New York.

Tomlinson, J., 2007, *The Culture of Speed: The Coming of Immediacy*, Sage, London.

Urry, J., 2002, *The Tourist Gaze* (2nd edn), Sage, London.

———, 2011, *The Tourist Gaze 3.0*, Sage, Los Angeles.

Vannini, P. and Williams, P., 2009, *Authenticity in Culture, Self and Society*, Ashgate Publishing, Burlington.

Zukin, S., 2008, 'Consuming authenticity', *Cultural Studies*, 22(5), 724–748.

———, 2010, *Naked City: The Death and Life of Authentic Urban Places*, Oxford University Press, Oxford.

Index